SEVEN PRACTICE TESTS

ACHIEVING HIGHER TOEIC® TEST SCORES

VOLUME 1

SEVEN PRACTICE TESTS

ACHIEVING HIGHER TOEIC® TEST SCORES

VOLUME 1

STEVEN A. STUPAK

Published by
Longman Asia ELT
2/F Cornwall House
Taikoo Place
979 King's Road
Quarry Bay
Hong Kong

fax: +852 2856 9578
e-mail: aelt@pearsoned.com.hk
website: www.longman-elt.com

and Associated Companies throughout the world.

First published 1997
Reprinted 2001

Produced by Pearson Education North Asia Limited, Hong Kong
SWTC/06

ISBN 0 13 619933 X

Acquisitions editor: Nancy Baxer
Copy editors: J. Johnston / Nicola Miller
Editorial manager: Ang Lee Ming
Production manager: Oliver Lam
Cover design coordinator: Merle Krumper

The
publisher's
policy is to use
paper manufactured
from sustainable forests

CONTENTS

FOREWORD

Any person who sits down to take a test needs to know in advance what the test is like. TOEIC examinees are no exception. They need to know what the question formats are and where their own strengths and weaknesses lie. Having nearly thirty years of experience in the field of language testing, and having been director of the TOEIC program at Educational Testing Service during the years of the TOEIC's most rapid expansion, 1982 through 1990, Steven A. Stupak is uniquely prepared to inform readers about the TOEIC. A recognized expert in the field of language testing, Mr. Stupak conducts workshops internationally in both test development and oral proficiency testing. In this book, he shares with the reader his knowledge of the TOEIC and testing. A special section on the Language Proficiency Interview (LPI) and the Oral Proficiency Interview (OPI) will be of particular interest to teachers who prepare students for the LPI or for students who want to inform themselves about the LPI.

Nancy Baxer
Certified LPI Interviewer
ESL/EFL Instructor

INTRODUCTION

Steven A. Stupak was the director of the TOEIC Program at Educational Testing Service from 1982–1990. Prior to holding that position he had held positions in and had consulted in Test Development, Research Administration, Occupational and Professional Licensing, and other areas of ETS. Because of his over a quarter of a century in testing, at ETS and elsewhere, and specifically because of his experience with the TOEIC, Mr. Stupak is the person best qualified to bring this material to the TOEIC public.

This book contains one test that was calibrated against the TOEIC test and six other tests on which statistical data was compiled and for which mean part and section scores characteristic of a TOEIC total score of 500 are provided.

The purpose of this book is not to teach English. Its purpose is to familiarize TOEIC examinees with item formats that are found on the TOEIC, TOEIC vocabulary, test content, difficulty level, and administration. In short, it is to provide the TOEIC examinee with a TOEIC experience, such that when the examinee takes the test, both the material and the process will be familiar.

Just as the study of English is a lifelong process, the TOEIC is a test that one should take many times over a lifetime. It should serve as an ongoing measure of a person's English language capability, tracking progress as a person's English improves. It is designed for the serious student, not for the sometime dabbler in language. By studying this book, as well as its sister volume, which contains the same number of but different tests, the author hopes that the student will come to regard the TOEIC a familiar friend, and that meeting it again and again will be a welcome experience.

ACKNOWLEDGMENTS

In my earlier book, *The Prentice Hall Regents Prep Book for the TOEIC Test,* I acknowledged the contribution to my career of my mentors and colleagues at Educational Testing Service, particularly Protase E. Woodford and Suzanne Stahl. Their efforts to mold me into a testing professional are no less reflected in this book than in that one and my appreciation of them, and others at ETS, including Dr. Rose Scheider, Dr. John L.D. Clark, and Jean Scanlon Sachs, is undiminished.

I would also like to express my appreciation to Stephen Troth, publishing director at Simon & Schuster (Asia), to my publisher, Nancy Baxer, to production manager, Oliver Lam, and to editorial manager, Ang Lee Ming. While any errors in the text are wholly my own, I must recognize the great contribution of my copy editor, Janet S. Johnston. Words, or at least my words, cannot express my admiration for what she is able to do with a manuscript. Senior editor Nicola Miller applied her keen eye to the manuscript and spotted a number of problems that might have slipped through the cracks, had she not done so.

Certainly, the project would not have been initiated without on-going professional encouragement from a variety of sources, including Yasuo Kitaoka, Hisao Noguchi, Osamu Sakai, and Junichi Chida, in Japan, K.C. Kang, Glen Penrod, of the Samsung Human Resources Development Center, and T. Dean Snyder, of LG Academy, in Korea, and Sammy Takahashi, at Pacific Gateway International College, in Vancouver, British Columbia, Canada. Friends and colleagues at my former employer, ASPECT, in San Francisco and at America Cultural Exchange in Seattle, World Learning in Brattleboro, and ELS Educational Services Inc. in Culver City are a continuing source of professional support that I much appreciate.

Special thanks go to Y.B. Min and to S.S. Min, chairman and president, respectively, of YBM/Si-sa-yong-o-sa, Inc., the company for which I work, for making it possible for me to publish this and other books for the international TOEIC community.

And finally, I dedicate this book to the memory of Dr. J. Davis Applewhite, a kind, generous, and loving person who is greatly missed by all who knew him. I met Dr. Applewhite when I was an undergraduate at the University of Redlands and he a professor of American history. It was Dr. Applewhite who initiated the chain of events that formed my academic and professional life and who, with his wife, Rhea Dana Applewhite, followed my peregrinations from one college or university to another (eight in all), to study abroad, to the Peace Corps and finally to the responsibilities of adulthood, never with judgment but always with support and loving counsel. I was greatly privileged to have known him.

Steven A. Stupak
Seoul, Korea

TOEIC®
PRACTICE TEST

TEST OF ENGLISH FOR INTERNATIONAL COMMUNICATION

General Directions

This is a test of your ability to use the English language. The total time for the test is approximately two hours. It is divided into seven parts. Each part of the test begins with a set of specific directions. Be sure you understand what you are to do before you begin work on a part.

You will find that some of the questions are harder than others, but you should try to answer every one. There is no penalty for guessing. Do not be concerned if you cannot answer all of the questions.

Do not mark your answers in this book. You must put all of your answers on the separate answer sheet that you have been given. When putting your answer to a question on your answer sheet, be sure to fill in the answer space corresponding to the letter of your choice. Fill in the space so that the letter inside the oval cannot be seen, as shown in the example below.

Mr. Jones ——— to his accountant yesterday.

(A) talk
(B) talking
(C) talked
(D) to talk

Sample Answer

Ⓐ Ⓑ ● Ⓓ

The sentence should read, "Mr. Jones talked to his accountant yesterday." Therefore, you should choose answer (C). Notice how this has been done in the example given.

Mark only one answer for each question. If you change your mind about an answer after you have marked it on your answer sheet, completely erase your old answer and then mark your new answer. You must mark the answer sheet carefully so that the test-scoring machine can accurately record your test score.

LISTENING COMPREHENSION

In this section of the test, you will have the chance to show how well you understand spoken English. There are four parts to this section, with special directions for each part.

Part I

Directions: For each question, you will see a picture in your test book and you will hear four short statements. The statements will be spoken just one time. They will not be printed in your test book, so you must listen carefully to understand what the speaker says.

When you hear the four statements, look at the picture in your test book and choose the statement that best describes what you see in the picture. Then, on your answer sheet, find the number of the question and mark your answer.

Look at the sample below.

Now listen to the four statements.

Sample Answer

Statement (B), "They're having a meeting," best describes what you see in the picture. Therefore, you should choose answer (B).

GO ON TO THE NEXT PAGE

1.

2.

3. 

4. 

GO ON TO THE NEXT PAGE

5.

6.

7.

8.

GO ON TO THE NEXT PAGE

9.

10.

11.

12.

GO ON TO THE NEXT PAGE

13.

14.

15.

16.

GO ON TO THE NEXT PAGE

17. 

18. 

19.

20.

GO ON TO THE NEXT PAGE

Part II

Directions: In this part of the test you will hear a question spoken in English, followed by three responses, also spoken in English. The question and the responses will be spoken just one time. They will not be printed in your test book, so you must listen carefully to understand what the speakers say. You are to choose the best response to each question.

Now listen to a sample question:

You will hear:

You will also hear:

Sample Answer

● Ⓑ Ⓒ

The best response to the question "How are you?" is choice (A) "I am fine, thank you." Therefore, you should choose answer (A).

21. Mark your answer on your answer sheet.
22. Mark your answer on your answer sheet.
23. Mark your answer on your answer sheet.
24. Mark your answer on your answer sheet.
25. Mark your answer on your answer sheet.
26. Mark your answer on your answer sheet.
27. Mark your answer on your answer sheet.
28. Mark your answer on your answer sheet.
29. Mark your answer on your answer sheet.
30. Mark your answer on your answer sheet.
31. Mark your answer on your answer sheet.
32. Mark your answer on your answer sheet.
33. Mark your answer on your answer sheet.
34. Mark your answer on your answer sheet.
35. Mark your answer on your answer sheet.
36. Mark your answer on your answer sheet.
37. Mark your answer on your answer sheet.
38. Mark your answer on your answer sheet.
39. Mark your answer on your answer sheet.
40. Mark your answer on your answer sheet.
41. Mark your answer on your answer sheet.
42. Mark your answer on your answer sheet.
43. Mark your answer on your answer sheet.
44. Mark your answer on your answer sheet.
45. Mark your answer on your answer sheet.
46. Mark your answer on your answer sheet.
47. Mark your answer on your answer sheet.
48. Mark your answer on your answer sheet.
49. Mark your answer on your answer sheet.
50. Mark your answer on your answer sheet.

Part III

Directions: In this part of the test, you will hear 30 short conversations between two people. The conversations will not be printed in your test book. You will hear the conversations only once, so you must listen carefully to understand what the speakers say.

In your test book you will read a question about each conversation. The question will be followed by four answers. You are to choose the best answer to each question and mark it on your answer sheet.

51. What does the woman want to buy?

(A) Food
(B) Coffee
(C) Tickets
(D) Clothing

52. Why is the man going outside?

(A) To take a walk
(B) To buy supplies
(C) To meet a friend
(D) To have a cigarette

53. What problem does the woman have?

(A) She has lost her key.
(B) Her bicycle is broken.
(C) Her car will not start.
(D) She has missed her bus.

54. What is out of order?

(A) A car
(B) A computer
(C) An elevator
(D) A garage door

55. What has the woman requested?

(A) A menu
(B) A telephone
(C) A plate of fruit
(D) Something to drink

56. What is the woman looking for?

(A) A school
(B) A pharmacy
(C) The bus terminal
(D) The police station

57. What does the woman want to do?

(A) Get a credit card
(B) Interview for a job
(C) Enter a university
(D) Buy something expensive

58. Why does the man need a ride?

(A) His car is out of gas.
(B) His car has a flat tire.
(C) He has been in an accident.
(D) He locked his keys in his car.

59. What happened to Mary's father?

(A) He died.
(B) He took a trip.
(C) He was promoted.
(D) He lost his job.

60. With whom is the woman speaking?

(A) A friend
(B) A clerk
(C) A salesman
(D) A relative

GO ON TO THE NEXT PAGE

61. What business are the speakers in?

(A) Medicine
(B) Clothing
(C) Publishing
(D) Construction

62. What did the man want to do?

(A) Change his seat
(B) Take an earlier flight
(C) Exchange his airplane ticket
(D) Smoke on board the airplane

63. Where does this conversation take place?

(A) In a hotel lobby
(B) In an office
(C) In a restaurant
(D) In a furniture store

64. What has the doctor told the man he may do?

(A) Eat soft foods
(B) Work half-days
(C) Have more liquids
(D) Go out for exercise

65. What are the speakers discussing?

(A) A new market area
(B) An effort to cut costs
(C) A change in supervisors
(D) A successful new product

66. Where does this conversation take place?

(A) In a bank
(B) At a hotel
(C) On the telephone
(D) In a department store

67. Where will the men meet?

(A) In a restaurant
(B) At the theater
(C) At the office
(D) In an auditorium

68. What is the woman worried about?

(A) She lost a present.
(B) She must go out of town.
(C) She missed an important date.
(D) She forgot the date of a birthday.

69. What type of report has the woman prepared?

(A) Stock
(B) Weather
(C) Sales
(D) News

70. What is being discussed?

(A) A letter of complaint
(B) A payment that is due
(C) A purchase order
(D) A phone message

71. What accommodation can the hotel provide?

(A) Two single rooms
(B) Two double rooms
(C) One single room
(D) One double room

72. What has happened during the winter?

(A) Temperatures have been the lowest ever.
(B) Ice has broken water pipes.
(C) There has been a lot of snow.
(D) The woman's heater had to be replaced.

73. What did the woman receive?

(A) A pen
(B) Jewelry
(C) A plant
(D) A ceramic

74. What problem do the speakers have?

(A) A shipment has been lost.
(B) Five employees have resigned.
(C) They cannot find a qualified applicant.
(D) A shipment is late in going out.

75. Why does the man have to wait?

(A) The woman has to attend a meeting.
(B) The woman still has work she must do.
(C) The woman is looking for a lost file.
(D) The woman cannot leave for 15 or 20 minutes.

76. What happened in the lobby?

(A) Some guests arrived.
(B) An interview took place.
(C) A meeting was held.
(D) A bulletin was posted.

77. What job has Mrs. Wilson agreed to accept?

(A) Chair a committee
(B) Prepare a dinner
(C) Serve on the board
(D) Take notes at a meeting

78. What does the couple want to do?

(A) Buy a house
(B) Buy new furniture
(C) Sell their house
(D) Paint their house

79. What are the speakers looking for?

(A) Classroom space
(B) Study materials
(C) More trainees
(D) A teacher

80. What was the subject of the lecture?

(A) How to train supervisors
(B) A get-rich-quick scheme
(C) How to sell real estate
(D) Ways to enter the entertainment field

GO ON TO THE NEXT PAGE

Part IV

Directions: In this part of the test, you will hear several short talks. Each will be spoken just one time. They will not be printed in your test book, so you must listen carefully to understand and remember what is said.

In your test book you will read two or more questions about each short talk. The questions will be followed by four answers. You are to choose the best answer to each question and mark it on your answer sheet.

81. What sport is the announcer talking about?

(A) Soccer
(B) Tennis
(C) Baseball
(D) Basketball

82. When will the championship be determined?

(A) The next day
(B) The following Saturday
(C) The following Sunday
(D) Two weeks later

83. What television channel will report the game?

(A) Two
(B) Four
(C) Nine
(D) Eleven

84. What has flooded?

(A) A bridge
(B) An Expressway entrance
(C) An underpass
(D) A main intersection

85. Where are people being rerouted?

(A) Onto Third Avenue
(B) Onto the Expressway
(C) Onto Thirtieth Street
(D) Onto Oak Street

86. What position is Ms. Sindall running for?

(A) Chairperson
(B) Treasurer
(C) President
(D) Director

87. What has Ms. Sindall promised to do if elected?

(A) Organize fund-raising activities
(B) Construct a new headquarters building
(C) Hire additional staff
(D) Increase membership

88. When will the bus reach the Canadian border?

(A) It is about to arrive.
(B) In five miles.
(C) In a few hours.
(D) The next day.

89. Who are the passengers told they must see before entering Canada?

(A) National Police
(B) Immigration and Naturalization
(C) Canadian Border Patrol
(D) Customs

90. What will the bus do before crossing the border?

(A) Go over a bridge
(B) Go through a tunnel
(C) Pass through a toll booth
(D) Go down into a gorge

91. What have the passengers been told?

(A) That a flight has been canceled
(B) That a flight has been delayed
(C) To assemble after leaving the aircraft
(D) That the plane must make an emergency landing

92. What should passengers do who were booked on the WestSky flight to Seattle?

(A) Wait in the boarding area for further instructions
(B) See the WestSky attendant
(C) Go to baggage claim area 20
(D) Report to the WestSky ticket counter

93. What is about to take place at Scott Arena?

(A) A prize fight
(B) A bowling match
(C) A volleyball game
(D) A basketball game

94. What type of music is Beverly Hart known for?

(A) Opera
(B) Country
(C) Jazz
(D) Pop

95. What is Oatlands Plantation used for today?

(A) A museum
(B) A restaurant
(C) A farm
(D) A hotel

96. Who currently owns Oatlands Plantation?

(A) Mary Rebecca Kilton
(B) Matthew Friedlander
(C) Mary Fedders
(D) The Friedlander family

97. Who did Governor Friedlander want to inherit the plantation?

(A) The Fedders family
(B) The eldest son in the Friedlander family
(C) Any descendant with the name Friedlander
(D) The estate owner's eldest daughter

98. Who is making the announcement?

(A) The purser
(B) The captain
(C) A flight attendant
(D) The first officer

99. Why is the seat belt sign turned on?

(A) The plane is about to land.
(B) The plane is losing altitude.
(C) The plane is taking off.
(D) The plane is entering a storm.

100. Under what circumstances can a passenger leave the seat?

(A) To use the rest room
(B) Only when told to do so
(C) To get off the plane when parked
(D) To fasten a child's seat belt

This is the end of the Listening Comprehension portion of the test. Turn to Part V in your test book.

GO ON TO THE NEXT PAGE

YOU WILL HAVE ONE HOUR AND FIFTEEN MINUTES TO COMPLETE PARTS V, VI, AND VII OF THE TEST.

READING

In this section of the test, you will have a chance to show how well you understand written English. There are three parts to this section, with special directions for each part.

Part V

Directions: Questions 101–140 are incomplete sentences. Four words or phrases, marked (A), (B), (C), (D), are given beneath each sentence. You are to choose the one word or phrase that best completes the sentence. Then, on your answer sheet, find the number of the question and mark your answer.

Example

Because the equipment is very delicate, it must be handled with ———.

(A) caring
(B) careful
(C) care
(D) carefully

Sample Answer

Ⓐ Ⓑ ● Ⓓ

The sentence should read, "Because the equipment is very delicate, it must be handled with care." Therefore, you should choose answer (C).

As soon as you understand the directions, begin work on the questions.

101. Throughout the tour, the ——— provided the group with technical information on the facility's operation.

(A) act
(B) steer
(C) point
(D) guide

102. All laboratory visitors were asked to ——— protective eye cover.

(A) wash
(B) hold
(C) wear
(D) look

103. Doctors work for many years to establish ——— practice.

(A) some
(B) their
(C) another
(D) general

104. A meeting was held to ——— the effects of chemical waste disposal on the local environment.

(A) dissuade
(B) distract
(C) discuss
(D) dispute

105. The house was built on a ——— of concrete.

(A) foundation
(B) position
(C) company
(D) support

106. The phones were ——— after the office went out of business.

(A) discontinued
(B) disconnected
(C) disembarked
(D) dislocated

107. ——— the economy was in a recession, the family business was still making money.

(A) Nevertheless
(B) Therefore
(C) Although
(D) However

108. The secretary neglected to ——— the letter before sending it.

(A) seal
(B) smell
(C) steal
(D) scale

109. Before television was introduced, people ——— their idle time listening to the radio.

(A) spent
(B) held
(C) often
(D) sitting

110. It is not easy to find a vacation place that is interesting and is still ———.

(A) visited
(B) uncrowded
(C) unreasonable
(D) unrestrained

111. After completing her event, the gymnast ——— told she had won a medal.

(A) is
(B) was
(C) are
(D) were

112. The customer ——— a credit card to purchase the appliance.

(A) used
(B) made
(C) have
(D) give

113. A topographical map ——— elevations of bodies of water and landmasses.

(A) stays
(B) draws
(C) shows
(D) finds

114. The new equipment was so ——— that staff referred regularly to the instruction manual.

(A) educated
(B) saturated
(C) excavated
(D) complicated

GO ON TO THE NEXT PAGE

115. All departments are expected to submit a ——— budget.

(A) even
(B) time
(C) costly
(D) balanced

116. The report is a mass of inconsistencies, which leaves the reader very ———.

(A) confused
(B) refused
(C) amused
(D) reused

117. A storm on the mountain ——— ski resort management to close the facility.

(A) making
(B) having
(C) forced
(D) snowed

118. Water cannot run ———.

(A) at all
(B) uphill
(C) into
(D) around

119. Young people have always been willing to leave a comfortable home to seek ——— elsewhere.

(A) away
(B) wealthy
(C) opportunity
(D) adventuresome

120. The group ——— to go out for pizza after the movie.

(A) agreed
(B) insisted
(C) discussed
(D) suggested

121. The judge ——— his glasses before putting them on.

(A) drank
(B) folded
(C) cleaned
(D) broke

122. The man fired his subordinate with no ———.

(A) relation
(B) agitation
(C) reputation
(D) hesitation

123. Computer networks are ——— common in businesses.

(A) being
(B) becoming
(C) beginning
(D) believing

124. Good records are necessary for the ——— of any enterprise.

(A) surpassing
(B) surcharge
(C) surrender
(D) survival

125. The photocopier was not capable of ——— pages into separate stacks.

(A) having
(B) sorting
(C) turning
(D) molding

126. The main processing unit was faulty, which caused the ——— system to be out of service.

(A) hole
(B) enter
(C) single
(D) entire

127. Doing business in a foreign country can ——— be very difficult.

(A) many
(B) often
(C) usual
(D) nearly

128. The post office is ——— the corner.

(A) in
(B) over
(C) upon
(D) around

129. The woman's hands had become ———, due to a severe case of arthritis.

(A) designed
(B) deformed
(C) detailed
(D) detached

130. There were several ——— of the story, none of which was true.

(A) verses
(B) verdicts
(C) versions
(D) verticals

131. It ——— most of the day to finish the exam.

(A) was
(B) has
(C) took
(D) needs

132. The girl did not ——— anything like her pictures.

(A) see
(B) look
(C) dresses
(D) appeared

133. The candidate delivered his speech ——— thousands of cheering voters.

(A) above
(B) during
(C) before
(D) about

134. The parties ——— a way out of the impasse.

(A) work
(B) sought
(C) played
(D) enjoyed

GO ON TO THE NEXT PAGE

135. Their policy was ——— all inquiries the same day.

(A) to tell
(B) talking about
(C) called upon
(D) to reply to

136. A ——— was imposed to stop looting.

(A) curfew
(B) meeting
(C) closing
(D) decision

137. Some angry residents threatened to ——— the reappointment of the apartment manager.

(A) proceed
(B) provide
(C) protect
(D) protest

138. The sample product was distributed widely ——— two provincial cities.

(A) in
(B) on
(C) to
(D) at

139. Libraries are a good ——— for hard-to-find information.

(A) place
(B) house
(C) source
(D) opportunity

140. After the storm, the fields were covered with snow, and the roads were ———.

(A) immovable
(B) impossible
(C) impassable
(D) implausible

Part VI

Directions: In Questions 141–160 each sentence has four words or phrases underlined. The four underlined parts of the sentence are marked (A), (B), (C), (D). You are to identify the one underlined word or phrase that should be corrected or rewritten. Then, on your answer sheet, find the number of the question and mark your answer.

Example

All employee (A) are required to wear (B) their identification (C) badges while (D) at work.

Sample Answer

● Ⓑ Ⓒ Ⓓ

Choice (A), the underlined word "employee," is not correct in this sentence. This sentence should read, "All employees are required to wear their identification badges while at work." Therefore, you should choose answer (A).

As soon as you understand the directions, begin work on the questions.

141. Because (A) her watch had stopped (B) and she did not (C) know the time, the woman was late for she (D) interview.

142. The proposed (A) legislation would liberalized (B) voter registration and aid (C) the opposition party in the next general (D) election.

143. A budget are (A) a guide that (B) helps businesses and individuals monitor (C) income and expenses (D).

144. The rowing team practices (A) daily (B) on the river, even because (C) the weather is (D) cold and rainy.

145. The light (A) bulb was burnt (B) up (C) so the lamp could (D) not be used.

146. The office manager (A) gives (B) a presentation, requiring (C) that the staff meeting be postponed (D).

GO ON TO THE NEXT PAGE

147. Registration of the certificates was
A
mandatory, but nothing in the law

said that the owner's real name
B C
being used.
D

148. Although the industry is only

a few year old, international air cargo
A
companies today compete for their share
B C
of a very large and growing shipping
D
market.

149. The hostess greeted her guests on the
A B
door, then showed them to the dinner
C D
buffet.

150. Under new management, the business
A B
undergo a complete reorganization.
C D

151. Spring came early this year and stayed
A
late, makes it risky for farmers to plant
B C D
crops with a long growing season.

152. The company expects to have greater
A B
employee turning over in the
C
coming months.
D

153. Texas is a state in the southcentral

United States that is known for it
A B C
colorful early history as an independent
D
territory.

154. The suspension bridge was
A B
in desperation need of repair.
C D

155. Computer programs are now being
A
developed that are said to be
B C
used-friendly.
D

156. Because of an early snowstorm, the
A
forests wildlife searched frantically
B C D
for food.

157. Part-time employees should discuss every changes (A) in (B) work schedules with Mr. J. Smythe, who (C) can be reached (D) on extension 310.

158. The local residence (A) were (B) busy preparing (C) for the town's (D) annual festival.

159. Except (A) for Sundays, (B) the store is open (C) for business everyday. (D)

160. The computer hardware was (A) never (B) functioned (C) properly. (D)

GO ON TO THE NEXT PAGE

Part VII

Directions: Questions 161–200 are based on a variety of reading material (for example, announcements, paragraphs, advertisements, and the like). You are to choose the one best answer, (A), (B), (C), or (D), to each question. Then, on your answer sheet, find the number of the question and mark your answer. Answer all questions following a passage on the basis of what is stated or implied in that passage.

Read the following example.

> The Museum of Technology is a "hands-on" museum, designed for people to experience science at work. Visitors are encouraged to use, test, and handle the objects on display. Special demonstrations are scheduled for the first and second Wednesdays of each month at 1:30 P.M. Open Tuesday–Friday, 2:30–4:30 P.M., Saturday 11:00 A.M.–4:30 P.M., and Sunday 1:00–4:30 P.M.
>
> When during the month can visitors see special demonstrations?
>
> (A) Every weekend
> (B) The first two Wednesdays
> (C) One afternoon a week
> (D) Every other Wednesday

Sample Answer

Ⓐ ● Ⓒ Ⓓ

The passage says that the demonstrations are scheduled for the first and second Wednesdays of the month. Therefore, you should choose answer (B).

As soon as you understand the directions, begin work on the questions.

Questions 161–163 refer to the following newspaper report.

Weather: Saturday, January 12

Today : Cloudy, afternoon flurries.
High 46. Low 30. Wind 8–16 mph.
Sunday : Partly sunny, windy, cold.
High 44. Low 29. Wind 15–30 mph.
Monday: Temp. range 28–41. Wind 10 mph.
Tuesday: Temp. range 27–40. Snow possible.

Details on page B2.

161. Of the days reported, for which day is the highest temperature expected?

(A) Saturday
(B) Sunday
(C) Monday
(D) Tuesday

162. What will the temperature be for the days reported?

(A) Temperatures will drop fast.
(B) Temperatures will gradually go down.
(C) Temperatures will remain stable.
(D) Temperatures will warm slightly.

163. What should the reader do for more information on the weather?

(A) Telephone the newspaper
(B) Listen to the weather report on radio
(C) Watch the weather report on television
(D) Look elsewhere in the newspaper

Questions 164–166 refer to the following announcement.

FIRST NATIONAL ANNOUNCES EMPLOYEES OF THE MONTH

Customer Service Representatives (CSRs) in our First National Bank community are usually so busy they don't have an opportunity to work beyond their immediate assignments. So it's especially noteworthy when not just one but two CSRs are recognized for their contribution of exceptional service.

Carol Gretch and Joni Katchuk are both CSRs at the First National downtown branch. When only a part-time employee, Carol identified an error in the system regarding notification of late mortgage payments and took the initiative to resolve it, avoiding delays in issuing notices that could have resulted in substantial late fees to customers.

Joni was recognized for her mastery of information on on-line bank programs and her prompt and courteous customer service.

Congratulations to Carol and Joni on their efforts!

164. In what activity are the women involved?

(A) Retailing
(B) Banking
(C) Real Estate
(D) Public relations

165. For what were the two women recognized?

(A) Secretarial skills
(B) Sales ability
(C) High test scores
(D) Exceptional service

166. According to the announcement, what is special about Carol?

(A) She works only part time.
(B) She has worked in the same office for 25 years.
(C) She has received the honor twice before.
(D) She is the mother of two.

Questions 167–169 refer to the following advertisement.

> **For Sale:** 1993 two-door hatchback. Good condition. Check this one. Runs smoothly, four new tires, brakes, shocks, and exhaust. Needs minor work on fenders and door panels, paint. Reliable transportation for student or as second car. Asking $2000 or best cash offer. Call Joe, 738-9990 days.

167. According to the advertisement, what part of the car needs repair?

    (A) The exhaust system
    (B) The engine
    (C) The body
    (D) The brakes

168. What form of payment does the seller want?

    (A) Cash
    (B) Personal check
    (C) Money order
    (D) Bank check

169. To whom will the seller sell the car?

    (A) To the person who makes the first offer
    (B) To the person who first offers $200
    (C) To the person who makes the highest offer
    (D) To the person who makes the last offer

GO ON TO THE NEXT PAGE

Questions 170–172 refer to the following announcement.

MOVIES AT THE BIJOU

Out of the Darkness (1985). Drama. Martin Sheen, Hector Elizondo. Monday, 6:00 P.M.

Paris Blues (1961). Drama. Paul Newman, Joanne Woodward. Tuesday, 8:00 P.M.

Phantom Valley (1948). Western. Charles Starrett, Smiley Burnette. Wednesday, 6:00 P.M.

Queen's Logic (1990). Comedy. Christian Slater, Samantha Mathis. Monday through Wednesday, 3:00 P.M.

170. How many movies can be seen on each of the days advertised?

(A) One
(B) Two
(C) Three
(D) Four

171. Which movie is the oldest?

(A) *Out of the Darkness*
(B) *Paris Blues*
(C) *Phantom Valley*
(D) *Queen's Logic*

172. Which two movies are the same type?

(A) *Out of the Darkness* and *Phantom Valley*
(B) *Queen's Logic* and *Paris Blues*
(C) *Queen's Logic* and *Phantom Valley*
(D) *Out of the Darkness* and *Paris Blues*

Questions 173–175 refer to the following letter.

D.M. Frames Co.
P.O. Box 773
Campbell, Idaho
Tel: (718) 546-3355 Fax: (718) 546-3390

Mr. F.A. Marley
Optical Specialties, Inc.
Box 1072
Seattle, WA

Dear Mr. Marley:

Thank you for sending me a copy of your latest eyeglass catalog. I am interested in an eyeglass frame with a strong copper core. According to the catalog, models in your 450 series are made of copper. Before I place an order, however, I would like the exact specifications on weight, size, and color for frames in this series.

There is some urgency to this order, and I would appreciate receiving the information by fax. Upon receipt, I will contact you with any additional questions I may have.

I look forward to hearing from you.

Sincerely,

D.M. Shin

173. What does the letter request?

(A) Additional information
(B) The latest catalog
(C) A pair of eyeglasses
(D) A replacement part

174. How is Mr. Marley asked to respond to the request?

(A) By overnight mail
(B) By telephone
(C) By facsimile transmission
(D) By telegraph

175. What should the eyeglass frames that Mr. Shin is looking for be like?

(A) Fashionable
(B) Inexpensive
(C) Lightweight
(D) Copper cored

GO ON TO THE NEXT PAGE

Questions 176–179 refer to the following advertisement.

From the Lillian Benton Catalog ...
$5 Off Solid Brass Exclusives!

Item H. Personalized Dice Paperweights—A sure bet for any executive or your favorite "high roller." Each gold-plated, solid brass 1 1/4" cube weighs a hefty 9 oz. Holds papers and organizes a crowded desk. Price includes custom engraving of up to three initials. Velour drawstring gift pouch. Was $17.98, now only $12.98. Use order #66754.

176. What is the sale price of a paperweight?

(A) $5.00
(B) $12.98
(C) $17.98
(D) $22.98

177. How can the paperweights be personalized?

(A) With a monogrammed velour pouch
(B) With a certificate of origin
(C) With stamped initials on a wooden box
(D) With custom engraving

178. How much does one paperweight weigh?

(A) 1.25 ounces
(B) 9 ounces
(C) 1.25 pounds
(D) 100 grams

179. What identification should be used when ordering the paperweights?

(A) #66754
(B) Item H
(C) The customer's initials
(D) The words "Brass paperweights"

Questions 180–183 refer to the following article.

Explosion Partially Destroys Factory

Albany: May 10. An explosion earlier this week caused extensive damage in the new multi-million dollar factory of Lisboa, Ltd., an Albany-based glass products manufacturer. There were no injuries. A preliminary investigation points to a faulty central heating system as responsible for the explosion that removed nearly half of the roof, leaving the rest of the facility intact.

The company that built and installed the heating unit, Beta AG of Austria, was contacted by Lisboa more than six weeks ago about strange noises coming from the unit. Lisboa received a reply, but Beta took no action. A Lisboa spokesman has said that Lisboa will take legal action against Beta AG, seeking total compensation for the loss.

Meanwhile, Lisboa is closing its doors until it can provide adequate working conditions for its employees. This will cost the company about $50,000 per day in lost production.

180. What is Lisboa's business?

(A) Textiles
(B) Explosives
(C) Glass products
(D) Building supplies

181. What do Lisboa's plans include?

(A) Filing for bankruptcy
(B) Moving operations to Albany
(C) Closing the plant for repairs
(D) Continuing with reduced production capacity

182. What is Beta AG?

(A) An industrial insurer
(B) A construction company
(C) A legal firm hired by Lisboa
(D) A manufacturer of heating systems

183. What part of Lisboa's facility was affected most by the explosion?

(A) The roof
(B) Corporate offices
(C) Production equipment
(D) The shipping department

GO ON TO THE NEXT PAGE

Questions 184–186 refer to the following memorandum.

Memorandum for: All Employees
cc: John Tower/President

From: Tom Perales/VP Personnel
Date: July 3, 19—

Once again this year, we will put in place for the month of August our summer short-week work schedule. As in the past, each Friday during the month of August, full-time on-site employees will be allowed to go home at 3:00 P.M., rather than the usual 5:00 P.M. Employees will be paid for the entire day. Regular employees who are ill or on vacation on any of the August Fridays, or who for some other reason are off-site, will not be able to take advantage of this benefit.

During this period, employees who are eligible for this benefit will mark their weekly time sheets as time-off-with-pay, or TOWP, for two hours each Friday. If time sheets are not properly marked, employees will not be paid for the time. If you have any questions concerning this matter, please contact your supervisor.

Enjoy your summer.

184. How many hours per week are affected by this policy?

(A) 2
(B) 3
(C) 5
(D) 10

185. Which of the following employees is affected by this policy?

(A) An employee who is on vacation
(B) A temporary employee
(C) A regular employee who will retire on August 15
(D) A part-time employee who has worked for the company for ten years

186. How may eligible employees take advantage of the policy?

(A) By submitting a request in writing
(B) By contacting the Personnel Department
(C) By getting permission from their supervisor
(D) By marking their time sheets appropriately

Questions 187–190 refer to the following report.

Quillim Corporation Quarterly Expenses

Second Quarter

Employee Name	APR	MAY	JUN	Qtr. Total
John	165.00	142.00	150.00	457.00
Bill	132.00	100.00	121.00	353.00
Gail	75.00	98.00	101.00	274.00
Linda	100.00	00.00	00.00	100.00
TOTAL	**$472.00**	**$340.00**	**$372.00**	**$1184.00**

Third Quarter

Employee Name	JUL	AUG	SEP	Qtr. Total
John	243.00	187.00	132.00	562.00
Bill	125.00	130.00	118.00	373.00
Gail	68.00	94.00	77.00	239.00
Linda	00.00	135.00	147.00	282.00
TOTAL	**$436.00**	**$546.00**	**$474.00**	**$1456.00**

187. Which Quillim employee had lower expenses in the third quarter than in the second quarter?

(A) John
(B) Bill
(C) Gail
(D) Linda

188. Which Quillim employee was either on leave or unable to work for a three-month period?

(A) John
(B) Bill
(C) Gail
(D) Linda

189. Which Quillim employee consistently averaged the lowest monthly expenses for the reporting period?

(A) John
(B) Bill
(C) Gail
(D) Linda

190. What was the highest reported total of company expenses for a single month?

(A) $243.00
(B) $546.00
(C) $562.00
(D) $1456.00

GO ON TO THE NEXT PAGE

Questions 191–192 refer to the following advertisement.

VACATIONS IN THAILAND

Buy into the world's premier vacation destination—Thailand. Take advantage of the booming Thai tourism market.

Experts predict a continuing global expansion of tourism through the decade, and emphasize Southeast Asia as the region that will experience the greatest development.

As large as our tourism market already is, this is only the beginning. There are plenty of opportunities for investment in beachfront development, in hotel and entertainment construction, and in sports facilities.

If you want to participate in the expanding Southeast Asia market, this is the future-oriented industry to invest in.

191. What does the advertisement urge people to do?

(A) Vacation in Thailand
(B) Promote Thai tourism
(C) Find work in the Thai hotel industry
(D) Invest in Thai tourism

192. What is the status of Thai tourism?

(A) It is a mature industry.
(B) It is in the development stage.
(C) It is dominated by international hotel chains.
(D) It is very popular with Europeans.

Questions 193–196 refer to the following letter.

Fiduciary Trust Mortgage Corporation
One Fiduciary Center
Buffalo, NY 12456

March 5, 19—

William K. Ponds
Kelly S. Ponds
2055 Dupont Sq.
Remont, DE 22901 Re: Loan No. 925239-1

Dear Mr. and Mrs. Ponds:

We are returning to you the enclosed hazard insurance documents. This is because you recently paid off your mortgage, which had been held by Fiduciary Trust. You are now responsible for all hazard insurance premiums on the property.

Please inform your insurance company, State Farm of America, to remove Fiduciary Trust Company as mortgagee. We thank you for your patronage.

Sincerely,

Felicia Mellerson
Hazard Insurance Section
Mortgage Loan Servicing Department

193. To whom is this letter written?

(A) Felicia Mellerson
(B) State Farm of America
(C) William and Kelly Ponds
(D) Fiduciary Trust Company

194. What documents are enclosed with the letter?

(A) Hazard insurance papers
(B) Certification of occupancy
(C) Mortgage payoff notice
(D) Mortgage loan application forms

195. Where is the Mortgage Loan Servicing Department located?

(A) Dupont Square
(B) New York City
(C) Remont, Delaware
(D) Fiduciary Center

196. What two requests does the letter make?

(A) That all future premiums be paid by the customer and that Fiduciary Trust be removed as mortgagee
(B) That the mortgage loan be paid in full and that the insurance company be notified
(C) That insurance on the property be filed for and that the mortgagee be notified
(D) That the hazard insurance on the property be canceled and that Fiduciary Trust be removed as mortgagee

Questions 197–200 refer to the following article.

> FRONT LINE. Tuesday at 8 P.M. on Public Television. Three years after the brutal 1993 suppression of the Dumar student pro-democracy movement, Dumar-watcher Irv Drasnin returned to find out what was happening. His report, based on five weeks of filming and interviewing, found a people in ferment, as the nation's aging leadership squares off against its youth—three-quarters of the nation's university-educated population are under 35 years of age. "There is a growing gap between rhetoric and reality," says Drasnin. Watch this week to learn more.

197. What is the name of the program that will be aired?

  (A) The Pro-democracy Movement
  (B) Front Line
  (C) Dumar Watch
  (D) This Week

198. When was the show filmed?

  (A) 1990
  (B) 1993
  (C) 1995
  (D) 1996

199. According to the article, what percentage of Dumar's university-educated population is OVER 35 years of age?

  (A) 10%
  (B) 25%
  (C) 35%
  (D) 75%

200. What is the show about?

  (A) Dumar's educated elite
  (B) A student uprising
  (C) Dumar's political situation
  (D) Investment opportunities in a new Dumar

Stop! This is the end of the test. If you finish before time is called, you can go back to Parts V, VI, and VII and check your work.

Answer Sheet—TOEIC® Practice Test

Listening (Parts I–IV)

1. Ⓐ Ⓑ Ⓒ Ⓓ
2. Ⓐ Ⓑ Ⓒ Ⓓ
3. Ⓐ Ⓑ Ⓒ Ⓓ
4. Ⓐ Ⓑ Ⓒ Ⓓ
5. Ⓐ Ⓑ Ⓒ Ⓓ
6. Ⓐ Ⓑ Ⓒ Ⓓ
7. Ⓐ Ⓑ Ⓒ Ⓓ
8. Ⓐ Ⓑ Ⓒ Ⓓ
9. Ⓐ Ⓑ Ⓒ Ⓓ
10. Ⓐ Ⓑ Ⓒ Ⓓ
11. Ⓐ Ⓑ Ⓒ Ⓓ
12. Ⓐ Ⓑ Ⓒ Ⓓ
13. Ⓐ Ⓑ Ⓒ Ⓓ
14. Ⓐ Ⓑ Ⓒ Ⓓ
15. Ⓐ Ⓑ Ⓒ Ⓓ
16. Ⓐ Ⓑ Ⓒ Ⓓ
17. Ⓐ Ⓑ Ⓒ Ⓓ
18. Ⓐ Ⓑ Ⓒ Ⓓ
19. Ⓐ Ⓑ Ⓒ Ⓓ
20. Ⓐ Ⓑ Ⓒ Ⓓ
21. Ⓐ Ⓑ Ⓒ
22. Ⓐ Ⓑ Ⓒ
23. Ⓐ Ⓑ Ⓒ
24. Ⓐ Ⓑ Ⓒ
25. Ⓐ Ⓑ Ⓒ
26. Ⓐ Ⓑ Ⓒ
27. Ⓐ Ⓑ Ⓒ
28. Ⓐ Ⓑ Ⓒ
29. Ⓐ Ⓑ Ⓒ
30. Ⓐ Ⓑ Ⓒ
31. Ⓐ Ⓑ Ⓒ
32. Ⓐ Ⓑ Ⓒ
33. Ⓐ Ⓑ Ⓒ
34. Ⓐ Ⓑ Ⓒ
35. Ⓐ Ⓑ Ⓒ
36. Ⓐ Ⓑ Ⓒ
37. Ⓐ Ⓑ Ⓒ
38. Ⓐ Ⓑ Ⓒ
39. Ⓐ Ⓑ Ⓒ
40. Ⓐ Ⓑ Ⓒ
41. Ⓐ Ⓑ Ⓒ
42. Ⓐ Ⓑ Ⓒ
43. Ⓐ Ⓑ Ⓒ
44. Ⓐ Ⓑ Ⓒ
45. Ⓐ Ⓑ Ⓒ
46. Ⓐ Ⓑ Ⓒ
47. Ⓐ Ⓑ Ⓒ
48. Ⓐ Ⓑ Ⓒ
49. Ⓐ Ⓑ Ⓒ
50. Ⓐ Ⓑ Ⓒ
51. Ⓐ Ⓑ Ⓒ Ⓓ
52. Ⓐ Ⓑ Ⓒ Ⓓ
53. Ⓐ Ⓑ Ⓒ Ⓓ
54. Ⓐ Ⓑ Ⓒ Ⓓ
55. Ⓐ Ⓑ Ⓒ Ⓓ
56. Ⓐ Ⓑ Ⓒ Ⓓ
57. Ⓐ Ⓑ Ⓒ Ⓓ
58. Ⓐ Ⓑ Ⓒ Ⓓ
59. Ⓐ Ⓑ Ⓒ Ⓓ
60. Ⓐ Ⓑ Ⓒ Ⓓ
61. Ⓐ Ⓑ Ⓒ Ⓓ
62. Ⓐ Ⓑ Ⓒ Ⓓ
63. Ⓐ Ⓑ Ⓒ Ⓓ
64. Ⓐ Ⓑ Ⓒ Ⓓ
65. Ⓐ Ⓑ Ⓒ Ⓓ
66. Ⓐ Ⓑ Ⓒ Ⓓ
67. Ⓐ Ⓑ Ⓒ Ⓓ
68. Ⓐ Ⓑ Ⓒ Ⓓ
69. Ⓐ Ⓑ Ⓒ Ⓓ
70. Ⓐ Ⓑ Ⓒ Ⓓ
71. Ⓐ Ⓑ Ⓒ Ⓓ
72. Ⓐ Ⓑ Ⓒ Ⓓ
73. Ⓐ Ⓑ Ⓒ Ⓓ
74. Ⓐ Ⓑ Ⓒ Ⓓ
75. Ⓐ Ⓑ Ⓒ Ⓓ
76. Ⓐ Ⓑ Ⓒ Ⓓ
77. Ⓐ Ⓑ Ⓒ Ⓓ
78. Ⓐ Ⓑ Ⓒ Ⓓ
79. Ⓐ Ⓑ Ⓒ Ⓓ
80. Ⓐ Ⓑ Ⓒ Ⓓ
81. Ⓐ Ⓑ Ⓒ Ⓓ
82. Ⓐ Ⓑ Ⓒ Ⓓ
83. Ⓐ Ⓑ Ⓒ Ⓓ
84. Ⓐ Ⓑ Ⓒ Ⓓ
85. Ⓐ Ⓑ Ⓒ Ⓓ
86. Ⓐ Ⓑ Ⓒ Ⓓ
87. Ⓐ Ⓑ Ⓒ Ⓓ
88. Ⓐ Ⓑ Ⓒ Ⓓ
89. Ⓐ Ⓑ Ⓒ Ⓓ
90. Ⓐ Ⓑ Ⓒ Ⓓ
91. Ⓐ Ⓑ Ⓒ Ⓓ
92. Ⓐ Ⓑ Ⓒ Ⓓ
93. Ⓐ Ⓑ Ⓒ Ⓓ
94. Ⓐ Ⓑ Ⓒ Ⓓ
95. Ⓐ Ⓑ Ⓒ Ⓓ
96. Ⓐ Ⓑ Ⓒ Ⓓ
97. Ⓐ Ⓑ Ⓒ Ⓓ
98. Ⓐ Ⓑ Ⓒ Ⓓ
99. Ⓐ Ⓑ Ⓒ Ⓓ
100. Ⓐ Ⓑ Ⓒ Ⓓ

Reading (Parts V–VII)

101. Ⓐ Ⓑ Ⓒ Ⓓ
102. Ⓐ Ⓑ Ⓒ Ⓓ
103. Ⓐ Ⓑ Ⓒ Ⓓ
104. Ⓐ Ⓑ Ⓒ Ⓓ
105. Ⓐ Ⓑ Ⓒ Ⓓ
106. Ⓐ Ⓑ Ⓒ Ⓓ
107. Ⓐ Ⓑ Ⓒ Ⓓ
108. Ⓐ Ⓑ Ⓒ Ⓓ
109. Ⓐ Ⓑ Ⓒ Ⓓ
110. Ⓐ Ⓑ Ⓒ Ⓓ
111. Ⓐ Ⓑ Ⓒ Ⓓ
112. Ⓐ Ⓑ Ⓒ Ⓓ
113. Ⓐ Ⓑ Ⓒ Ⓓ
114. Ⓐ Ⓑ Ⓒ Ⓓ
115. Ⓐ Ⓑ Ⓒ Ⓓ
116. Ⓐ Ⓑ Ⓒ Ⓓ
117. Ⓐ Ⓑ Ⓒ Ⓓ
118. Ⓐ Ⓑ Ⓒ Ⓓ
119. Ⓐ Ⓑ Ⓒ Ⓓ
120. Ⓐ Ⓑ Ⓒ Ⓓ
121. Ⓐ Ⓑ Ⓒ Ⓓ
122. Ⓐ Ⓑ Ⓒ Ⓓ
123. Ⓐ Ⓑ Ⓒ Ⓓ
124. Ⓐ Ⓑ Ⓒ Ⓓ
125. Ⓐ Ⓑ Ⓒ Ⓓ
126. Ⓐ Ⓑ Ⓒ Ⓓ
127. Ⓐ Ⓑ Ⓒ Ⓓ
128. Ⓐ Ⓑ Ⓒ Ⓓ
129. Ⓐ Ⓑ Ⓒ Ⓓ
130. Ⓐ Ⓑ Ⓒ Ⓓ
131. Ⓐ Ⓑ Ⓒ Ⓓ
132. Ⓐ Ⓑ Ⓒ Ⓓ
133. Ⓐ Ⓑ Ⓒ Ⓓ
134. Ⓐ Ⓑ Ⓒ Ⓓ
135. Ⓐ Ⓑ Ⓒ Ⓓ
136. Ⓐ Ⓑ Ⓒ Ⓓ
137. Ⓐ Ⓑ Ⓒ Ⓓ
138. Ⓐ Ⓑ Ⓒ Ⓓ
139. Ⓐ Ⓑ Ⓒ Ⓓ
140. Ⓐ Ⓑ Ⓒ Ⓓ
141. Ⓐ Ⓑ Ⓒ Ⓓ
142. Ⓐ Ⓑ Ⓒ Ⓓ
143. Ⓐ Ⓑ Ⓒ Ⓓ
144. Ⓐ Ⓑ Ⓒ Ⓓ
145. Ⓐ Ⓑ Ⓒ Ⓓ
146. Ⓐ Ⓑ Ⓒ Ⓓ
147. Ⓐ Ⓑ Ⓒ Ⓓ
148. Ⓐ Ⓑ Ⓒ Ⓓ
149. Ⓐ Ⓑ Ⓒ Ⓓ
150. Ⓐ Ⓑ Ⓒ Ⓓ
151. Ⓐ Ⓑ Ⓒ Ⓓ
152. Ⓐ Ⓑ Ⓒ Ⓓ
153. Ⓐ Ⓑ Ⓒ Ⓓ
154. Ⓐ Ⓑ Ⓒ Ⓓ
155. Ⓐ Ⓑ Ⓒ Ⓓ
156. Ⓐ Ⓑ Ⓒ Ⓓ
157. Ⓐ Ⓑ Ⓒ Ⓓ
158. Ⓐ Ⓑ Ⓒ Ⓓ
159. Ⓐ Ⓑ Ⓒ Ⓓ
160. Ⓐ Ⓑ Ⓒ Ⓓ
161. Ⓐ Ⓑ Ⓒ Ⓓ
162. Ⓐ Ⓑ Ⓒ Ⓓ
163. Ⓐ Ⓑ Ⓒ Ⓓ
164. Ⓐ Ⓑ Ⓒ Ⓓ
165. Ⓐ Ⓑ Ⓒ Ⓓ
166. Ⓐ Ⓑ Ⓒ Ⓓ
167. Ⓐ Ⓑ Ⓒ Ⓓ
168. Ⓐ Ⓑ Ⓒ Ⓓ
169. Ⓐ Ⓑ Ⓒ Ⓓ
170. Ⓐ Ⓑ Ⓒ Ⓓ
171. Ⓐ Ⓑ Ⓒ Ⓓ
172. Ⓐ Ⓑ Ⓒ Ⓓ
173. Ⓐ Ⓑ Ⓒ Ⓓ
174. Ⓐ Ⓑ Ⓒ Ⓓ
175. Ⓐ Ⓑ Ⓒ Ⓓ
176. Ⓐ Ⓑ Ⓒ Ⓓ
177. Ⓐ Ⓑ Ⓒ Ⓓ
178. Ⓐ Ⓑ Ⓒ Ⓓ
179. Ⓐ Ⓑ Ⓒ Ⓓ
180. Ⓐ Ⓑ Ⓒ Ⓓ
181. Ⓐ Ⓑ Ⓒ Ⓓ
182. Ⓐ Ⓑ Ⓒ Ⓓ
183. Ⓐ Ⓑ Ⓒ Ⓓ
184. Ⓐ Ⓑ Ⓒ Ⓓ
185. Ⓐ Ⓑ Ⓒ Ⓓ
186. Ⓐ Ⓑ Ⓒ Ⓓ
187. Ⓐ Ⓑ Ⓒ Ⓓ
188. Ⓐ Ⓑ Ⓒ Ⓓ
189. Ⓐ Ⓑ Ⓒ Ⓓ
190. Ⓐ Ⓑ Ⓒ Ⓓ
191. Ⓐ Ⓑ Ⓒ Ⓓ
192. Ⓐ Ⓑ Ⓒ Ⓓ
193. Ⓐ Ⓑ Ⓒ Ⓓ
194. Ⓐ Ⓑ Ⓒ Ⓓ
195. Ⓐ Ⓑ Ⓒ Ⓓ
196. Ⓐ Ⓑ Ⓒ Ⓓ
197. Ⓐ Ⓑ Ⓒ Ⓓ
198. Ⓐ Ⓑ Ⓒ Ⓓ
199. Ⓐ Ⓑ Ⓒ Ⓓ
200. Ⓐ Ⓑ Ⓒ Ⓓ

PRACTICE TEST—SCRIPT

In this section of the test, you will have the chance to show how well you understand spoken English. There are four parts to this section, with special directions for each part.

Part I

Directions: For each question, you will see a picture in your test book and you will hear four short statements. The statements will be spoken just one time. They will not be printed in your test book, so you must listen carefully to understand what the speaker says.

When you hear the four statements, look at the picture in your test book and choose the statement that best describes what you see in the picture. Then, on your answer sheet, find the number of the question and mark your answer. Look at the sample below.

Now listen to the four statements.

(Woman)
(A) They're looking out the window.
(B) They're having a meeting.
(C) They're eating in a restaurant.
(D) They're moving the furniture.

Statement (B), "They're having a meeting," best describes what you see in the picture. Therefore, you should choose answer (B).

Now let us begin Part I with question number 1.

1. (Man B)
(A) The boat is far from land.
(B) The boat is being turned over.
(C) The boat is on a lake.
(D) The boat is chained to a tree.

2. (Woman)
(A) The fence needs to be repaired.
(B) The gates are being closed.
(C) The fence is made of wood.
(D) The gates open to the woods.

3. (Man B)
(A) The bride has gone outside.
(B) The bird is standing on a rock.
(C) The boards are against the wall.
(D) The birds are flying out to sea.

4. (Woman)
(A) The car is going through water.
(B) The driver is late.
(C) The road goes through the trees.
(D) The trees are in the way.

5. (Man B)
(A) The woman is washing the window.
(B) The woman is rocking a cradle.
(C) The woman is setting the table.
(D) The woman is giving a speech.

6. (Man B)
(A) Three people are in a race.
(B) People are eating on the lawn.
(C) The woman has parked on the lawn.
(D) Food is being served on the grass.

7. (Woman)
(A) The boy is running in the sand.
(B) The boys are playing on the beach.
(C) The boy is not happy.
(D) The boys are talking to one another.

8. (Man B)
(A) People are about to go up on the stage.
(B) People are about to leave the stage.
(C) People are sitting in rows to watch.
(D) People are watching an outdoor performance.

9. (Woman)
(A) The boys have been sent away.
(B) Children are sitting on the lawn.
(C) The children left the park.
(D) The players are having a meeting.

10. (Woman)
(A) The audience is listening to an after-dinner speaker.
(B) Dinner is being served.
(C) The speaker is eating his dinner.
(D) People are standing to applaud the speaker.

11. (Woman)
(A) It's fifteen to ten.
(B) It's five to five.
(C) It's fifteen after eleven.
(D) It's a quarter to one.

12. (Man B)
(A) The worker is sweeping the floor.
(B) The tree is in bloom.
(C) The man is working on the roof.
(D) The man is sleeping on the floor.

13. (Man B)
(A) People are counting the stock.
(B) The women are talking at the counter.
(C) The woman is counting the snacks.
(D) The people are all standing around.

14. (Man B)
(A) The man is leaning on the wall.
(B) The man is standing in water.
(C) The man has fallen in the water.
(D) The man is getting a drink.

15. (Woman)
(A) The man is looking at his golf club.
(B) The men are waiting to go golfing.
(C) The man is about to hit the ball.
(D) The men are on the golf course.

16. (Man B)
(A) The gardeners are standing in the park.
(B) The men are adding flour to the mix.
(C) The workers are planting the flower bed.
(D) The men are walking on the flowers.

17. (Man B)
(A) The car has been left along the road.
(B) The car is about to make a stop.
(C) The car is about to have an accident.
(D) The car has run into the tree.

18. (Woman)
(A) The heavy trunk is being taken off the truck.
(B) The truck has backed over the box.
(C) The man is sitting on the trunk.
(D) The boxes are ready to be put on the truck.

19. (Woman)
(A) The man is holding up the car.
(B) The man is getting out of the car.
(C) The man is looking in the car window.
(D) The man is rolling up the car window.

20. (Man B)
(A) The cars have run into each other.
(B) The man is reaching into the car.
(C) The boy is getting into the car.
(D) The man is opening the car door.

Part II

Directions: In this part of the test you will hear a question spoken in English, followed by three responses, also spoken in English. The question and the responses will be spoken just one time. They will not be printed in your test book, so you must listen carefully to understand what the speakers say. You are to choose the best response to each question.

Now listen to a sample question:

You will hear:	(Woman)	Good morning, John. How are you?
You will also hear:	(Man B)	(A) I am fine, thank you. (B) I am in the living room. (C) My name is John.

The best response to the question "How are you?" is choice (A) "I am fine, thank you." Therefore, you should choose answer (A).

Now let us begin Part II with question number 21.

21. (Man A) Where're you going?
    (Man B)
    (A) I like to dance.
    (B) I'm going to the store.
    (C) I'm at the bank.

22. (Man B) When is the next council meeting?
    (Man A)
    (A) In the main conference room.
    (B) At the president's home.
    (C) On Monday, July twelfth.

23. (Man A) What time do you plan to arrive?
    (Woman)
    (A) No, I really don't.
    (B) I should be there by eight.
    (C) I delivered the plans yesterday.

24. (Man A) How long will your marketing presentation last?
    (Man B)
    (A) About forty-five minutes.
    (B) Environmental issues.
    (C) In the auditorium.

25. (Man A) Are you ready to leave?
    (Woman)
    (A) No, it's too big to carry.
    (B) Yes, let's go.
    (C) Yes, I've already been there.

26. (Man B) Is it time to go to lunch yet?
(Woman) (A) I think he just arrived.
(B) It was held at the new restaurant.
(C) No, it's only eleven o'clock.

27. (Man B) May I use your computer tomorrow to print out my report?
(Woman) (A) Sure, I'll be out of the office all morning and won't be needing it.
(B) Here, let me get the number for you.
(C) It's scheduled for early tomorrow morning.

28. (Man B) What would you like to drink?
(Man A) (A) Yes, it's hot.
(B) Just a glass of water, please.
(C) I take two spoonfuls of sugar.

29. (Woman) Can you read this letter and tell me if you think it sounds o.k.?
(Man B) (A) Sure, I'd be glad to look at it.
(B) I'll take it on the other phone, if it's all right with you.
(C) Here, let me carry that.

30. (Woman) Would you like something to drink?
(Man B) (A) Could I have three copies?
(B) Yes, I need a pair of work gloves.
(C) No, thank you. I'm about to leave.

31. (Man A) Where's the staff meeting going to be held?
(Man B) (A) In Conference Room C.
(B) At one o'clock this afternoon.
(C) In just a few minutes.

32. (Man B) I don't know what's wrong with my car; it stopped and refuses to start.
(Man A) (A) Have you checked the fuel gauge?
(B) You shouldn't refuse until you're sure.
(C) Perhaps you should look it up in the dictionary.

33. (Man B) Will you be traveling first class?
(Woman) (A) No, my ticket's for business class.
(B) No, I'm on my way to Europe first.
(C) Even so, I wouldn't like to fly.

34. (Man A) Do you have an extra floppy disk I can use?
(Woman) (A) I don't have time right now.
(B) I have some extras. Help yourself.
(C) No, my computer's down, and I can't do a thing.

35. (Man B) When did you last get a raise?
(Woman)
(A) In a month.
(B) At the shop, earlier today.
(C) It's been more than two years.

36. (Man B) What flight are you on?
(Woman)
(A) Four-eight-two, to Rome.
(B) I fly on a regular basis.
(C) Of course I'm afraid. Aren't you?

37. (Man A) Did your sister get that job she wanted at the bank?
(Woman)
(A) She's been working here for more than five years.
(B) She went to the Caribbean on her honeymoon.
(C) Yes, she started this week and really likes it.

38. (Man B) Why weren't you at the staff meeting this morning?
(Man A)
(A) I know. The whole office is expected.
(B) I was working on the Sintex bid.
(C) I've rescheduled it for 9:00 A.M., Monday.

39. (Woman) Do you have the phone number for the Accounting Department?
(Man B)
(A) No, I just came from there.
(B) Yes. I've already gone over my expenses.
(C) No, they're moving this week and can't be reached by phone.

40. (Man B) Will the zoo be open over the holiday?
(Man A)
(A) No. It's still closed for renovations.
(B) No, the exhibit isn't new.
(C) I don't plan to visit them anytime soon.

41. (Woman) I hear we finally put in a fax machine.
(Man B)
(A) Perhaps you should speak to the manager.
(B) Yes, it was connected this morning.
(C) I'm sorry if they make a lot of noise.

42. (Woman) I'd like to order some parts for my car.
(Man A)
(A) Give me the make and year, and a list of what you need.
(B) Would you like something to eat with that?
(C) Hold on. I'll see if they came in.

43. (Man B) Do you want to see this report before I distribute it?
(Man A)
(A) No, I don't have any.
(B) Yes, I'd like to go with you.
(C) Yes, I'd like to take a look at it.

44. (Man B) How many children do you have?
(Man A)
(A) Yes, I really like kids.
(B) One, and another on the way.
(C) Just the two of us.

45. (Man B) Are there any product brochures left?
(Woman)
(A) Let me see if she's still here.
(B) I'm sorry, we're all out.
(C) Yes, I'll be staying late.

46. (Woman) How are you feeling?
(Man B)
(A) That'll be fine, thank you.
(B) Yes, I would like to go.
(C) Much better, thanks. My cold seems to be clearing up.

47. (Man B) Charlie, what did you have to do to get the Niemann account?
(Man A)
(A) It's a new company with a lot of potential.
(B) I told them their image could benefit from a young firm with new ideas.
(C) They're always on time with their payments.

48. (Man A) Is there any news on his condition?
(Woman)
(A) I don't think we ought to do it.
(B) All right, but only if they make the changes.
(C) We haven't heard anything this morning.

49. (Man B) How is Ibsen Electric doing these days?
(Man A)
(A) They filed for bankruptcy recently.
(B) The Ibsen representative called to get some information.
(C) Yes, they did a very good job on it.

50. (Man A) Does your computer still work after that storm we had?
(Woman)
(A) No, I'm on break right now.
(B) Yes, it's an IBM-compatible.
(C) No, the lightning knocked it out.

Part III

Directions: In this part of the test, you will hear 30 short conversations between two people. The conversations will not be printed in your test book. You will hear the conversations only once, so you must listen carefully to understand what the speakers say.

In your test book you will read a question about each conversation. The question will be followed by four answers. You are to choose the best answer to each question and mark it on your answer sheet.

Now let us begin Part III with question number 51.

51. (Woman) I'd like tickets for the eight o'clock show.
(Man A) I'm sorry, we're sold out. Would you like to see the six o'clock show?
(Woman) Yes, if that's all that's available. I'll need two, please.

52. (Man B) Do you mind if I smoke?
(Man A) Yes, I really do.
(Man B) I'll just go outside then. Please excuse me for a few minutes.

53. (Woman) Excuse me, sir. Can you help me with my bicycle chain? I don't understand the problem.
(Man B) Yes ... uh ... A link seems to have broken. Unless you have a spare, you'll need to take it to a repair shop.
(Woman) I was afraid of that. I don't have one, so I guess I'll just have to be late for class.

54. (Man B) You'll have to take the stairs. The elevator isn't working.
(Man A) It was out yesterday, too. How long do you expect it to be down?
(Man B) Just one more day. Nobody is happy about having to climb the stairs, but we're doing the best we can.

55. (Woman) I'd like an iced tea with my meal.
(Man A) Would you like it with lemon and sugar?
(Woman) With lemon only, please.

56. (Woman) I'm supposed to pick up a prescription at National Drugs. Is it around here somewhere?
(Man B) Yes, it's just around the corner. You shouldn't miss it, but it's closed. I just came past it.
(Woman) Oh, no! I was supposed to pick up my son's medicine.

57. (Woman) I'd like to apply for a credit card. What do I have to do?
(Man B) Do you have any other credit cards, or have you ever applied for one?
(Woman) No. I've only just begun to work. I was a student before.

58. (Man B) I have a flat tire. Can you give me a lift?
(Man A) Sure. Where would you like to go?
(Man B) To the nearest service station.

59. (Woman) Did you hear about Mary's father?
(Man B) Yes. He passed away this morning.
(Woman) It's so sad. He was only fifty-two. The funeral is tomorrow.

60. (Woman) I need to buy a used car.
(Man B) Wonderful! Right now we have a very good deal on a nearly new four-door sedan. It has four new tires, radio, air conditioner, and a lot more.
(Woman) No, I was thinking of something a little less grand.

61. (Man B) Do you know whether this manuscript has been approved for publication?
(Man A) You'll have to check with John. He makes all the editorial decisions.
(Man B) I was afraid of that. John's out for a week and we need to go to press.

62. (Man B) I'd like three seats, please, in the smoking section.
(Woman) I'm sorry. This is a domestic flight, and no smoking is permitted.
(Man B) Oh, that's right. I'd like three seats together, if possible.

63. (Man A) Waiter, can you please show us to another table?
(Man B) Certainly. Is something wrong with this one?
(Man A) Yes. There's a draft coming from the front door, and we're cold.

64. (Man B) Doctor, it's been two weeks since my operation. Can I begin taking something other than liquids?
(Woman) Yes, I think it'd be o.k. if you have something bland, such as rice, boiled potatoes, or bean curd.
(Man B) Thanks, Doctor. I'm starving.

65. (Man A) They say that to contain costs, during the next year we'll be moving all of our international production to Malaysia.
(Woman) I haven't heard about it, but that would sure cut down on expenses.
(Man A) It's still just a rumor, but people seem to like the idea.

66. (Man B) I'd like to make a withdrawal from my savings account.
(Woman) Of course. May I have your confidential access number?
(Man B) Yes. It's 3-2-7-6.

67. (Man A) The awards ceremony starts in a few minutes. Let's go down and see where we're supposed to sit.
(Man B) I have one more idea I want to put in my speech. You go ahead. I'll catch up.
(Man A) I'll meet you on the stage, but hurry. We don't want to be late.

68.	(Woman)	Do you know when Mr. Evans' birthday is?
	(Man A)	Yes. It's coming up on the seventeenth.
	(Woman)	Oh, my! That's next Tuesday! Is anybody planning a party for him?
69.	(Woman)	Here are the sales figures you asked for.
	(Man A)	Are they for the month we just finished, or for last month?
	(Woman)	They're for both. In fact, they're for the last three months, and they cover all product lines.
70.	(Woman)	Did we pay on that invoice from Abercrombie?
	(Man A)	No. I need to check it, and I've been too busy.
	(Woman)	It's due tomorrow. Please see to it right away.
71.	(Man A)	I'd like two single rooms, please.
	(Man B)	I'm sorry. All we have left are double rooms, but I can give them to you for the same rate. Would that be o.k.?
	(Man A)	Of course. Thank you.
72.	(Man B)	We're having an awfully cold winter this year.
	(Woman)	I understand you are. I hear that record lows have been set almost twenty times.
	(Man B)	That sounds about right. I don't remember anything like it.
73.	(Woman)	Thank you for the lovely flowering cactus you sent me for my birthday.
	(Man A)	You're welcome. I thought you'd like it, and it doesn't need watering.
	(Woman)	Oh, I do like it, and it so brightens my desk.
74.	(Woman)	Has anybody applied for the open position in the Shipping Department?
	(Man B)	Yes. We've had five people apply, but no one who has experience in shipping, and we need an experienced person.
	(Woman)	Let's run some more ads. Emphasize the need for experience and the company benefits.
75.	(Man B)	Are you ready to go yet?
	(Woman)	No. I have to sign these checks before I can leave. There're fifteen or twenty of them.
	(Man B)	I'll wait. I have plenty of time.
76.	(Man B)	Where did they post the notice about the new lunch hours?
	(Man A)	On the bulletin board in the main lobby.
	(Man B)	Good. Everyone'll see it there, and be sure to announce it over the PA system.

77. (Man B) Mrs. Wilson, the executive board would like to invite you to serve as chairperson of the Annual Banquet Committee. Would you accept?
(Woman) It would be a lot of work, but yes, I would accept.
(Man B) Good. Please see me after the meeting, and I'll give you my notes from last year.

78. (Man A) That house we've always wanted is up for sale.
(Woman) Let's make an offer on it.
(Man A) I thought you'd say that, so this morning I asked a Realtor to draw up the papers for us to put in a bid.

79. (Woman) The new session starts next week, and we still need one more teacher.
(Man A) I spoke with a fellow yesterday who has teaching experience. He says he's interested in the position.
(Woman) That's good news. If you give me his name and telephone number, I'll call to set up an interview.

80. (Man B) I enjoyed the lecture. Thanks for inviting me. But what did he say?
(Woman) It sounded to me like it was more entertainment than substance.
I'm not convinced that people can use somebody else's money, get rich in real estate, and run no risk.
(Man B) Yes, he's trying to convince us we can get something for nothing.

Part IV

Directions: In this part of the test, you will hear several short talks. Each will be spoken just one time. They will not be printed in your test book, so you must listen carefully to understand and remember what is said.

In your test book you will read two or more questions about each short talk. The questions will be followed by four answers. You are to choose the best answer to each question and mark it on your answer sheet.

(Man A) Questions 81 through 83 refer to the following announcement.

(Man A) Hello, sports fans! Next Sunday the Falcons travel to Chicago to take on the Bears in the final round of the race for the fall American Soccer Confederation championship. Channel Four will bring you complete coverage of this sure-to-be-exciting match-up. That's next Sunday, fans, at one o'clock, right here on Channel Four, as the Falcons take on the Bears for the ASC conference championship.

(Man A) Now read question 81 in your test book and answer it.

(Man A) Now read question 82 in your test book and answer it.

(Man A) Now read question 83 in your test book and answer it.

(Man A) Questions 84 and 85 refer to the following traffic bulletin.

(Woman) Attention, motorists! Due to heavy rains in the area, the underpass at Oak Street has been flooded. Traffic is being rerouted onto Third Avenue. Motorists who normally use the Oak Street underpass to get to the Expressway should use the Third Avenue entrance.

(Man A) Now read question 84 in your test book and answer it.

(Man A) Now read question 85 in your test book and answer it.

(Man A) Questions 86 and 87 refer to the following speech.

(Woman) If I am elected president of the Interior Design Association, my first goal will be to increase membership by at least 50 percent. As you all know, increased membership means increased revenues from dues and greater investment in professional development programs for members. If I am successful, we will be able to pay off the association's debts. We can then work to restore all of our old programs, as well as initiate new ones. Cast your ballot for Trish Sindall for president and help bring this organization back to life!

(Man A) Now read question 86 in your test book and answer it.

(Man A) Now read question 87 in your test book and answer it.

(Man A) Questions 88 through 90 refer to the following announcement.

(Man B) May I have your attention, please! We're only five miles from the Canadian border. Before being allowed to cross over the Rainbow Bridge and into Canada, we'll have to pass through Canadian customs. You may be asked to get off the bus. Please have your passport ready and be prepared to declare any items you are bringing into the country. After we clear customs, we will continue over the bridge. If you look down into the gorge, you will see only mist rising from the river below, because of an atmospheric phenomenon. The river itself cannot be seen.

(Man A) Now read question 88 in your test book and answer it.

(Man A) Now read question 89 in your test book and answer it.

(Man A) Now read question 90 in your test book and answer it.

(Man A) Questions 91 and 92 refer to the following announcement.

(Man B) Attention, passengers! The captain has just been notified that WestSky flight number two-o to Seattle has been canceled. If you are scheduled to make that connection out of Tokyo, please see the WestSky attendant as you deplane. The attendant will inform you of space available on other Tokyo–Seattle flights today and will make reservations for you. Thank you for your cooperation.

(Man A) Now read question 91 in your test book and answer it.

(Man A) Now read question 92 in your test book and answer it.

(Man A) Questions 93 and 94 refer to the following announcement.

(Man B) Good evening, everyone, and welcome to Scott Arena! The women's championship volleyball game between the Howlin' Bulldogs and the Fire-Breathing Dragons is about to get under way here at Scott Arena. And with us today to sing a modern rendition of our national anthem is avid volleyball player and fan, pop star Beverly Hart! Will everyone please rise.

(Man A) Now read question 93 in your test book and answer it.

(Man A) Now read question 94 in your test book and answer it.

(Man A) Questions 95 through 97 refer to the following introduction.

(Woman) Welcome to Oatlands Plantation, the ancestral home of our state's first governor, Matthew Friedlander. The plantation home sits on 180 acres of rich southern farmland that even today is tilled by descendants of the governor. The home was built by Mr. Friedlander in 1802 as a gift for his bride-to-be, Mary Fedders. On the day of their wedding, out of regard for his new wife, Mr. Friedlander asked that after his death, the plantation always pass on to the eldest daughter in the family holding the estate. For nearly 200 years there has always been a daughter to inherit the plantation. Currently, the home is occupied by the governor's ninth-generation granddaughter, Mary Rebecca Kilton, and her family.

(Man A) Now read question 95 in your test book and answer it.

(Man A) Now read question 96 in your test book and answer it.

(Man A) Now read question 97 in your test book and answer it.

(Man A) Questions 98 through 100 refer to the following announcement.

(Man B) This is your captain speaking. We're about to pass through a storm front and may experience turbulence. The seat belt sign has been turned on. Please return to your seat and fasten your seat belt, and please remain seated until I tell you it is safe to move about. If you need a flight attendant, press the call button located in your armrest.

(Man A) Now read question 98 in your test book and answer it.

(Man A) Now read question 99 in your test book and answer it.

(Man A) Now read question 100 in your test book and answer it.

This is the end of the Listening Comprehension portion of the test. Turn to Part V in your test book.

PRACTICE TEST—SCORE CONVERSION TABLE

Coverting raw score to scaled score: Count the number of correct answers for the Listening section of the test to obtain a listening score. Then count the number of correct answers for the Reading section of the test to obtain a reading score. The sum of the two provides a total score.

Raw score	L/C	R/C	Raw score	L/C	R/C	Raw score	L/C	R/C
0	5	5	34	135	115	68	335	310
1	5	5	35	140	120	69	340	320
2	5	5	36	145	130	70	345	325
3	5	5	37	150	135	71	350	330
4	5	5	38	160	140	72	355	335
5	5	5	39	165	145	73	360	340
6	5	5	40	170	150	74	365	345
7	5	5	41	175	155	75	375	350
8	5	5	42	180	165	76	380	360
9	5	5	43	185	170	77	385	365
10	5	5	44	195	175	78	390	370
11	10	5	45	200	180	79	395	375
12	10	5	46	205	185	80	400	380
13	15	5	47	210	195	81	405	385
14	20	5	48	215	200	82	410	395
15	25	5	49	220	205	83	415	400
16	30	10	50	225	210	84	420	405
17	40	20	51	230	215	85	425	410
18	45	25	52	240	220	86	430	415
19	50	30	53	245	225	87	435	420
20	55	35	54	255	230	88	445	430
21	60	40	55	260	235	89	450	435
22	65	45	56	265	240	90	455	440
23	70	55	57	270	245	91	460	445
24	75	60	58	275	255	92	465	450
25	85	65	59	280	260	93	470	455
26	90	70	60	285	265	94	475	460
27	95	75	61	295	270	95	480	470
28	100	80	62	300	280	96	485	475
29	105	85	63	305	285	97	490	480
30	110	95	64	310	290	98	495	485
31	115	100	65	315	295	99	495	490
32	125	105	66	320	300	100	495	495
33	130	110	67	330	305			

Standard error of measurement (SEM) for the total TOEIC score is plus/minus 35 points. Thus, an obtained score of 450 points would give a true score of between 415 and 485. While this appears to be a wide range, when considering the spread of scores on the TOEIC covers a range of 980 points, the SEM comes to only 7%.

ANSWER KEY FOR PRACTICE TEST—LISTENING

Key: Part I

1. (D) The boat is chained to a tree.
2. (D) The gates open to the woods.
3. (B) The bird is standing on a rock.
4. (A) The car is going through water.
5. (C) The woman is setting the table.
6. (B) People are eating on the lawn.
7. (C) The boy is not happy.
8. (D) People are watching an outdoor performance.
9. (B) Children are sitting on the lawn.
10. (A) The audience is listening to an after-dinner speaker.
11. (D) It's a quarter to one.
12. (A) The worker is sweeping the floor.
13. (B) The women are talking at the counter.
14. (D) The man is getting a drink.
15. (D) The men are on the golf course.
16. (C) The workers are planting the flower bed.
17. (A) The car has been left along the road.
18. (A) The heavy trunk is being taken off the truck.
19. (C) The man is looking in the car window.
20. (B) The man is reaching into the car.

Key: Part II

21. (B) I'm going to the store.
22. (C) On Monday, July twelfth.
23. (B) I should be there by eight.
24. (A) About forty-five minutes.
25. (B) Yes, let's go.
26. (C) No, it's only eleven o'clock.
27. (A) Sure, I'll be out of the office all morning and won't be needing it.
28. (B) Just a glass of water, please.
29. (A) Sure, I'd be glad to look at it.
30. (C) No, thank you. I'm about to leave.
31. (A) In Conference Room C.
32. (A) Have you checked the fuel gauge?
33. (A) No, my ticket's for business class.
34. (B) I have some extras. Help yourself.
35. (C) It's been more than two years.
36. (A) Four-eight-two, to Rome.
37. (C) Yes, she started this week and really likes it.
38. (B) I was working on the Sintex bid.
39. (C) No, they're moving this week and can't be reached by phone.
40. (A) No. It's still closed for renovations.
41. (B) Yes, it was connected this morning.
42. (A) Give me the make and year, and a list of what you need.
43. (C) Yes, I'd like to take a look at it.
44. (B) One, and another on the way.
45. (B) I'm sorry, we're all out.
46. (C) Much better, thanks. My cold seems to be clearing up.
47. (B) I told them their image could benefit from a young firm with new ideas.
48. (C) We haven't heard anything this morning.
49. (A) They filed for bankruptcy recently.
50. (C) No, the lightning knocked it out.

Key: Part III

51. (C) Tickets
52. (D) To have a cigarette
53. (B) Her bicycle is broken.
54. (C) An elevator
55. (D) Something to drink
56. (B) A pharmacy
57. (A) Get a credit card
58. (B) His car has a flat tire.
59. (A) He died.
60. (C) A salesman
61. (C) Publishing
62. (D) Smoke on board the airplane
63. (C) In a restaurant
64. (A) Eat soft foods
65. (B) An effort to cut costs
66. (A) In a bank
67. (D) In an auditorium
68. (D) She forgot the date of a birthday.
69. (C) Sales
70. (B) A payment that is due
71. (B) Two double rooms
72. (A) Temperatures have been the lowest ever.
73. (C) A plant
74. (C) They cannot find a qualified applicant.
75. (B) The woman still has work she must do.
76. (D) A bulletin was posted.
77. (A) Chair a committee
78. (A) Buy a house
79. (D) A teacher
80. (B) A get-rich-quick scheme

Key: Part IV

81. (A) Soccer
82. (C) The following Sunday
83. (B) Four
84. (C) An underpass
85. (A) Onto Third Avenue
86. (C) President
87. (D) Increase membership
88. (B) In five miles
89. (D) Customs
90. (A) Go over a bridge
91. (A) That a flight has been canceled
92. (B) See the WestSky attendant
93. (C) A volleyball game
94. (D) Pop
95. (C) A farm
96. (A) Mary Rebecca Kilton
97. (D) The estate owner's eldest daughter
98. (B) The captain
99. (D) The plane is entering a storm.
100. (B) Only when told to do so

ANSWER KEY FOR PRACTICE TEST—READING

Key: Part V

101. (D) guide
102. (C) wear
103. (B) their
104. (C) discuss
105. (A) foundation
106. (B) disconnected
107. (C) Although
108. (A) seal
109. (A) spent
110. (B) uncrowded
111. (B) was
112. (A) used
113. (C) shows
114. (D) complicated
115. (D) balanced
116. (A) confused
117. (C) forced
118. (B) uphill
119. (C) opportunity
120. (A) agreed
121. (C) cleaned
122. (D) hesitation
123. (B) becoming
124. (D) survival
125. (B) sorting
126. (D) entire
127. (B) often
128. (D) around
129. (B) deformed
130. (C) versions
131. (C) took
132. (B) look
133. (C) before
134. (B) sought
135. (D) to reply to
136. (A) curfew
137. (D) protest
138. (A) in
139. (C) source
140. (C) impassable

Key: Part VI

141. (D) her
142. (B) would liberalize
143. (A) is
144. (C) even when
145. (C) out
146. (B) gave
147. (D) had to be used
148. (A) a few years old
149. (B) at
150. (C) underwent
151. (B) making
152. (C) turnover
153. (C) its
154. (C) in desperate
155. (D) user-friendly
156. (B) forest, forest's
157. (A) any changes, any change, all changes
158. (A) residents
159. (D) every day
160. (A) has, had

Key: Part VII

161. (A) Saturday
162. (B) Temperatures will gradually go down.
163. (D) Look elsewhere in the newspaper
164. (B) Banking
165. (D) Exceptional service
166. (A) She works only part time.
167. (C) The body
168. (A) Cash
169. (C) To the person who makes the highest offer
170. (B) Two
171. (C) *Phantom Valley*
172. (D) *Out of the Darkness* and *Paris Blues*
173. (A) Additional information
174. (C) By facsimile transmission
175. (D) Copper cored
176. (B) $12.98
177. (D) With custom engraving
178. (B) 9 ounces
179. (A) #66754
180. (C) Glass products
181. (C) Closing the plant for repairs
182. (D) A manufacturer of heating systems
183. (A) The roof
184. (A) 2
185. (C) A regular employee who will retire on August 15
186. (D) By marking their time sheets appropriately
187. (C) Gail
188. (D) Linda
189. (C) Gail
190. (B) $546.00
191. (D) Invest in Thai tourism
192. (B) It is in the development stage.
193. (C) William and Kelly Ponds
194. (A) Hazard insurance papers
195. (D) Fiduciary Center
196. (A) That all future premiums be paid by the customer and that Fiduciary Trust be removed as mortgagee
197. (B) Front Line
198. (D) 1996
198. (B) 25%
200. (C) Dumar's political situation

TOEIC®
TEST 1

LISTENING COMPREHENSION

In this section of the test, you will have the chance to show how well you understand spoken English. There are four parts to this section, with special directions for each part.

Part I

Directions: For each question, you will see a picture in your test book and you will hear four short statements. The statements will be spoken just one time. They will not be printed in your test book, so you must listen carefully to understand what the speaker says.

When you hear the four statements, look at the picture in your test book and choose the statement that best describes what you see in the picture. Then, on your answer sheet, find the number of the question and mark your answer.

Look at the sample below.

Now listen to the four statements.

Sample Answer

Statement (B), "They're having a meeting," best describes what you see in the picture. Therefore, you should choose answer (B).

1.

2.

GO ON TO THE NEXT PAGE

3. 

4. 

5. 

6. 

GO ON TO THE NEXT PAGE

7. 

8. 

9.

10.

GO ON TO THE NEXT PAGE

11.

12.

13.

14.

GO ON TO THE NEXT PAGE

15.

16.

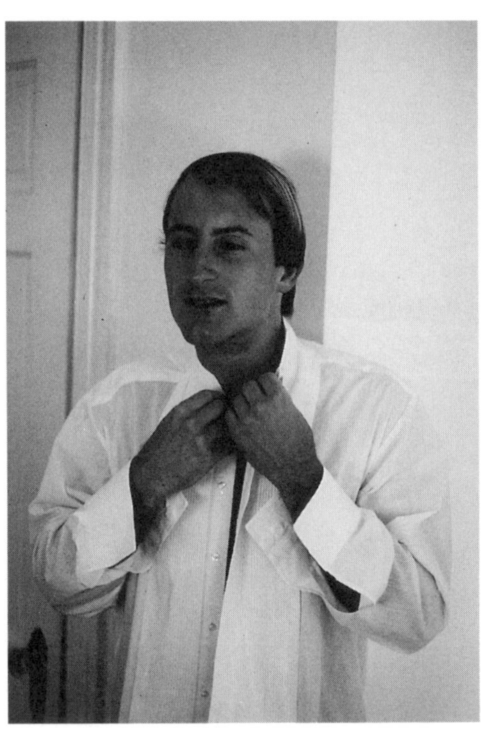

17.

18.

GO ON TO THE NEXT PAGE

19.

20.

Part II

Directions: In this part of the test you will hear a question spoken in English, followed by three responses, also spoken in English. The question and the responses will be spoken just one time. They will not be printed in your test book, so you must listen carefully to understand what the speakers say. You are to choose the best response to each question.

Now listen to a sample question:

You will hear:

You will also hear:

Sample Answer

● Ⓑ Ⓒ

The best response to the question "How are you?" is choice (A) "I am fine, thank you." Therefore, you should choose answer (A).

21. Mark your answer on your answer sheet.

22. Mark your answer on your answer sheet.

23. Mark your answer on your answer sheet.

24. Mark your answer on your answer sheet.

25. Mark your answer on your answer sheet.

26. Mark your answer on your answer sheet.

27. Mark your answer on your answer sheet.

28. Mark your answer on your answer sheet.

29. Mark your answer on your answer sheet.

30. Mark your answer on your answer sheet.

31. Mark your answer on your answer sheet.

32. Mark your answer on your answer sheet.

33. Mark your answer on your answer sheet.

34. Mark your answer on your answer sheet.

35. Mark your answer on your answer sheet.

36. Mark your answer on your answer sheet.

37. Mark your answer on your answer sheet.

38. Mark your answer on your answer sheet.

39. Mark your answer on your answer sheet.

40. Mark your answer on your answer sheet.

41. Mark your answer on your answer sheet.

42. Mark your answer on your answer sheet.

43. Mark your answer on your answer sheet.

44. Mark your answer on your answer sheet.

45. Mark your answer on your answer sheet.

46. Mark your answer on your answer sheet.

47. Mark your answer on your answer sheet.

48. Mark your answer on your answer sheet.

49. Mark your answer on your answer sheet.

50. Mark your answer on your answer sheet.

GO ON TO THE NEXT PAGE

Part III

Directions: In this part of the test, you will hear 30 short conversations between two people. The conversations will not be printed in your test book. You will hear the conversations only once, so you must listen carefully to understand what the speakers say.

In your test book you will read a question about each conversation. The question will be followed by four answers. You are to choose the best answer to each question and mark it on your answer sheet.

51. What does the man want to buy?

    (A) A new car
    (B) A toy for his son
    (C) A gift for his wife
    (D) A jacket for himself

52. What did the man lose?

    (A) A pen
    (B) A camera
    (C) An address book
    (D) A pair of glasses

53. What is taking place?

    (A) There has been an accident.
    (B) A party is about to begin.
    (C) Bill wants to borrow money.
    (D) The men are leaving to go to dinner.

54. Where is the hotel in relation to the meeting place?

    (A) Across town
    (B) Around the corner
    (C) Across the street
    (D) A few blocks away

55. What advice has the woman given the man?

    (A) To exercise
    (B) To take medicine
    (C) To get some rest
    (D) To eat a good meal

56. How will the woman travel?

    (A) By bus
    (B) By boat
    (C) By plane
    (D) By train

57. With what is the woman having difficulty?

    (A) Finding a box for shipping
    (B) Calculating a charge
    (C) Finding something in the warehouse
    (D) Lifting some boxes

58. Why will the man leave work early?

    (A) He is leaving on vacation.
    (B) He has a dental appointment.
    (C) He has to catch an airplane.
    (D) He is going to meet a friend.

59. What is the man expecting?

(A) He wants money to arrive.
(B) He wants to take a telephone call.
(C) He wants some goods to be shipped.
(D) He wants to see an inspection report.

60. What kind of company does the man work for?

(A) Trade
(B) Travel
(C) Finance
(D) Manufacturing

61. What are the speakers talking about?

(A) A film
(B) A comedian
(C) A film star
(D) A television show

62. Why do the men need a repairman?

(A) A window is broken.
(B) The electricity is off.
(C) Their computer is down.
(D) The phone is out of order.

63. Why will the couple go early to the event?

(A) To meet some friends
(B) To get a parking place
(C) To take some photographs
(D) To choose the best place to sit

64. What will Miss Raymond do at the meeting?

(A) Take notes
(B) Give a presentation
(C) Make an announcement
(D) Seat the participants

65. What happened to the bank?

(A) It was robbed.
(B) It had to be closed.
(C) It has been renovated.
(D) It was destroyed by fire.

66. What do the prospects look like?

(A) Ore quality will improve.
(B) The patient may not survive.
(C) The man has to abandon his studies.
(D) Bad weather may shut down the operation.

67. Why is the woman giving the man a ride?

(A) His car is out of gasoline.
(B) His car needs to be repaired.
(C) He is late for an appointment.
(D) He does not have a driver's license.

68. What are the men discussing?

(A) A new employee
(B) A baseball team
(C) Election results
(D) A friend's illness

GO ON TO THE NEXT PAGE

69. Why was the man not allowed into the hall?

(A) He was not properly dressed.
(B) He had not registered for the conference.
(C) He did not have proper identification.
(D) He did not have a ticket to the show.

70. What has happened to the carpet?

(A) It got dirty.
(B) The woman cleaned it.
(C) It has to be replaced.
(D) The woman left it to be cleaned.

71. What will the couple do?

(A) Go to Italy
(B) Visit a friend
(C) Take a cooking class
(D) Have lunch together

72. What will the speakers do?

(A) Go to the theater
(B) Meet to discuss a project
(C) Talk on the telephone
(D) Meet with the president

73. Why is the man going to the Easton plant?

(A) He will make a sales call.
(B) He will review office practices.
(C) He has been sent there by his company.
(D) He has to appraise it for insurance purposes.

74. For what occasion is the woman buying a gift?

(A) A wedding
(B) A birthday
(C) A graduation
(D) An anniversary

75. What was the woman supposed to pick up?

(A) A camera
(B) Some film
(C) Photographs
(D) Some frames

76. What will expire at the end of the month?

(A) A lease agreement
(B) The man's license
(C) An offer on a sale
(D) An insurance policy

77. What has happened to Ilian?

(A) It has sold its newspaper.
(B) It is going out of business.
(C) It is hiring new layout people.
(D) It has become the largest publisher.

78. About what is the community concerned?

(A) A proposed landfill
(B) Littering of town streets
(C) Poor waste disposal services
(D) Toxic gas from a nearby plant

79. What has the man asked for?

(A) Directions
(B) An address
(C) An appointment
(D) A registration form

80. What problem are the men discussing?

(A) They are lost and worried.
(B) Their work has been slowed down.
(C) Some friends are returning late.
(D) Weather is keeping them from traveling.

GO ON TO THE NEXT PAGE

Part IV

Directions: In this part of the test, you will hear several short talks. Each will be spoken just one time. They will not be printed in your test book, so you must listen carefully to understand and remember what is said.

In your test book you will read two or more questions about each short talk. The questions will be followed by four answers. You are to choose the best answer to each question and mark it on your answer sheet.

81. What is about to happen?

(A) A play will begin.
(B) A movie will be shown.
(C) A speech will be heard.
(D) An orchestra and dancers will perform.

82. What is NOT allowed during the function?

(A) Eating
(B) Talking
(C) Smoking
(D) Drinking

83. What agreement was made between Tilton and CBD International?

(A) To merge
(B) To sell Tilton
(C) To settle a lawsuit
(D) To share office space

84. What will happen to Tilton employees as a result of the agreement?

(A) All will be temporarily laid off.
(B) All will become employees of CBDI.
(C) Some will lose their jobs permanently.
(D) Some will be asked to take early retirement.

85. What is being held on the back lawn of the Imperial Inn?

(A) A barbecue
(B) A reception
(C) A company party
(D) A buffet dinner

86. What type of entertainment is being featured?

(A) A comedian
(B) A magic show
(C) Asian dancing
(D) Traditional music

87. What can guests do in the parlor of the Imperial Inn?

(A) Play cards
(B) Have coffee
(C) Watch a movie
(D) Enjoy the view

88. What is wrong with the truck?

(A) Its lights are on.
(B) It has rolled down a hill.
(C) It is parked in a no-parking zone.
(D) It has been hit by another vehicle.

89. Where is the truck?

(A) At an intersection
(B) On a nearby street
(C) Near the store entrance
(D) In an underground parking area

90. What color is the truck?

(A) Yellow
(B) Green
(C) Black
(D) Blue

91. When will passengers be allowed to board?

(A) In one hour
(B) After refueling
(C) After the decks are cleaned
(D) After disembarkation of arriving passengers

92. What are passengers holding tickets for the upper level to do?

(A) Keep to the right
(B) Board at the forward gate
(C) Go to the head of the line
(D) Wait until all other passengers have boarded

93. Who is making the announcement?

(A) A mother
(B) Mrs. White
(C) The store manager
(D) A security officer

94. Who is said to be lost?

(A) A family
(B) A mother
(C) Two children
(D) Three children

95. Why must guests of the Coral Reef Resort carry identification?

(A) To be permitted in the pool area
(B) In case they are stopped by guards
(C) To receive discounts in stores and shops
(D) To reenter the resort grounds at night

96. What are Coral Reef identification holders entitled to?

(A) Discounts at area restaurants
(B) Free swimming lessons at the pool
(C) Reduced room rates at the resort
(D) Free towels and chairs for the beach

97. What are investors doing?

(A) Selling stocks at a profit
(B) Buying bonds at low prices
(C) Selling high-interest bonds
(D) Buying stocks at low prices

98. What does the speaker recommend?

(A) Investment in gold
(B) That investors wait
(C) The purchase of real estate
(D) That investors sell nothing

GO ON TO THE NEXT PAGE

99. Why are the units being shut down?

(A) To add new machines
(B) To inventory the stock
(C) To program the computer
(D) To install electric lines

100. What are Units Three and Four operators to do?

(A) Stay home from work
(B) Report to other units
(C) Report to their units
(D) Report to the maintenance supervisor

This is the end of the Listening Comprehension portion of the test. Turn to Part V in your test book.

YOU WILL HAVE ONE HOUR AND FIFTEEN MINUTES TO COMPLETE PARTS V, VI, AND VII OF THE TEST.

READING

In this section of the test, you will have a chance to show how well you understand written English. There are three parts to this section, with special directions for each part.

Part V

Directions: Questions 101–140 are incomplete sentences. Four words or phrases, marked (A), (B), (C), (D), are given beneath each sentence. You are to choose the one word or phrase that best completes the sentence. Then, on your answer sheet, find the number of the question and mark your answer.

Example

Because the equipment is very delicate, it must be handled with ———.

(A) caring
(B) careful
(C) care
(D) carefully

Sample Answer

Ⓐ Ⓑ ● Ⓓ

The sentence should read, "Because the equipment is very delicate, it must be handled with care." Therefore, you should choose answer (C).

As soon as you understand the directions, begin work on the questions.

101. The manager requested two ——— of the monthly report.

(A) captions
(B) copies
(C) copes
(D) caps

102. The traffic moved slowly ——— of construction.

(A) about
(B) always
(C) because
(D) therefore

103. The power supply was ——— by a computer breakdown.

(A) magnet
(B) tolled
(C) holding
(D) disrupted

104. Everyone in the art community was ——— to the opening of the exhibition.

(A) invited
(B) delighted
(C) expressed
(D) surprised

105. Bananas are a good ——— of carbohydrates.

(A) source
(B) course
(C) place
(D) area

106. Television was ——— to American mass audiences in the 1950s.

(A) introduce
(B) introduced
(C) introducing
(D) introduction

107. With no regard for the welfare of others, the ——— went through the red light.

(A) single
(B) office
(C) driver
(D) delivery

108. Word processing software had been ——— on all of the company's computers.

(A) bought
(B) buying
(C) instilled
(D) installed

109. The region was known for its ——— production.

(A) farmers
(B) working
(C) planting
(D) agricultural

110. The event went off so well that the organizer was ——— a commendation for her good work.

(A) awarded
(B) allowed
(C) printed
(D) achieved

111. Sales figures for the year were up 50 percent, and the staff ——— larger than usual year-end bonuses.

(A) renamed
(B) recalled
(C) received
(D) reclaimed

112. There is some question about where on earth man first ———.

(A) lived
(B) leaned
(C) lied
(D) lay

113. The wood is old and ——— to be replaced.

(A) will
(B) needs
(C) must
(D) should

114. The cars approached the signal and ——— for it to turn green.

(A) waited
(B) called
(C) stalled
(D) hurried

115. The man was asked to wait while the bank manager ——— his loan application.

(A) retired
(B) reviewed
(C) reunited
(D) retracted

116. A membership card was ——— to enter the club.

(A) invited
(B) showing
(C) required
(D) determined

117. Reimbursement for business expenses is ——— made by the Accounting Department.

(A) utility
(B) usually
(C) untimely
(D) uselessly

118. Employees receive their promotions ——— before the annual plant maintenance shutdown.

(A) even so
(B) quite
(C) very
(D) just

119. The vice-president's ——— arrived early to get a head start on his work.

(A) registrant
(B) applicant
(C) assailant
(D) assistant

120. Once each year the main office ——— an employee dinner.

(A) hosted
(B) hoisted
(C) hastened
(D) happened

121. All hotel guests are ——— to register on arrival.

(A) inquired
(B) required
(C) related
(D) desired

122. The bridge ——— under the weight of the load.

(A) quake
(B) breaks
(C) collided
(D) collapsed

123. Poor sales forced the company to ——— bankruptcy.

(A) say
(B) state
(C) restore
(D) declare

124. Dynamic marketing was ——— as the reason for the increase in sales.

(A) name
(B) gave
(C) cited
(D) saying

GO ON TO THE NEXT PAGE

125. The contract terms were ———.

(A) clearly
(B) clarity
(C) spelled
(D) unclear

126. Because of the holiday, the trade center was operating with a ——— staff.

(A) relied
(B) recited
(C) reduced
(D) rejected

127. Firms use marketing surveys to ——— the needs of their customers.

(A) determine
(B) dissuade
(C) digest
(D) defeat

128. Employees were not ——— in the building until the work was finished.

(A) allowed
(B) permits
(C) sending
(D) worked

129. The package will not arrive for ——— two days.

(A) many
(B) other
(C) another
(D) several

130. Elections are held on a regular basis to allow the ——— public to vote for national, state, and local leaders.

(A) great
(B) general
(C) common
(D) real

131. The bank ——— was handled quickly and efficiently.

(A) transaction
(B) register
(C) bargain
(D) amount

132. After closing the door, it ——— to Mrs. Martin that she had left her keys inside.

(A) appeared
(B) occurred
(C) seemed
(D) became

133. Cider is made by ——— fresh apples.

(A) dividing
(B) crushing
(C) hitting
(D) cutting

134. The secretary worked ——— the pile of correspondence, answering every inquiry.

(A) near
(B) around
(C) through
(D) between

135. Traffic was often ——— around the city center, creating problems for motorists many blocks away.

(A) conjured
(B) corrected
(C) conspired
(D) congested

136. The sign ——— not to walk on the grass.

(A) say
(B) talk
(C) said
(D) wrote

137. With the breakdown of many forms of government, constitutional monarchy sometimes ——— an acceptable alternative.

(A) grows
(B) becomes
(C) elected
(D) establish

138. On careful inspection, it was established that the press pass was ———.

(A) falls
(B) unknown
(C) unqualified
(D) counterfeit

139. The luncheon was held on the ——— behind the hotel.

(A) façade
(B) garden
(C) terrace
(D) furnace

140. The chairman called the meeting to order ——— at nine o'clock.

(A) opening
(B) promptly
(C) every
(D) timely

GO ON TO THE NEXT PAGE

Part VI

Directions: In Questions 141–160 each sentence has four words or phrases underlined. The four underlined parts of the sentence are marked (A), (B), (C), (D). You are to identify the one underlined word or phrase that should be corrected or rewritten. Then, on your answer sheet, find the number of the question and mark your answer.

Example

All employee (A) are required to wear (B) their identification (C) badges while (D) at work.

Sample Answer

● (B) (C) (D)

Choice (A), the underlined word "employee," is not correct in this sentence. This sentence should read, "All employees are required to wear their identification badges while at work." Therefore, you should choose answer (A).

As soon as you understand the directions, begin work on the questions.

141. Most (A) of the company staffs (B) were (C) dedicated (D) workers.

142. Their (A) is a lot of paperwork to complete (B) before (C) a loan can be secured (D).

143. Policemen (A) directing (B) traffic around (C) the construction (D) site.

144. He studied economics when their (A) study was not common, and he later went (B) on to (C) distinguish himself in the field (D).

145. The company (A) uses (B) a telephone answering service off (C) normal working (D) hours.

146. The meeting was hastily (A) called (B) for four o'clock, which left few (C) time for people to rearrange their schedules (D).

147. Some (A) federal programs faces (B) budget cuts (C) of up to (D) 100 percent.

148. The debate was lively and interesting,
A B
but agreement was never reach.
C D

149. During the recess, the union
representatives met in the hallway and
A
disgust their position on the issue.
B C D

150. Many visits were lining the streets
A B C
to watch the parade.
D

151. The reasons for which some people
choose his profession are often
A B
unfathomable to those who do not
C
know them.
D

152. The patent law became strengthening
A
with the introduction of criminal
B
penalties for offenders who submit false
C D
documents to support their claims.

153. The community asked the Township
A
Committee to built a center for senior
B
citizens to use as a meeting place.
C D

154. The door is locked securely, but the
A B
robber still managed to get in.
C D

155. After finished the painting, the artist was
A
very pleased with the work she
B C
had created.
D

156. A national strike halted all rail
A
transportation, causing industry to ask
B
the government of intervention before
C
raw materials were exhausted.
D

157. It is impossible to tell from the
A
applicant's résumé whether he
B
would able to perform the tasks
C
expected of him in this position.
D

158. The dry goods store does not open
A
until noon, which was unusual for
B C
retail establishments in that particular
D
market.

GO ON TO THE NEXT PAGE

159. Voters were concerned <u>about</u> (A) the <u>budget deficit,</u> (B) <u>when</u> (C) they voted for candidates <u>who shared</u> (D) their views.

160. <u>Delivering</u> (A) <u>were</u> (B) <u>scheduled</u> (C) for <u>Tuesdays and Thursdays.</u> (D)

Part VII

Directions: Questions 161–200 are based on a variety of reading material (for example, announcements, paragraphs, advertisements, and the like). You are to choose the one best answer, (A), (B), (C), or (D), to each question. Then, on your answer sheet, find the number of the question and mark your answer. Answer all questions following a passage on the basis of what is stated or implied in that passage.

Read the following example.

> The Museum of Technology is a "hands-on" museum, designed for people to experience science at work. Visitors are encouraged to use, test, and handle the objects on display. Special demonstrations are scheduled for the first and second Wednesdays of each month at 1:30 P.M. Open Tuesday–Friday, 2:30–4:30 P.M., Saturday 11:00 A.M.–4:30 P.M., and Sunday 1:00–4:30 P.M.
>
> When during the month can visitors see special demonstrations?
>
> (A) Every weekend
> (B) The first two Wednesdays
> (C) One afternoon a week
> (D) Every other Wednesday

Sample Answer

The passage says that the demonstrations are scheduled for the first and second Wednesdays of the month. Therefore, you should choose answer (B).

As soon as you understand the directions, begin work on the questions.

GO ON TO THE NEXT PAGE

Questions 161–163 refer to the following set of instructions.

HOW TO ORDER BACK ISSUES

If you know the date of the issue you wish to purchase, send a check or money order for $3.75 for each issue requested to: *Bankers' Review*, c/o Mid-Atlantic Book Service, 5 Lawton Ave., Bloomtown, NJ.

If you do not know the issue date, but want to find a specific issue or issues, you must send sixty cents for each issue and a self-addressed stamped envelope with your request to John McCarthy, *Bankers' Review*, 5 West 25th St., New York, NY. (Sorry, no self-addressed stamped envelope, no reply.)

161. How much does it cost to order one back issue of *Bankers' Review* if the date of the issue is known?

(A) $0.60
(B) $1.20
(C) $3.75
(D) $4.35

162. Who can assist customers in identifying issues of *Bankers' Review* when the date of publication is not known?

(A) Mid-Atlantic Book Service
(B) *Bankers' Review* offices
(C) John McCarthy
(D) The National Consumer Connection

163. Which of the following must the customer do to get assistance in finding back issues with unknown publication dates?

(A) Send in a check or money order for $3.75
(B) Submit a completed subscription form
(C) Show proof of membership in the association
(D) Send a self-addressed stamped envelope

Questions 164–166 refer to the following advertisement.

> The Boy Scouts of America is seeking applications for the position of part-time store manager. Hours of employment are 11:00–4:00, Monday through Saturday. All applicants must have good communication skills, bookkeeping experience, and a friendly attitude toward customers. Applications are available from the Boy Scout office, 10 Main Street, opposite the Central University library.

164. Why is this job said to be part time?

    (A) The employee will not work a full day.
    (B) The employee will not work a full week.
    (C) The employee will work as a substitute.
    (D) The employee will work on weekends only.

165. What skills must applicants possess?

    (A) Word processing
    (B) Typing and dictation
    (C) Bookkeeping and communication
    (D) Sales and leadership

166. Where is the Boy Scout office located?

    (A) Off Main Street
    (B) On the Central University campus
    (C) Next to a library
    (D) Across from a library

GO ON TO THE NEXT PAGE

Questions 167–170 refer to the following directions.

Awapuhi for Your Hair

Directions for use: After shampooing and conditioning hair with Jackie Laine Salon Hair Care Products, apply to the hair a dab of Awapuhi Gel (the size of a dime for short hair, a quarter for long hair). Apply gel to damp or dry clean hair. Blow-dry, comb, or finger-place hair in desired style and dry under lamps, with a hair dryer, in the sun, or naturally. Natural drying will produce a non-oily wet look. Simply run a brush through the hair to create a dry, fluffy look and hair full of body and shine.

167. For what product are directions being given?

(A) Mousse
(B) Shampoo
(C) Conditioner
(D) Gel

168. When should Awapuhi be applied to the hair?

(A) After styling
(B) After shampooing
(C) Before conditioning
(D) After perming

169. How large a dab of Awapuhi should a person with short hair use?

(A) The size of an egg
(B) The size of a quarter
(C) The size of a dime
(D) The size of a pea

170. How should hair be dried using Awapuhi to create the wet look?

(A) With a hair dryer
(B) Using lamps
(C) With towels
(D) Naturally

Questions 171–173 refer to the following notice.

NOTICE
PUBLIC HEARING

The Milton Homeowner Association's Board of Directors and Covenants Committee invite Milton homeowners to participate in a Public Hearing on the Use and Maintenance Guidelines and Covenants Committee Procedures on:

Wednesday, March 3, at 7:30 P.M.

The hearing will be held in the Milton Homeowner Association's main conference room at 1930 Isaac Newton Square. This will be an opportunity for public comment on the committee procedures and on the use and maintenance guidelines. The meeting agenda is available at the Covenants Administration Office and at 1930 Isaac Newton Square.

171. To whom is this notice directed?

(A) Covenants Committee members
(B) Milton homeowners
(C) Business owners in Milton
(D) Parents of school-age children

172. What will the hearing be about?

(A) Relocating the Administration Office
(B) Zoning laws in Milton
(C) Covenant enforcement
(D) Use and maintenance guidelines

173. What is available at 1930 Isaac Newton Square?

(A) The meeting agenda
(B) Copies of the Covenants
(C) Use and maintenance guidelines
(D) Directions to the hearing

GO ON TO THE NEXT PAGE

Questions 174 and 175 refer to the following notice.

DONOR INFORMATION

Competent adults may donate their entire body, or parts of it, in case of death. To do so, the donor must complete a donor card in duplicate and file one copy with the National Medical Foundation. The second copy is to be attached to the back of the donor's driver's license or permanent ID card, if the donor does not drive. The donor card can also be used to indicate one's wish not to be a donor.

174. What is required of all potential donors?

(A) That they visit the National Medical Foundation
(B) That they complete a donor card
(C) That they hold a driver's license
(D) That they agree to donate their entire body

175. What ought a donor do with the second copy of a card?

(A) File it with the National Medical Foundation
(B) Keep it with personal records
(C) Attach it to his driver's license or ID card
(D) Give it to his doctor

Questions 176–178 refer to the following notice.

TO OUR SUBSCRIBERS

On September 1, the single-copy price of the *Daily Record* will increase to $0.35, and the monthly subscription rate to $9.25. This increase is necessary because of rising production and delivery costs. The *Record's* daily single-copy price has been $0.25 for the past eighteen years, although in the same period the cost of newsprint has quadrupled. If you have any questions, please call the circulation telephone number in your area.

176. By how much will the price of the newspaper increase?

(A) $0.05
(B) $0.10
(C) $0.25
(D) $0.35

177. Why is the price of the newspaper being increased?

(A) Because of rising labor costs
(B) To raise capital to expand production facilities
(C) Because of an increase in taxes
(D) Because of higher material and delivery costs

178. How long has it been since the last price increase?

(A) Almost 5 years
(B) Almost 10 years
(C) Almost 20 years
(D) Almost 25 years

GO ON TO THE NEXT PAGE

Questions 179–182 refer to the following advertisement.

GREAT FISHING ABOARD THE *MYSTIC LADY*

Boat catches this year average 79 fish per day.

Best Catch—a 38-pound, 47-inch cobia caught June 21 by Kevin Barrett. Mr. Barrett, fishing with eight fellow employees from the First Maryland State Bank, also caught 11 blues.

Terms: Groups only. Minimum six people, maximum twelve.
Full day: $40/person weekdays; $50/person weekends.
Deposit of $150 required at time of reservation.

Proprietor/operator: Capt. Eugene D. Pittman

Contact: CHESAPEAKE CHARTERS, INC.
Reedville, MD

179. Who owns the *Mystic Lady*?

(A) Kevin Barrett
(B) Eugene Pittman
(C) First Maryland State Bank
(D) Chesapeake Charters, Inc.

180. How much would it cost a group of six to fish off the *Mystic Lady* all day on a Sunday?

(A) $200
(B) $300
(C) $360
(D) $450

181. What is said to be the average number of fish caught daily by groups fishing off the *Mystic Lady*?

(A) 50
(B) 79
(C) 110
(D) 189

182. What deposit must be paid to reserve the *Mystic Lady* for a full day of fishing for eight people on a weekday?

(A) $50
(B) $150
(C) $160
(D) $320

Questions 183–186 refer to the following advertisement.

ATTENTION, TRIVIA BUFFS

If you know the answer to the trivia question below, send it, along with your name and address, to Randy Scanlon, ITB Newspapers Movie Trivia Contest, 16 Regis Parkway, Regis, LA 23456. Allow four to six weeks for delivery of prizes.

TWO LUCKY WINNERS, drawn at random from all correct entries received, will win TWO PASSES to any Leeds theater.

Question: D.B. Sweat was featured in what popular TV series starring Robert Maxim?

Answer to last week's contest: The song "Pretty in Velvet." Winners were Julie Sussman, of Clayton, and Sherry Huge, of Chantale.

183. What did Julie Sussman and Sherry Huge do?

(A) They won passes to a Leeds theater.
(B) They knew who Robert Maxim was.
(C) They appeared in a film at a Leeds theater.
(D) They organized a movie trivia game.

184. According to this advertisement, how long will it take for winners to receive contest prizes?

(A) One week
(B) Two to three weeks
(C) Four to six weeks
(D) Six months

185. Who sponsors the movie trivia contest?

(A) Randy Scanlon
(B) ITB Newspapers
(C) Leeds theaters
(D) D.B. Sweat

186. How are contest winners selected?

(A) The first correct answers received win.
(B) All entries are eligible for a drawing.
(C) Random drawing of correct entries.
(D) Voting by contest judges.

GO ON TO THE NEXT PAGE

Questions 187–190 refer to the following notice.

Placing orders with Nick's Knacks Catalog Store

Do you want to receive your Nick's Knacks order sooner? Try SpeedMail air-delivery service. Here's how.

For just an extra eighteen dollars (in contiguous 48 states) per order, Nick's Knacks Catalog Store will guarantee overnight delivery or pay all shipping charges. Any order received by 2:00 P.M., Monday through Thursday, will be delivered the next day. Orders received by 2:00 P.M. Friday will be delivered the following Monday. Orders received over the weekend will be delivered the following Tuesday. Deliveries to Hawaii and Alaska require an additional day. SpeedMail cannot accommodate international shipments.

*Note: There is a $10 surcharge on SpeedMail of bulky items, such as furniture, identified in the catalog with an *.*

187. How much will Nick's Knacks customers normally be charged for SpeedMail?

(A) $10
(B) $18
(C) $28
(D) $48

188. What is SpeedMail?

(A) A personalized postal service
(B) A decentralized warehouse distribution system
(C) The delivery service using motorcycles and bicycles
(D) An overnight air-delivery service

189. On what day will an order be delivered by SpeedMail to a destination in Alabama if the order is received at Nick's Knacks Catalog Store late Friday afternoon?

(A) Saturday
(B) Sunday
(C) Monday
(D) Tuesday

190. What is SpeedMail NOT able to handle?

(A) International orders
(B) Furniture
(C) Overnight deliveries
(D) Weekend orders

Questions 191–194 refer to the following notice.

ATTENTION: RETAIL OUTLETS

SUBJECT: PRODUCT RECALLS

The following recalls have been instituted by the Consumer Product Safety Commission:

Liquid antacid: Gelusil, 6-ounce bottle, lot number K789, expiration date 8/96. Indisil, 24-ounce bottle, lot number S666, expiration date 9/96. Distributed nationwide by Genutell, Inc. Problem: Products may be contaminated with bacteria.

Fire extinguisher: TICO brand, manufactured by Badger between May and September of this year and distributed nationwide. Model number Z1000. Problem: Possible improper installation of the valve and nozzle assembly. Spray head could blow off with extreme force when used.

Suntan lotion: Bixan brand, distributed only in Texas, New Mexico, and Colorado. Four-ounce and six-ounce bottles are affected. Lot numbers 456 and 123, respectively. Problem: Inadequate amount of active ingredient, reducing lotion's effectiveness.

191. Where did the product recalls originate?

(A) Consumer Product Safety Commission
(B) Individual manufacturers
(C) Department of the Interior
(D) Stores selling the products

192. Which of the following is a reason for which one product was recalled?

(A) It was not properly refrigerated.
(B) It caused skin rashes.
(C) It was improperly assembled.
(D) It contained contaminated chemicals.

193. Which company was affected by recall of two different products?

(A) TICO
(B) Genutell
(C) Badger
(D) Bixan

194. What may happen if a consumer uses a fire extinguisher that has been recalled?

(A) A fire may start.
(B) A skin rash may develop.
(C) The valve and nozzle may blow off.
(D) The pressure gauge may fail.

Questions 195–197 refer to the following article.

ASSOCIATION APPROVES BUDGET

The local homeowners' association Board of Directors narrowly approved its biennial budget last Thursday, setting the next year's annual assessment at $306 and the following year's at $315.

The budget passed with a 4–3 vote, with Directors McGuire, Smith, and Hartnett voting against the budget, and Rogers, Williams, Ralston-Nichols, and Murray voting in favor (Wilkens abstaining).

195. How often does the Board of Directors prepare a budget?

(A) Once each year
(B) Twice a year
(C) Every other year
(D) Every three years

196. By how much will the annual assessment increase after next year?

(A) $4–5
(B) $9
(C) $306
(D) $315

197. Which member of the Board did not vote?

(A) Wilkens
(B) Hodges
(C) Williams
(D) McGuire

Questions 198–200 refer to the following news article.

There are rumors that the ailing state-owned Askocz Steel Works, in Prague, Czech Republic, is soon to be put on the block in open bidding. Total value of the facility is estimated at more than $190 million. These rumors have been circulating through the Czech Ministry of Industry and no one in a position to do so has denied them. If the rumors prove to be true, European Community nations could be the first to benefit, as they are well acquainted with the Czech market and have direct connections to the Czech government and its ministries.

198. What does this article discuss?

(A) Approaches to management
(B) New markets for Czech steel production
(C) A new type of steel
(D) Sale of state property

199. Who does the article say will benefit from developments it describes?

(A) The Czech Ministry of Industry
(B) European Community nations
(C) Private investors
(D) Factory workers

200. What is the source of the article's information?

(A) Rumors
(B) The Ministry of Industry
(C) Published documents
(D) A government spokesperson

Stop! This is the end of the test. If you finish before time is called, you can go back to Parts V, VI, and VII and check your work.

TEST 1—SCRIPT

Part I

1. (Man B)
   (A) The car has been in a wreck.
   (B) The men are getting in the car.
   (C) The car is rolling away.
   (D) The man is working on his car.

2. (Woman)
   (A) The wall is a good sign.
   (B) The road is closed to traffic.
   (C) The gate is being closed.
   (D) The signal is broken.

3. (Man A)
   (A) The dog is tied to a tree.
   (B) The dog is looking at the tree.
   (C) The dog is among the trees.
   (D) The dog is looking for a tree.

4. (Man B)
   (A) The trucks are being held back.
   (B) The man is loading his truck.
   (C) The trucks are waiting to pass.
   (D) The man is turning the truck.

5. (Woman)
   (A) The bicycle has fallen over on the car.
   (B) The bicycle is racing past the car.
   (C) The bicycle is on top of the car.
   (D) The bicycle has rolled over the car.

6. (Woman)
   (A) The woman is holding the flowers.
   (B) Flowers are growing all around.
   (C) Flowers are on the ground all about the woman.
   (D) The woman has a flower in her hair.

7. (Man B)
   (A) The cars are waiting for traffic.
   (B) A car crossed the road and hit the post.
   (C) The car is pulling out into traffic.
   (D) A car is blocking the highway.

8. (Man A)
   (A) A boat is displayed in front of a store.
   (B) A boat is being taken into the store.
   (C) A boat is going past the windows.
   (D) A boat is coming in for repairs.

9. (Man B)
(A) Luggage to be moved is on the cart.
(B) Bags have been left outside the hotel.
(C) Luggage is being loaded into the car.
(D) Bags are standing around in the lobby.

10. (Woman)
(A) Bananas are being picked for shipping.
(B) The bananas are in boxes on the table.
(C) Bananas are for sale at the stand.
(D) Some bananas have been left beside the road.

11. (Woman)
(A) The street is full of cars.
(B) Cars are parked along the curb, heading uphill.
(C) It's difficult for cars to go on the street.
(D) Cars are coming down the hill.

12. (Man B)
(A) The artist is drawing a girl's portrait.
(B) A girl is standing next to the artist.
(C) The man is taking a picture of the girl.
(D) The girl is too late for her picture.

13. (Woman)
(A) The woman is changing the lock on the door.
(B) The car door has closed on the woman's hand.
(C) The car has been left in front of the door.
(D) The woman is unlocking her car door.

14. (Woman)
(A) Flowers are blooming in the trash can.
(B) The broom and trash can are under the sign.
(C) The workers are leaving their tools to go home.
(D) Debris was left on the walk next to the trash can.

15. (Man B)
(A) The man's guitar is in the tree.
(B) The man is sitting in the tree.
(C) The man is looking at the three guitars.
(D) The man is playing his guitar in the shade of the tree.

16. (Man B)
(A) The man is cleaning his shirt.
(B) The man has removed his shirt.
(C) The man is buttoning his shirt.
(D) The man is looking for a shirt.

17. (Man A)
(A) The men threw the box.
(B) The box is too high for the men.
(C) The men are lifting the box.
(D) The box is being delivered to the men.

18. (Man B) (A) The swan is walking away from the woman.
(B) The woman is looking at the swan.
(C) The swans are attacking the woman.
(D) The women are picking up the swan.

19. (Man B) (A) The man is sitting on a stool reading.
(B) The man has put some books on the chair.
(C) The man is holding up the chair.
(D) The stool has given out under the man.

20. (Woman) (A) The boy is carrying the woman's bag.
(B) The woman has run into the boy.
(C) The boy is running after his mother.
(D) The woman has the boy by the hand.

Part II

21. (Man B) What time are you leaving for the airport?
(Woman) (A) Flight 208.
(B) At around two o'clock.
(C) Bill will take me.

22. (Man A) I need to use the phone. Do you have change for a dollar?
(Man B) (A) I'm on my way home. I'll drop you off.
(B) The phone is by the cash register.
(C) I'm sorry. I don't have any change at all.

23. (Man B) Can you tell me how to get to the center of town?
(Woman) (A) You have to measure it very carefully.
(B) Take that street, and turn right at the first light.
(C) I think you have to try much harder.

24. (Woman) May I get you something to drink?
(Man A) (A) Yes, I'll do it right away.
(B) Yes, please. I'd like an orange juice.
(C) No, I'm sorry I don't.

25. (Man A) Can you tell me where the nearest barbershop is?
(Man B) (A) No, I just had my hair cut.
(B) It closes at noon, today.
(C) There's one just down the block.

26. (Man B) May I use your car to go to the store?
(Man A) (A) Yes, it's a new sport convertible.
(B) Yes. The keys are on my desk.
(C) I don't want to sell it.

27. (Woman) What do you do for a living?
(Man B) (A) I'd like the green one.
(B) I usually take the bus.
(C) I'm a clothing salesman.

28. (Man A) When can we expect to turn a profit on this?
(Man B) (A) I'd say within the first six months.
(B) Yes, we all expect a profit.
(C) I'm afraid to turn it up very high.

29. (Man B) Do you think it's going to snow today?
(Woman) (A) Yes. We're supposed to get 40 centimeters.
(B) No, but I saw him late yesterday.
(C) We'll begin in a little while.

30. (Man A) Could you help me with this problem?
(Man B) (A) No, everything's fine.
(B) I'll wait for you.
(C) Sure, let's see what it is.

31. (Woman) Can you tell me where I can find a salesclerk?
(Man B) (A) I think we'll have a good second quarter.
(B) I'm sorry, but all of the parking lots are full.
(C) I can help you. What are you looking for?

32. (Man A) I'm really looking forward to our trip to Europe, aren't you?
(Woman) (A) I sure am. I've waited for this for years!
(B) Our flight leaves at 8.00 P.M.
(C) I think I'll be in France on the 18th.

33. (Man B) Is it raining out?
(Man A) (A) Not yet, but showers are forecast for later today.
(B) It was picked up an hour ago.
(C) Yes, but we have more on order.

34. (Man B) When do they plan to open their new office?
(Woman) (A) They needed more space.
(B) Later this month, they say.
(C) It's in the Pacific Building.

35. (Woman) Excuse me. Can you tell me where there's a pay phone?
(Man B)
(A) You should get plenty of sleep.
(B) No, I think the other one is larger.
(C) Yes. At the end of the hall, next to the stairs.

36. (Woman) Are you going to the office picnic on Friday?
(Man A)
(A) Yes, we're out of paper.
(B) Yes, I'll be in my office.
(C) Yes, I'm looking forward to it.

37. (Woman) Do you know how to use this new software?
(Man B)
(A) No, I'm afraid I can't be much help.
(B) No, I liked it the other way.
(C) I think it came in a big box.

38. (Man B) Did you hear about what happened to Mac?
(Man A)
(A) No, he forgot to tell me.
(B) Yes, I heard about it this morning.
(C) Yes, they came in a while ago.

39. (Man B) Will the park be closed for the holidays?
(Woman)
(A) No, it closes only for Christmas Day.
(B) No, it's a holiday.
(C) Yes, there's a river through the park.

40. (Man B) What time does your program come on?
(Woman)
(A) At nine o'clock.
(B) It's on Channel Seven.
(C) It'll be over by noon.

41. (Woman) Why do you look so worried?
(Man B)
(A) Really? I feel good, too.
(B) I just learned that my mother is ill.
(C) Yes, he looks that way to me, too.

42. (Man B) This diskette is full. Can you give me another?
(Man A)
(A) We don't have any more. Can't you erase some files to make room on it?
(B) Pour some out, but be careful where you do it.
(C) Yes, aren't they delicious?

43. (Woman) Did the accountant ever return your call?
(Man A)
(A) No. He says he wants to keep it.
(B) Yes, yesterday afternoon, and everything's been taken care of.
(C) He gave it to me to give to you.

44. (Man A) Were you able to find your glasses?
(Man B) (A) No. I don't think he's coming.
(B) Yes. They were on my dresser.
(C) Yes. I'd like to see that.

45. (Man A) Did you say you need to stop at the pharmacy?
(Man B) (A) Yes, we're all leaving early today.
(B) There's one just two blocks from here.
(C) Yes, I have to pick up a prescription.

46. (Woman) Where can I make a donation?
(Man B) (A) It's up the block, on your right.
(B) See the receptionist at the main entrance. She'll take it.
(C) I think it leaves in an hour.

47. (Man A) How's our application to refinance the Edison warehouse coming along?
(Man B) (A) We need only one more document to complete it.
(B) Our inventories are low and moving fast.
(C) They're sending over more stock.

48. (Man A) What's happening over there?
(Woman) (A) I'll be down in a minute.
(B) O.k. I'll cover it up.
(C) Some trash caught fire, but it's out now.

49. (Man B) How did your job interview go?
(Woman) (A) The job's going well, thanks.
(B) Great! I start work on Monday.
(C) No, I didn't see the interview.

50. (Man B) You must be Carol. Thank you for coming.
(Woman) (A) Yes, I am. May I ask who you are?
(B) Yes, it is a little early.
(C) No. I'm just fine, thank you.

Part III

51. (Man B) Can I help you find something?
(Man A) Yes, I need a birthday present for my wife.
(Man B) Well, a bottle of a good perfume always makes a nice gift.

52. (Man B) Have you seen my glasses anywhere?
(Woman) No. Did you lose them?
(Man B) Yes. And I can't see a thing without them.

53. (Man B) Mark, old buddy, old pal. Is it o.k. if I come in?
(Man A) Sure, Bill, but it sounds like you want something.
(Man B) Well, as a matter of fact, I'm in a bind. Can you lend me ten dollars until payday?

54. (Man A) Were we able to get hotel reservations for the meeting in Houston?
(Man B) Yes, I was finally able to get something at the airport High Top Inn. Everything else was completely booked.
(Man A) That's way on the other side of town from where we have to go. Let's make sure we can rent a car, and allow plenty of time.

55. (Woman) You look tired.
(Man B) I am. I was up all night.
(Woman) Well, be sure to go to bed early tonight.

56. (Woman) Is there a train leaving tonight for Memphis?
(Man B) There's one more express at, let's see ... at nine o'clock.
(Woman) Good. I'd like a round-trip ticket, returning tomorrow evening.

57. (Woman) Can you help me with this order?
(Man B) Sure. What's the problem?
(Woman) I don't understand how I'm supposed to figure the handling charge.

58. (Woman) I thought you were going to leave early today so you could stop at the dentist's.
(Man B) I'm still planning to, but he can't take me until three.
(Woman) That's too bad. I hope your tooth isn't bothering you too much.

59. (Man B) When will that shipment of bananas go out to Pittsburgh?
(Woman) I was told it'll go out by this evening.
(Man B) I certainly hope so. I don't want the whole shipment to ripen here on the pier.

60. (Woman) What kind of work does your company do?
(Man B) We're a general trading company. Last year we were number three, but this year we slipped to the fifth position.
(Woman) Selling on the world market is not an easy business.

61. (Man B) Did you see the new host of the "Sunday Variety Hour"?
(Woman) No, why? Is he good?
(Man B) He's young, but he'll do fine. The show was very good this week.

62. (Man B) The phone isn't working, and I have to make some calls.
(Man A) I didn't know it was out. I'll get a repairman in right away.
(Man B) When you do, try to find out when we can expect the line to be operating again.

63. (Woman) What time is the parade on Saturday?
(Man A) At one o'clock, but we should get there early so we get seats in the shade.
(Woman) I agree, but we also want to have a good view.

64. (Man A) Who'll be taking notes at today's meeting?
(Man B) Miss Raymond, our secretary. She'll be here in just a few minutes.
(Man A) O.k. When she gets here, please let me know. I need to tell her the format we require.

65. (Man B) Did you hear about the fire at the bank?
(Woman) Yes. They say the building is in ruins.
(Man B) That's right. It went up like a matchbox. There was nothing they could do to save it.

66. (Man B) How is that manganese operation going?
(Man A) To tell the truth, we're coming up with only low-grade ore. It doesn't look promising.
(Man B) Don't worry about it. We're just beginning. The geologists are sure it'll get better.

67. (Man B) My car has a flat tire.
(Woman) I see it has. Can I give you a ride to a gas station?
(Man B) Yes, thanks. I think there's one about three miles up ahead.

68. (Man B) Did you ever think that Jerry would win the election?
(Man A) Not in a hundred years. I don't know how he did it.
(Man B) I didn't think he would, either. And I doubt that he'll do a very good job.

69. (Man A) Sorry, sir. You'll need to register for the conference before I can let you into the exhibition hall.
(Man B) Sure. Where do I sign up?
(Man A) At that desk over there.

70. (Woman) Look. The children got dirt on the carpet! I'm going to have to call in the carpet cleaners.
(Man B) Did you try to get it out with spot remover?
(Woman) Yes, but I only made it worse. I should have known better.

71. (Man A) Where should we go for lunch?
(Woman) I think I'd like Italian food, for a change.
(Man A) Fine. I know a great little Italian restaurant.

72. (Woman) I'd like to schedule a meeting on the Unix project for nine o'clock tomorrow. Are you available?
(Man A) No, I'll be in a meeting with the president all morning. How about right after lunch?
(Woman) That'll be fine. I'll see you in my office at one.

73. (Man A) Did you know that I've been transferred?
(Man B) No! Where to?
(Man A) To the Easton plant. I've been made head of Purchasing.

74. (Woman) I need to buy a wedding gift for Joan and Paul.
(Man B) Should we stop at the gift shop?
(Woman) I suppose so. The wedding's not until next week, but I won't have time later to get them anything.

75. (Man B) Were you able to stop by the photo shop to pick up those prints for me?
(Woman) No, I'm sorry. I just haven't been able to find the time.
(Man B) I'm worried that most of the shots won't come out. I used the wrong exposure.

76. (Woman) When does our insurance expire?
(Man A) At the end of the month.
(Woman) Then I'll need to submit a claim form for our accident right away.

77. (Man B) Did you hear that Ilian just filed for bankruptcy? That leaves only Wilson, City Publishing, and us.
(Man A) Yes. It was on the front page of today's paper. Do you think we can get some of their business?
(Man B) Maybe we can. I'd like to see if we can get some of their people, especially their layout team.

78. (Man B) Everybody I know is concerned about the proposed landfill. People are very upset.
(Woman) Of course, and they have reason to be.
(Man B) I suppose so, but nobody seems to understand the problems we have with waste disposal.

79. (Man A) Can you tell me where the Office of the Registrar is?
(Woman) Yes. It's down the hall and to your right. Do you have an appointment?
(Man A) Yes. I was supposed to be there twenty minutes ago, but I got lost.

80. (Man B) Did we get the field reports we were expecting from Irian Jaya?
(Man A) No. We haven't been able to get in because of heavy rains. There aren't any rivers any more, only gushing cascades.
(Man B) This is setting us back. I hope we can make up for it later.

Part IV

(Man A) Questions 81 and 82 refer to the following announcement.

(Woman) Good evening, ladies and gentlemen! We are about to begin tonight's feature presentation, *The Crossing*, from film's golden age and starring Mary Pickford, Douglas Fairbanks, and many other old-movie greats. You might begin to take your seats. Out of consideration for others, all food and drinks should be purchased before the showing begins or during intermission. Municipal fire regulations prohibit smoking anywhere in the theater, except in designated smoking areas. Thank you, and enjoy the film.

(Man A) Now read question 81 in your test book and answer it.

(Man A) Now read question 82 in your test book and answer it.

(Man A) Questions 83 and 84 refer to the following announcement.

(Man B) Good morning, Tilton employees! I will not bore you with formalities, as I am sure you're all anxious to know the results of yesterday's merger meeting with CBD International. I am pleased to report that last night at seven o'clock, Tilton and CBD International signed an agreement merging Tilton into CBD International, effective the first of next month. The agreement brings all Tilton divisions into CBDI. There will be some restructuring in support areas because of duplication of functions, but there will be NO layoffs and, operationally, no plant closings. There will be a freeze on hiring while things sort themselves out, so tell your brother-in-law he'll have to wait. I'm sure you all find this welcome news. Now, let's go back to work. We have pumps to build.

(Man A) Now read question 83 in your test book and answer it.

(Man A) Now read question 84 in your test book and answer it.

(Man A) Questions 85 through 87 refer to the following announcement.

(Man B) Welcome to the Imperial Inn. We invite you, our guests this evening, to a buffet dinner and dance show on the back lawn of the inn. We're sure you'll enjoy the many delicacies prepared by our chef. After the buffet, we hope you'll stay and enjoy an exhibition by our classical Asian dancers. Later this evening, please stroll around the grounds of the inn or join us in the parlor for a cup of coffee. We hope you enjoy your stay here at the Imperial Inn.

(Man A) Now read question 85 in your test book and answer it.

(Man A) Now read question 86 in your test book and answer it.

(Man A) Now read question 87 in your test book and answer it.

(Man A) Questions 88 through 90 refer to the following announcement.

(Man B) Attention, shoppers! There is a blue pick-up truck, license number H-A-2-2-0, parked in underground Area C, with its lights on. That's a blue truck, in underground parking Area C with its lights on.

(Man A) Now read question 88 in your test book and answer it.

(Man A) Now read question 89 in your test book and answer it.

(Man A) Now read question 90 in your test book and answer it.

(Man A) Questions 91 and 92 refer to the following announcement.

(Man B) Attention! The Lucky Ferry has just arrived from Kowloon and is now in the deboarding process. Passengers with tickets for the trip to Hong Kong Island will be allowed to board after all passengers have disembarked. Ticketed passengers with seats on the upper deck should stay to the right. Please watch your step. Upper-deck passengers to the right, lower deck to the left.

(Man A) Now read question 91 in your test book and answer it.

(Man A) Now read question 92 in your test book and answer it.

(Man A) Questions 93 and 94 refer to the following announcement.

(Woman) Attention, all White's customers. This is the store manager. The mother of a five-year-old boy, who says his name is Bobby, and Jane, his three-year-old sister, is reported to be lost in the store. Will the lost mother of Bobby and Jane please come to the manager's office?

(Man A) Now read question 93 in your test book and answer it.

(Man A) Now read question 94 in your test book and answer it.

(Man A) Questions 95 and 96 refer to the following announcement.

(Woman) Guests visiting Coral Reef Resort will need both their pool pass and resort identification for full access to services. If you plan to spend the day away from the resort sightseeing or enjoying one of the region's many fine public beaches, your identification will gain you reentry to the grounds at night. Your ID also entitles you to discounts in area restaurants. Pool passes are always required for entrance to the resort's indoor and outdoor pool areas. Thank you.

(Man A) Now read question 95 in your test book and answer it.

(Man A) Now read question 96 in your test book and answer it.

(Man A) Questions 97 and 98 refer to the following stock market report.

(Woman) Year-end profit taking has investors selling with one hand and looking for bargains with the other. The sad fact is, they aren't finding any. The market has taken an upturn, with prices in all sectors unexpectedly high. The bond market, usually an attractive alternative in such cases, offers little incentive to investors because of an expected rise in interest rates. You might say that investors are all dressed up with nowhere to go this season. Our advice is to stay home, have a party, and come out after January first.

(Man A) Now read question 97 in your test book and answer it.

(Man A) Now read question 98 in your test book and answer it.

(Man A) Questions 99 and 100 refer to the following notice.

(Man B) Your attention, please. Production Units Three and Four will shut down at noon, Saturday, for system modifications. Feeder lines with greater capacity are being installed to accommodate the power needs of additional equipment. Unit operators are asked to report to work as usual, at which time you will be temporarily reassigned.

(Man A) Now read question 99 in your test book and answer it.

(Man A) Now read question 100 in your test book and answer it.

This is the end of the Listening Comprehension portion of the test. Turn to Part V in your test book.

TEST 1 COMPARISON SCORES

The score range for the TOEIC is 10 to 990, 5 to 495 for listening and 5 to 495 for reading. This is a converted score, otherwise known as a scaled score, arrived at by converting an examinee's raw score by a formula that changes with every test. The raw score is merely the number of questions answered correctly. On the TOEIC, there is no penalty for answering a question incorrectly.

Converted scores are reported, rather than raw scores, because the developers of the TOEIC make a statistical adjustment for the relative ease or difficulty of each test. This procedure ensures that scores are equivalent over time and do not fluctuate because one or another test may be easier or more difficult than others.

The raw scores that appear below, for this test and for this test only, correspond to a total mean converted TOEIC score of 500, 250 for listening and 250 for reading. Other tests in this book have mean scores calculated on different formulas.

These scores are provided so, if they like, students can compare their performance on this test with a performance that would produce a total converted score of 500. Raw part scores of above the scores provided here would convert to a score of above 500, while raw part scores of below the scores provided here would convert to a score of below 500.

Part	**Mean Raw Score**
I	14
II	21
III	19
IV	12
Mean Listening	66
V	28
VI	12
VII	29
Mean Reading	69
Mean Total	135

Converted Scores for Above Mean Scores

Mean Listening	250
Mean Reading	250
Mean Total	500

ANSWER KEY FOR TEST 1—LISTENING

Key: Part I

1. (D) The man is working on his car.
2. (B) The road is closed to traffic.
3. (A) The dog is tied to a tree.
4. (B) The man is loading his truck.
5. (C) The bicycle is on top of the car.
6. (D) The woman has a flower in her hair.
7. (C) The car is pulling out into traffic.
8. (A) A boat is displayed in front of a store.
9. (A) Luggage to be moved is on the cart.
10. (C) Bananas are for sale at the stand.
11. (B) Cars are parked along the curb, heading uphill.
12. (A) The artist is drawing a girl's portrait.
13. (D) The woman is unlocking her car door.
14. (B) The broom and trash can are under the sign.
15. (D) The man is playing his guitar in the shade of the tree.
16. (C) The man is buttoning his shirt.
17. (C) The men are lifting the box.
18. (B) The woman is looking at the swan.
19. (A) The man is sitting on a stool reading.
20. (D) The woman has the boy by the hand.

Key: Part II

21. (B) At around two o'clock.
22. (C) I'm sorry. I don't have any change at all.
23. (B) Take that street, and turn right at the first light.
24. (B) Yes, please. I'd like an orange juice.
25. (C) There's one just down the block.
26. (B) Yes. The keys are on my desk.
27. (C) I'm a clothing salesman.
28. (A) I'd say within the first six months.
29. (A) Yes. We're supposed to get 40 centimeters.
30. (C) Sure, let's see what it is.
31. (C) I can help you. What are you looking for?
32. (A) I sure am. I've waited for this for years!
33. (A) Not yet, but showers are forecast for later today.
34. (B) Later this month, they say.
35. (C) Yes. At the end of the hall, next to the stairs.
36. (C) Yes, I'm looking forward to it.
37. (A) No, I'm afraid I can't be much help.
38. (B) Yes, I heard about it this morning.
39. (A) No, it closes only for Christmas Day.
40. (A) At nine o'clock.
41. (B) I just learned that my mother is ill.
42. (A) We don't have any more. Can't you erase some files to make room on it?
43. (B) Yes, yesterday afternoon, and everything's been taken care of.
44. (B) Yes. They were on my dresser.
45. (C) Yes, I have to pick up a prescription.
46. (B) See the receptionist at the main entrance. She'll take it.
47. (A) We need only one more document to complete it.
48. (C) Some trash caught fire, but it's out now.
49. (B) Great! I start work on Monday.
50. (A) Yes, I am. May I ask who you are?

Key: Part III

51. (C) A gift for his wife
52. (D) A pair of glasses
53. (C) Bill wants to borrow money.
54. (A) Across town
55. (C) To get some rest
56. (D) By train
57. (B) Calculating a charge
58. (B) He has a dental appointment.
59. (C) He wants some goods to be shipped.
60. (A) Trade
61. (D) A television show
62. (D) The phone is out of order.
63. (D) To choose the best place to sit
64. (A) Take notes
65. (D) It was destroyed by fire.
66. (A) Ore quality will improve.
67. (B) His car needs to be repaired.
68. (C) Election results
69. (B) He had not registered for the conference.
70. (A) It got dirty.
71. (D) Have lunch together
72. (B) Meet to discuss a project
73. (C) He has been sent there by his company.
74. (A) A wedding
75. (C) Photographs
76. (D) An insurance policy
77. (B) It is going out of business.
78. (A) A proposed landfill
79. (A) Directions
80. (B) Their work has been slowed down.

Key: Part IV

81. (B) A movie will be shown.
82. (C) Smoking
83. (A) To merge
84. (B) All will become employees of CBDI.
85. (D) A buffet dinner
86. (C) Asian dancing
87. (B) Have coffee
88. (A) Its lights are on.
89. (D) In an underground parking area
90. (D) Blue
91. (D) After disembarkation of arriving passengers
92. (A) Keep to the right
93. (C) The store manager
94. (B) A mother
95. (D) To reenter the resort grounds at night
96. (A) Discounts at area restaurants
97. (A) Selling stocks at a profit
98. (B) That investors wait
99. (D) To install electric lines
100. (C) Report to their units

ANSWER KEY FOR TEST 1—READING

Key: Part V

101. (B) copies
102. (C) because
103. (D) disrupted
104. (A) invited
105. (A) source
106. (B) introduced
107. (C) driver
108. (D) installed
109. (D) agricultural
110. (A) awarded
111. (C) received
112. (A) lived
113. (B) needs
114. (A) waited
115. (B) reviewed
116. (C) required
117. (B) usually
118. (D) just
119. (D) assistant
120. (A) hosted
121. (B) required
122. (D) collapsed
123. (D) declare
124. (C) cited
125. (D) unclear
126. (C) reduced
127. (A) determine
128. (A) allowed
129. (C) another
130. (B) general
131. (A) transaction
132. (B) occurred
133. (B) crushing
134. (C) through
135. (D) congested
136. (C) said
137. (B) becomes
138. (D) counterfeit
139. (C) terrace
140. (B) promptly

Key: Part VI

141. (B) company staff
142. (A) There
143. (B) directed
144. (A) its
145. (C) after
146. (C) little
147. (B) face, faced
148. (D) reached
149. (B) discussed
150. (A) visitors
151. (B) their
152. (A) strengthened
153. (B) to build
154. (A) was
155. (A) finishing
156. (C) to intervene
157. (C) would be able to perform
158. (A) did not open
159. (C) and
160. (A) Deliveries

Key: Part VII

161. (C) $3.75
162. (C) John McCarthy
163. (D) Send a self-addressed stamped envelope
164. (A) The employee will not work a full day.
165. (C) Bookkeeping and communication
166. (D) Across from a library
167. (D) Gel
168. (B) After shampooing
169. (C) The size of a dime
170. (D) Naturally
171. (B) Milton homeowners
172. (D) Use and maintenance guidelines
173. (A) The meeting agenda
174. (B) That they complete a donor card
175. (C) Attach it to his driver's license or ID card
176. (B) $0.10
177. (D) Because of higher material and delivery costs
178. (C) Almost 20 years
179. (B) Eugene Pittman
180. (B) $300
181. (B) 79
182. (B) $150
183. (A) They won passes to a Leeds theater.
184. (C) Four to six weeks
185. (B) ITB Newspapers
186. (C) Random drawing of correct entries.
187. (B) $18
188. (D) An overnight air-delivery service
189. (D) Tuesday
190. (A) International orders
191. (A) Consumer Product Safety Commission
192. (C) It was improperly assembled.
193. (B) Genutell
194. (C) The valve and nozzle may blow off.
195. (C) Every other year
196. (B) $9
197. (A) Wilkens
198. (D) Sale of state property
199. (B) European Community nations
200. (A) Rumors

TOEIC®
TEST 2

LISTENING COMPREHENSION

In this section of the test, you will have the chance to show how well you understand spoken English. There are four parts to this section, with special directions for each part.

Part I

Directions: For each question, you will see a picture in your test book and you will hear four short statements. The statements will be spoken just one time. They will not be printed in your test book, so you must listen carefully to understand what the speaker says.

When you hear the four statements, look at the picture in your test book and choose the statement that best describes what you see in the picture. Then, on your answer sheet, find the number of the question and mark your answer.

Look at the sample below.

Now listen to the four statements.

Sample Answer

Statement (B), "They're having a meeting," best describes what you see in the picture. Therefore, you should choose answer (B).

1. 

2. 

GO ON TO THE NEXT PAGE

3. 

4. 

5. 

6. 

GO ON TO THE NEXT PAGE

7. 

8. 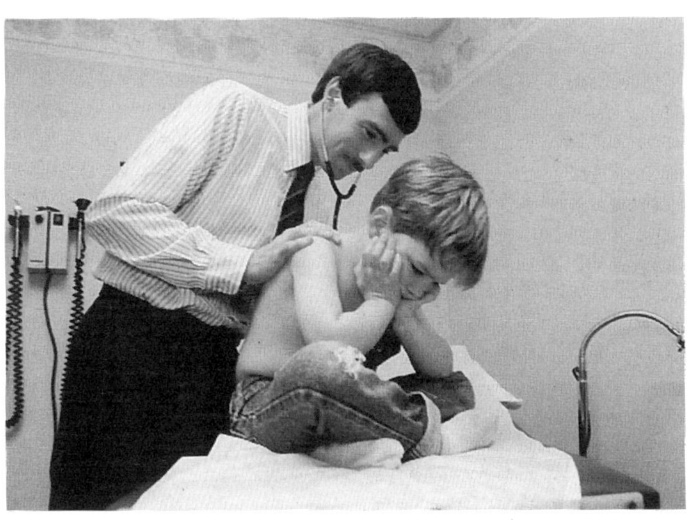

9. 

10. 

GO ON TO THE NEXT PAGE

11. 

12. 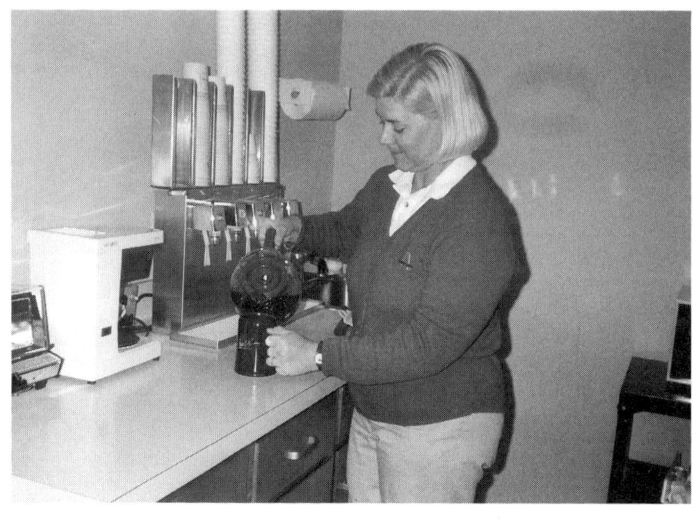

13.

14.

GO ON TO THE NEXT PAGE

15.

16.

17.

18.

GO ON TO THE NEXT PAGE

19.

20.

Part II

Directions: In this part of the test you will hear a question spoken in English, followed by three responses, also spoken in English. The question and the responses will be spoken just one time. They will not be printed in your test book, so you must listen carefully to understand what the speakers say. You are to choose the best response to each question.

Now listen to a sample question:

You will hear:

You will also hear:

Sample Answer

● Ⓑ Ⓒ

The best response to the question "How are you?" is choice (A) "I am fine, thank you." Therefore, you should choose answer (A).

21. Mark your answer on your answer sheet.
22. Mark your answer on your answer sheet.
23. Mark your answer on your answer sheet.
24. Mark your answer on your answer sheet.
25. Mark your answer on your answer sheet.
26. Mark your answer on your answer sheet.
27. Mark your answer on your answer sheet.
28. Mark your answer on your answer sheet.
29. Mark your answer on your answer sheet.
30. Mark your answer on your answer sheet.
31. Mark your answer on your answer sheet.
32. Mark your answer on your answer sheet.
33. Mark your answer on your answer sheet.
34. Mark your answer on your answer sheet.
35. Mark your answer on your answer sheet.
36. Mark your answer on your answer sheet.
37. Mark your answer on your answer sheet.
38. Mark your answer on your answer sheet.
39. Mark your answer on your answer sheet.
40. Mark your answer on your answer sheet.
41. Mark your answer on your answer sheet.
42. Mark your answer on your answer sheet.
43. Mark your answer on your answer sheet.
44. Mark your answer on your answer sheet.
45. Mark your answer on your answer sheet.
46. Mark your answer on your answer sheet.
47. Mark your answer on your answer sheet.
48. Mark your answer on your answer sheet.
49. Mark your answer on your answer sheet.
50. Mark your answer on your answer sheet.

GO ON TO THE NEXT PAGE

Part III

Directions: In this part of the test, you will hear 30 short conversations between two people. The conversations will not be printed in your test book. You will hear the conversations only once, so you must listen carefully to understand what the speakers say.

In your test book you will read a question about each conversation. The question will be followed by four answers. You are to choose the best answer to each question and mark it on your answer sheet.

51. What are the speakers looking for?
    (A) A hotel
    (B) A restaurant
    (C) A parking lot
    (D) A gas station

52. What has Carter done?
    (A) He retired.
    (B) He resigned.
    (C) He began work.
    (D) He was promoted.

53. What does the woman want to do?
    (A) Apply for a patent
    (B) Request more information
    (C) Sue a company for infringing patents
    (D) Avoid offending the other company

54. What is the man doing?
    (A) Reserving a seat on a train
    (B) Planning a conference call
    (C) Setting up a meeting
    (D) Scheduling an appointment

55. What is the woman buying?
    (A) Meat
    (B) Fruit
    (C) Bread
    (D) Vegetables

56. What will the man do on his way to work?
    (A) Stop at a store to buy coffee
    (B) Return some books to the library
    (C) Let the woman off at the library
    (D) Take the woman to the store

57. How does the man feel?
    (A) Excited
    (B) Calm
    (C) Unhappy
    (D) Nervous

58. What does the man want to do?
    (A) Attend a concert
    (B) Organize a benefit
    (C) Speak with companies
    (D) Give money to the homeless

59. What has the woman been asked to do?
    (A) Distribute the man's report
    (B) Review a financial statement
    (C) Report on a project in Mexico
    (D) Explain the man's absence from the meeting

60. What does the man want to do?
    (A) See a dentist
    (B) Take a management course
    (C) Attend a conference
    (D) Reserve a flight

61. What is this conversation about?

(A) An automobile
(B) Telephone service
(C) Shipping schedules
(D) Office equipment

62. Why does the woman recommend Red Fire perfume?

(A) Price
(B) Scent
(C) Popularity
(D) Brand name

63. What does the man want to do?

(A) Take his son for a boat ride
(B) Rent an apartment in the city
(C) Go somewhere for a vacation
(D) Have the tailor make him a suit

64. What does the woman need to do?

(A) Buy shoes
(B) Pay a fine
(C) Mail a letter
(D) Buy vegetables

65. What problem do the men have?

(A) They are lost.
(B) They are cold.
(C) They lost their map.
(D) They are out of gas.

66. What do the people say they are afraid of?

(A) Flying
(B) Sky diving
(C) Scuba diving
(D) Downhill skiing

67. What are the speakers talking about?

(A) A gift
(B) A child
(C) Travel
(D) Clothing

68. How do the speakers rate their English ability?

(A) Adequate only for survival
(B) Adequate for simple conversation
(C) Adequate for professional discussions
(D) Adequate for anything they want to do

69. What do the speakers say about the dinner guests?

(A) They arrived late.
(B) They were important.
(C) They were well-dressed.
(D) There were many of them.

70. What are the speakers discussing?

(A) Stock purchases
(B) Foreign investment
(C) Rates of inflation
(D) Rising interest rates

71. Why is the woman upset?

(A) Her bonus was less than expected.
(B) She was told she is not a good worker.
(C) Her salary was not increased.
(D) She did not get a promotion she expected

GO ON TO THE NEXT PAGE

72. Why does Mark NOT want to take the call?

(A) He is meeting with a customer.
(B) He is about to leave the office.
(C) He is talking on another telephone.
(D) He wants to avoid talking to the caller.

73. What is the topic of this conversation?

(A) Political developments
(B) Travel opportunities
(C) A company's overseas expansion
(D) Failed investments

74. What are the men discussing?

(A) Some of their clients
(B) The kinds of cars they drive
(C) The routes they take to get to work
(D) A construction project they are planning

75. What does the man want?

(A) He wants to write a letter.
(B) He is asking to read a letter.
(C) He wants a letter to be rewritten.
(D) He asks to have a letter read to him.

76. What are the speakers talking about?

(A) Worker demands
(B) High labor costs
(C) Company financing
(D) Founding a new company

77. What is the man worried about?

(A) Being able to find Sue
(B) Where to have breakfast
(C) Getting lost on the way
(D) Being able to leave early

78. For what did the man win an award?

(A) For his writing
(B) For his art work
(C) For community service
(D) For rescuing someone

79. What has happened?

(A) People are feeling good because of the weather.
(B) Rain is preventing people from going outside.
(C) The man has given the woman some flowers.
(D) The man wants to plant flowers in the garden.

80. How do the speakers describe Jake?

(A) Cautious
(B) Energetic
(C) Disciplined
(D) Unconventional

Part IV

Directions: In this part of the test, you will hear several short talks. Each will be spoken just one time. They will not be printed in your test book, so you must listen carefully to understand and remember what is said.

In your test book you will read two or more questions about each short talk. The questions will be followed by four answers. You are to choose the best answer to each question and mark it on your answer sheet.

81. With what does the Legitimate Business Office deal?

    (A) Business licensing
    (B) Business credit
    (C) Business research
    (D) Business crime

82. Who is said to be most responsible in the fight against fraud?

    (A) Banks
    (B) Police
    (C) Potential victims
    (D) The Legitimate Business Office

83. What volume of trade occurred on Monday?

    (A) 20 million shares
    (B) 100 million shares
    (C) 120 million shares
    (D) 200 million shares

84. What will happen on Tuesday?

    (A) Investors will return to the market.
    (B) Trading will be suspended briefly.
    (C) The Dow Jones Industrials will use a new system to report.
    (D) Leading economic indicators will be announced.

85. What is Foodtown announcing?

    (A) New hours
    (B) Temporary low prices
    (C) Opening the new store
    (D) Its new bakery department

86. What is Foodtown giving away?

    (A) Brewed coffee
    (B) Pizza samples
    (C) Special prizes
    (D) Frozen seafood

87. For what does Foodtown apologize?

    (A) Ongoing construction
    (B) Its need to charge high prices
    (C) A limited supply of fresh seafood
    (D) The quality of its fruits and vegetables

88. What type of music will be heard on WICM?

    (A) Rock
    (B) Jazz
    (C) Country
    (D) Classical

GO ON TO THE NEXT PAGE

89. What special feature will be presented during the evening on WICM?

(A) A new band
(B) A live interview
(C) A new disk jockey
(D) A tape of a concert

90. What has the D.J. told listeners about a concert at the Arena Stage?

(A) Tickets cost fifteen dollars.
(B) No more tickets are available.
(C) Several bands will be playing.
(D) The concert starts at eight o'clock.

91. What does the woman say about the restaurant?

(A) It is about to open.
(B) It is very busy on weekends.
(C) It does not take reservations.
(D) It was the scene of an unfortunate incident.

92. What choice is offered to people entering the restaurant?

(A) They may wait for a while.
(B) They may change their table.
(C) They may place a special order.
(D) They may order food to take out.

93. Where is the caller calling from?

(A) From Paris.
(B) From outside Paris.
(C) It is not clear from the message.
(D) From a country other than France.

94. What is the caller advised to do?

(A) Press a number
(B) Hang up and call again
(C) Telephone for information
(D) Wait for an operator to answer

95. How many guests are announced to appear on the show?

(A) One
(B) Two
(C) Three
(D) Four

96. Who is said to have written a book on travel?

(A) Bevo Bill
(B) John Wilson
(C) Charles Fagan
(D) Millicent Beatty

97. What will happen before the program is presented?

(A) The studio band will play.
(B) There will be an advertisement.
(C) An announcer will read the news.
(D) The audience is invited to write out questions.

98. How old must a child be to be on his own during the tour?

(A) Ten
(B) Eleven
(C) Twelve
(D) Thirteen

99. What will happen to people who disobey the tour rules?

(A) They will receive a warning.
(B) They will be escorted off the grounds.
(C) They will be questioned by authorities.
(D) They will have to leave the tour and wait for the others to finish.

100. Where do people walk while in the restricted area?

(A) On a marked pathway
(B) On a special elevated walkway
(C) Through galleries around the edge
(D) In nuclear-free zones away from the reactor

This is the end of the Listening Comprehension portion of the test. Turn to Part V in your test book.

GO ON TO THE NEXT PAGE

YOU WILL HAVE ONE HOUR AND FIFTEEN MINUTES TO COMPLETE PARTS V, VI, AND VII OF THE TEST.

READING

In this section of the test, you will have a chance to show how well you understand written English. There are three parts to this section, with special directions for each part.

Part V

Directions: Questions 101–140 are incomplete sentences. Four words or phrases, marked (A), (B), (C), (D), are given beneath each sentence. You are to choose the one word or phrase that best completes the sentence. Then, on your answer sheet, find the number of the question and mark your answer.

Example

Because the equipment is very delicate, it must be handled with ———.

(A) caring
(B) careful
(C) care
(D) carefully

Sample Answer

The sentence should read, "Because the equipment is very delicate, it must be handled with care." Therefore, you should choose answer (C).

As soon as you understand the directions, begin work on the questions.

101. ——— to several studies, 15 percent of the population under the age of 25 have taken up smoking.

(A) Accept
(B) Written
(C) According
(D) Determined

102. All keys for the store were ——— in a safe place behind the counter.

(A) kept
(B) guard
(C) holding
(D) displayed

103. The building was the ——— in the city.

(A) more
(B) most
(C) bigger
(D) tallest

104. The Marketing Department had no ——— plan for the new product.

(A) able
(B) statute
(C) specific
(D) in place

105. The student group asked to be left alone, to carry out their meeting without ———.

(A) fails
(B) boxes
(C) attitudes
(D) interruption

106. It is hard to find ——— people for low-paying positions.

(A) renewed
(B) invested
(C) valuable
(D) responsible

107. Air temperatures are ——— by wind and altitude, as well as by other factors.

(A) elements
(B) determine
(C) effective
(D) influenced

108. They ——— to the mountain town to visit friends.

(A) drove
(B) draft
(C) dried
(D) driven

109. Insurance providers strive to determine ways to ——— health plans.

(A) pay
(B) data
(C) repair
(D) improve

110. The ship entered port ——— three months at sea.

(A) for
(B) when
(C) after
(D) storms

111. The ——— matter is, the more it weighs.

(A) denser
(B) tighter
(C) older
(D) deeper

112. The young men were ——— for vandalism.

(A) quitted
(B) arrested
(C) finished
(D) stopped

113. Bicyclists ——— to ride in the park.

(A) is not
(B) cannot go
(C) not allowed
(D) are forbidden

114. The company ——— in 1970.

(A) founded
(B) were found
(C) was founded
(D) has been founded

115. Heavy rains ——— the tournament from continuing later in the afternoon.

(A) canceled
(B) included
(C) prevented
(D) organized

116. He was mature and ———, and his business decisions were sound.

(A) confidence
(B) confiding in
(C) self-confident
(D) self-confidently

117. Staff were asked to ——— for any contingency.

(A) predict
(B) preceded
(C) preparing
(D) be prepared

118. After ——— their tickets, the man and his family entered the ballpark.

(A) buying
(B) bought
(C) purchased
(D) acceptance

119. The company newspaper keeps staff ——— about matters that are of interest to everyone.

(A) told
(B) dated
(C) decided
(D) informed

120. The report said that everything was ——— control.

(A) on
(B) at
(C) over
(D) under

121. Swiss watches are known for their ——— workmanship.

(A) beauty
(B) exactly
(C) precision
(D) exception

122. The chairman saw no ——— revise the contract.

(A) reason
(B) reason to
(C) reason for
(D) reasonable

123. Out of courtesy, the council always asks whether we ——— its position.

(A) agree
(B) accept
(C) concur
(D) confer

124. The advertisement was less than ——— about the quality of the product.

(A) candid
(B) canned
(C) candor
(D) cannon

125. The company decided that to survive it would have to ——— to a building with lower rent.

(A) apply
(B) advance
(C) relocate
(D) movement

126. The company patented many products, but ——— marketed them successfully.

(A) not
(B) even
(C) rarely
(D) help

127. The association was ——— for refusing to cooperate with the investigation.

(A) tolled
(B) penalized
(C) experienced
(D) exacerbated

128. Return flights should be reconfirmed at least 72 hours ——— of departure.

(A) before
(B) in advance
(C) confirmation
(D) after leaving

129. He ——— he could go home this summer, but he cannot.

(A) hopes
(B) likes
(C) wishes
(D) will hope

130. The press release will be ready for ——— by noon.

(A) prints
(B) producer
(C) allocation
(D) distribution

131. After many years as director of the Accounting Department, the man ——— from the company.

(A) left
(B) took
(C) retired
(D) removed

132. Officials were afraid the matter would ——— into a major conflict.

(A) pass
(B) great
(C) concert
(D) escalate

133. The boy was not a good student, so he could ——— wait to tell his mother about his high marks.

(A) hard
(B) bare
(C) hardly
(D) definite

134. Unemployment ——— after a six-month period of decline.

(A) rose
(B) reducing
(C) went over
(D) goes down

135. This product ——— the market in early July.

(A) is
(B) were
(C) was up
(D) went on

136. Good employees should be ——— up quickly to encourage them to remain with the company.

(A) moved
(B) stood
(C) held
(D) raised

GO ON TO THE NEXT PAGE

137. The new policy on vacation time reduced ——— significantly.

(A) decision
(B) absolutism
(C) demolition
(D) absenteeism

138. He was very ——— to learn more about the product.

(A) bored
(B) motivated
(C) converted
(D) interesting

139. The government ——— a midnight-to-6 A.M. curfew.

(A) held
(B) imposed
(C) decided
(D) released

140. The deadline for ——— of bids is noon, July 1.

(A) to submit
(B) submission
(C) a submitting
(D) having submitted

Part VI

Directions: In Questions 141–160 each sentence has four words or phrases underlined. The four underlined parts of the sentence are marked (A), (B), (C), (D). You are to identify the one underlined word or phrase that should be corrected or rewritten. Then, on your answer sheet, find the number of the question and mark your answer.

Example

All employee (A) are required to wear (B) their identification (C) badges while (D) at work.

Sample Answer

● (B) (C) (D)

Choice (A), the underlined word "employee," is not correct in this sentence. This sentence should read, "All employees are required to wear their identification badges while at work." Therefore, you should choose answer (A).

As soon as you understand the directions, begin work on the questions.

141. The stars and the (A) moon has (B) always fascinated (C) man (D).

142. The Shipping Department did not seal (A) the cartons because (B) government officials wanted to inspect (C) the shipment since it went out (D).

143. Once (A) the condition is under controls (B), the patient must adhere (C) to a strict low-fat (D) diet.

144. Although (A) the reception was schedule (B) for six o'clock, the band did not arrive (C) until after seven (D).

145. High winds and heavy rain assaulted (A) the coast south of (B) the cape, and forcing (C) residents to find (D) refuge inland on higher ground.

146. It is seldom to (A) people find (B) the sounds of nature offensive (C), but sounds of civilization, particularly (D) in cities, are always bothersome.

GO ON TO THE NEXT PAGE

147. He had so much business to conduct in
A B
Tokyo that we did not expect he returns
C
until the twelfth.
D

148. Although four candidates ran for the
A
office, it was universally accepted that
B
only two of them stood any chance of
C
be elected.
D

149. The three childhood friends later went
everywhere together, included vacations
A B C
at the beach.
D

150. My brother was driving me to work
A
yesterday when our car was hitting
B C
a bus.
D

151. With the advent of satellite transmission
A
of photographs of the earth's atmosphere,
B
forecast the weather has become a
C D
relatively exact science.

152. I like to see a movie, but Bob would
A B C
rather go dancing at a disco club.
D

153. They asked what to find the restaurant
A B
at which they had made reservations.
C D

154. He is going to need of some time to
A B
train his replacement, and he
will remain with the company
C
until then.
D

155. Because they were very aware of the
A B
environment, they handled all waste
C
products with extremely carefully.
D

156. When going from country to country,
A B
travelers have always had to submit to
C
customers inspections of their baggage.
D

157. The fact that certainly public education
A
needs are being met by the private
B
sector does not sit well with liberal
C D
educators.

158. Employees are encouraged to discuss
A B
among themselves the advantages and
C
disadvantages to participate in the
D
company health plan.

159. The producing schedule, established early in the project, was the only guideline the team was given.
(A: producing schedule; B: established; C: in; D: given)

160. Although the French are known to be hard workers and rugged individualists, every French would prefer to spend his time in conversation with friends over a leisurely dinner.
(A: are known to be; B: every French; C: his; D: over)

GO ON TO THE NEXT PAGE

Part VII

Directions: Questions 161–200 are based on a variety of reading material (for example, announcements, paragraphs, advertisements, and the like). You are to choose the one best answer, (A), (B), (C), or (D), to each question. Then, on your answer sheet, find the number of the question and mark your answer. Answer all questions following a passage on the basis of what is stated or implied in that passage.

Read the following example.

> The Museum of Technology is a "hands-on" museum, designed for people to experience science at work. Visitors are encouraged to use, test, and handle the objects on display. Special demonstrations are scheduled for the first and second Wednesdays of each month at 1:30 P.M. Open Tuesday–Friday, 2:30–4:30 P.M., Saturday 11:00 A.M.–4:30 P.M., and Sunday 1:00–4:30 P.M.
>
> When during the month can visitors see special demonstrations?
>
> (A) Every weekend
> (B) The first two Wednesdays
> (C) One afternoon a week
> (D) Every other Wednesday

Sample Answer

The passage says that the demonstrations are scheduled for the first and second Wednesdays of the month. Therefore, you should choose answer (B).

As soon as you understand the directions, begin work on the questions.

Questions 161–163 refer to the following list of shopping tips.

SMART MAIL-ORDER SHOPPING TIPS

* When comparing costs, remember to include applicable shipping costs and sales tax in the final price.

* Read all of the fine print, including the return policy. Look for companies that provide a no-questions-asked return policy.

* Keep careful records of your orders, including the catalog name, address, and telephone number, items ordered, order date, operator name, and expected delivery date. Also, try to get an order number for future reference.

* If you are having a problem with a mail-order company that you cannot resolve yourself, contact one of the HELP organizations.

161. When ordering products through a catalog, what should the final price include?

(A) Shipping insurance costs
(B) Sales tax and insurance
(C) Sales tax and shipping costs
(D) Import duties and all taxes

162. Which of the following should be done by a person ordering by mail?

(A) Buy several items, to get the best price
(B) Read the fine print and get an order number
(C) Send payment only after receiving the order
(D) Discard records of transactions once completed

163. What should a person do if a mail-order company sends substandard merchandise and will not accept a return or exchange?

(A) Report it to the police
(B) Contact a HELP organization
(C) Write to the Better Business Bureau
(D) Return the merchandise to a local store

GO ON TO THE NEXT PAGE

Questions 164 and 165 refer to the following advertisement.

> At the Madrid Chancellor Hotel you can expect the finest in luxury and convenience, with the business traveler's special needs in mind. Our tasty array of regional, national, and international dishes, prepared by the most skilled European chefs, are served on only the finest china. Our concierge is always a source of the most up-to-date information and, of course, anyone having business in Spain will appreciate our modern communication facilities, on line 24 hours per day, and available in every room.

164. At whom is the above advertisement directed?

    (A) Vacationers
    (B) Senior citizens
    (C) Business travelers
    (D) Convention organizers

165. What do the advertisers say they are good at doing?

    (A) Making doing business more convenient
    (B) Helping guests find entertainment
    (C) Directing people to good restaurants
    (D) Accommodating individual preferences

Questions 166 and 167 refer to the following advertisement.

The Helping Hand

Need some help? The Helping Hand can help your office by answering busy phones, sending faxes worldwide, or providing local courier services. The Helping Hand is efficient, reliable, and reasonably priced. We have all the equipment you need on our site. Call us today for a free consultation and price quote.

166. What are two major features of the Helping Hand?

 (A) Low price and reliability
 (B) Responsibility and years of experience
 (C) Many employees and courteous representatives
 (D) Equipment available and delivered to local job sites

167. What type of services does the Helping Hand provide?

 (A) Sales
 (B) Office
 (C) Medical
 (D) Mechanical

GO ON TO THE NEXT PAGE

Questions 168–171 refer to the following instructions.

Blue Star Junipers
Guide to Planting and Care

1. Dig a hole larger than earth ball of soil attached to roots.
2. Remove plant from its container or burlap before planting. Do not disturb root system.
3. Plant at least 3–4 feet from other plantings.
4. Set earth ball into ground so that the top of the ball is slightly below ground level.
5. Fill hole with good topsoil and peat moss. Pack firmly.
6. Soak thoroughly with water. (Thereafter water once/week.)
7. Fertilize soil around the plant with well-balanced plant food twice annually.

168. According to the instructions, what special care must be taken while planting a juniper?

(A) The root system must not be damaged.
(B) The plant must be watered before planting.
(C) The hole for the plant must be twice as large as the earth ball.
(D) The handler must wear protective gloves to avoid skin rash.

169. How deep should the hole be to plant the juniper?

(A) From three to four feet
(B) Deep enough to reach ground water
(C) Deep enough to encircle the entire plant
(D) Deep enough for the earth ball to be below ground level

170. How often should a juniper be fertilized?

(A) Every month
(B) Every three months
(C) Two times per year
(D) Once each year, in spring

171. After the juniper is planted and the roots are covered with soil, what is the next step?

(A) Pack the soil and water the plant
(B) Fertilize the plant with peat moss
(C) Cut branch ends to encourage plant growth
(D) Water the plant and cover base with burlap

Questions 172–174 refer to the following memorandum.

To : All Employees
From: Clayton T. Barnes, President
Re : Closing of facility

As of the end of this fiscal year, the Clarkson distribution facility will permanently cease doing business. All operations will be relocated to the Silent Springs plant.

Personnel at salary grade 7 and below will not be relocated. If you fall within that category, you will be paid through June 30, the end of the fiscal year, or, in the case of workers held over to close down the building, through October 31. No new orders will be received at the facility after June 30. All released employees will receive two weeks' severance pay and time off to seek employment.

All personnel at salary grade 8 and above will remain in place and report to the Silent Springs facility on November 1. At that time you will receive your future assignments.

All company directors are concerned that this facility must close and people will lose jobs. However, the recession, which has caused a sharp decline in sales, leaves us no alternative.

We wish each of you luck and prosperity in your future endeavors.

172. When will the plant stop taking orders?

(A) At the end of the fiscal year
(B) At the end of the calendar year
(C) On October 31
(D) Not specified

173. Which Clarkson personnel are to be laid off?

(A) All part-time employees
(B) Employees at salary grade 8 and above
(C) Employees at salary grade 7 and below
(D) Employees who have the least seniority

174. What will the people who are being laid off receive?

(A) One week's pay
(B) Two weeks' pay
(C) One month's pay
(D) Time off with pay until the plant closes

GO ON TO THE NEXT PAGE

Questions 175 and 176 refer to the following advertisement.

> Today the opportunity is yours to secure space in Sydney's, and possibly Australia's, premier office development site.
>
> This 125,330-square-meter site, situated in the heart of Sydney's financial district, still has prime space available for sale. The building accommodates all modern office communications equipment and also commands an excellent view of both the financial district and Sydney Harbor.
>
> Within the next five years, a serious office space shortage is forecast for the city of Sydney. Wise businesses have already applied for Building 53 space.
>
> If you plan to do business in Australia in the 21st century, there is no better place to do it than from Building 53.

175. For what is this advertisement?

(A) Finance
(B) Construction
(C) Australian tourism
(D) Commercial property

176. What reason is given for people to invest?

(A) Low price
(B) Personal service
(C) Future short supply
(D) Government restrictions

Questions 177–179 refer to the following memorandum.

To : All Regular Staff
From: Industrial Relations Office
Date: April 18

Subject: Introduction of hourly-rate employees

Effective May 4, thirty new employees will begin working in our production plant on an hourly-rate basis. This is an experiment to determine whether hourly employment would give better results for all aspects of our enterprise. The new employees know they are part of an experiment. Management encourages regular staff to discuss the program among themselves and with the new employees. After six months, we will assess the program to learn any lessons it may have for us. Meanwhile, we welcome staff comment.

177. What can be said about the new employees?

(A) They will be part of an experiment.
(B) They will be paid the same as regular staff.
(C) They will work longer hours than regular staff.
(D) They will work different hours from regular staff.

178. How are veteran employees asked to treat new employees?

(A) They are to compete with them for prizes.
(B) They are supposed to train them for their work.
(C) They are asked to discuss the program with them.
(D) They are supposed to function separately from them.

179. What will happen after six months?

(A) The program will be evaluated.
(B) Everybody will be given a test.
(C) The program will be discontinued.
(D) All employees will be put on the same status.

GO ON TO THE NEXT PAGE

Questions 180–183 refer to the following statement.

> Due to recent political developments, our nation is now in a position to develop its economy by emphasizing market mechanisms. We are in the process of privatizing many state-owned industries and expect to make our currency fully convertible soon. We welcome and encourage all foreign investment and have reduced greatly the former obstacles to investment. Indeed, today foreign investment need not be negotiated through government offices, but rather can take place on a direct basis. Ownership of foreign patent and copyrights is respected and strictly enforced, and technology licensing and transfer is on a voluntary basis. Come. See what we have learned in only a short time. You will be pleasantly surprised.

180. According to the statement, foreign investment is

(A) reduced.
(B) desired.
(C) respected.
(D) negotiable.

181. Currency in the country discussed will soon be

(A) devalued.
(B) inflated.
(C) left to float.
(D) made convertible.

182. How is foreign technology viewed in the country discussed?

(A) As private property
(B) As a government subsidy
(C) As a gift from other countries
(D) As an educational opportunity

183. What is the statement intended to do?

(A) Welcome tourists
(B) Invite investment
(C) Nationalize financial markets
(D) Warn the international business community

Questions 184–186 refer to the following advertisement.

WANTED Market Analyst: Capable and reliable individual to work in New York City headquarters of international firm. We are a fast-growing company dealing in consumer electronics. With established offices in North America and Western Europe, we have just opened offices in Eastern Europe, South America, and Japan. Bilingual skills are not necessary for this position, but the successful candidate must be able to communicate effectively with people of diverse ethnic/language backgrounds, with patience and respect. Management skills a must. This job is career track and carries a heavy workload with tight deadlines. For the hardworking, organized, ambitious young manager with good verbal skills, it presents a tremendous opportunity. Competitive salary and benefits. Phone Mr. Collins at (811) 555-7155.

184. Where will the market analyst be stationed?

(A) Japan
(B) New York
(C) South America
(D) Western Europe

185. Which of the following would be a product of the company that placed this advertisement?

(A) Travel
(B) Insurance
(C) Automobiles
(D) Television sets

186. Which of the following appears to be a requirement of the position advertised?

(A) Ability to travel abroad
(B) Ability to work with people
(C) Ability to work with numbers
(D) Ability to speak other languages

GO ON TO THE NEXT PAGE

Questions 187–189 refer to the following note.

> Charlie,
>
> Next fall, I think we'll see a dramatic change in women's fashions. They will opt for a more modest, intelligent look than last year. Bright and fancy outfits will be a thing of the past. I suggest we drop our current plans to market low-cut blouses, short skirts, and other less-conservative styles.
>
> This change in direction is based on the findings of an outside opinion survey company, as well as on my personal observation of directions for women's clothing preferences.
>
> We have to come to a decision on our fashion line for next fall no later than January 1. This date has been moved up two weeks, as you will note, because of reaction of buyers last year to holding expensive inventories. We should meet to discuss this matter as soon as possible.
>
> Hal

187. What does the writer expect fall fashions to be like?

(A) Exotic
(B) Youthful
(C) Colorful
(D) Conservative

188. What does the writer propose the company do with regard to its product line?

(A) Change it completely
(B) Continue with it as is
(C) Expand it to other designs
(D) Delay decisions until others act

189. What problem did buyers have the previous year?

(A) They ran out of stock.
(B) They returned many items.
(C) Their inventories were too expensive.
(D) Their customers complained about prices.

Questions 190–192 refer to the following notice.

Date: November 1, 19—

Notice to Commercial Customers

Because of the increased cost of commercial waste disposal, AAA Garbage will increase rates by $10/quarter, effective January 1. This rate increase will appear in your first quarterly bill for the year, which will be mailed the first week in April. Payments are due within three weeks of the billing date. Businesses located outside the city limits will not be affected by this increase because they automatically qualify for special state subsidies.

Thank you for your cooperation.

190. Who will be affected by the rate increase?

(A) All AAA city customers
(B) Private customers only
(C) Certain commercial customers only
(D) Only customers living outside city limits

191. Which of the following line items has required AAA to raise its prices?

(A) Disposal
(B) Personnel
(C) Production
(D) Collection

192. When will customers first be billed for the increase?

(A) In January
(B) In March
(C) In April
(D) With their next payment

GO ON TO THE NEXT PAGE

Questions 193 and 194 refer to the following instructions.

> Before beginning to assemble your new four-cup Fukima Thermal Rice Cooker, read all directions carefully. Wash all non-electrical parts of the cooker before using the first time.
>
> Use your rice cooker only as described in the enclosed recipe booklet. The three-thermal-layer Fukima Enamel Rice Cooker, model number FX3, is not intended for steam cooking vegetables. Particles and minerals that come off during cooking may damage the finish on the inside of the cooking bin. Only model number FX5 (six-cup capacity), with five thermal layers, is manufactured with a protective internal coating strong enough for steaming vegetables.

193. What should be done before assembling this appliance?

(A) Review the recipe book.
(B) Certain parts should be washed.
(C) The cooking bin should be coated.
(D) Electrical parts should be tested.

194. To steam vegetables in a Fukima rice cooker, the appliance must

(A) be coated with an enamel finish.
(B) hold four cups of raw vegetables.
(C) be constructed of three thermal layers.
(D) have a protective coating in the cooking bin.

Questions 195–198 refer to the following notice.

Post Office Request to Hold Mail
(Please Print)

Name: MARCY WALKER

Address: 15 S. ORANGE RD. OLEAN, NY 12345

Begin Date: OCT. 12 End Date: OCT. 19

☐ I will pick up mail at post office
☑ Resume delivery on End Date
☐ Other ______

Signature: Marcy L. Walker Date 9/30

For Post Office Use Only

Receiving Clerk's Initials JLE

Carrier's Initials MKF Route # 3

195. What has the Post Office asked its customers to do?

(A) Hold the mail
(B) Telephone the Post Office
(C) Print responses rather than write longhand
(D) Return the request form to the mail carrier

196. Which of the following could be the name of the mail carrier?

(A) Neal Y. Olean
(B) Marcy L. Walker
(C) James L. Everett
(D) Millie K. Friedman

197. For how long is the Post Office asked to hold the mail?

(A) One day
(B) Two days
(C) One week
(D) One month

198. When should the Post Office stop mail delivery?

(A) September 30
(B) October 1
(C) October 12
(D) October 19

GO ON TO THE NEXT PAGE

Questions 199 and 200 refer to the following advertisement.

JOIN US AT KORASIA BANK

Through size and strength, KorAsia Bank has long been a major player in the world's financial markets. A total capital base of more than US$800 billion and a fully integrated global network give us the financial muscle that banks entering the market today cannot rival.

Then, of course, there are the KorAsia people, people with expertise, product resources, and industry knowledge, all of which are important in devising imaginative financial solutions to financial problems. Expertise. Resources. Knowledge. There has never been a better time to go with KorAsia Bank.

199. Which of the following is given for patrons to bank with KorAsia?

(A) Bank location
(B) Bank security
(C) Staff knowledge
(D) Staff friendliness

200. How might KorAsia operations best be described?

(A) As building on old resources
(B) As establishing new frontiers
(C) As merging with new institutions
(D) As scaling back to survive a tight money market

Stop! This is the end of the test. If you finish before time is called, you can go back to Parts V, VI, and VII and check your work.

TEST 2—SCRIPT

Part I

1. (Woman)
(A) There are a lot of people in the park.
(B) They are leaving the park.
(C) The benches are unoccupied.
(D) The lamps are in the trenches.

2. (Man B)
(A) They are flying at night.
(B) She has opened the kit.
(C) The girl is flying a kite.
(D) She turned off the light.

3. (Woman)
(A) The girls have left the office.
(B) The women are looking in the file drawer.
(C) Some books are open on the table.
(D) Many people have been turned away.

4. (Man B)
(A) The bus has left the parking lot.
(B) People are looking for their bus.
(C) The buses are lined up in the lot.
(D) People are boarding the bus.

5. (Man B)
(A) Many bathers are enjoying the beach.
(B) The swim meet has already begun.
(C) The sky is overcast.
(D) People are hurrying to get into the water.

6. (Woman)
(A) The man is removing the wheels.
(B) The man is washing his hands.
(C) The man is too tired.
(D) The man is working on the wheels.

7. (Man B)
(A) The water has been turned off.
(B) The waiter has run away.
(C) The waiter cannot turn it on.
(D) Water is on the way.

8. (Woman)
 (A) The doctor is taking an exam.
 (B) The doctors are in the back.
 (C) The doctors are in the lab.
 (D) The doctor is examining the patient.

9. (Man B)
 (A) The men are trying to open the doors.
 (B) The man is locking the doors.
 (C) People are going through the doors.
 (D) The men are standing outside the door.

10. (Woman)
 (A) The police are approaching the man.
 (B) The policeman is next to his car.
 (C) The man is looking at the police.
 (D) The policeman is washing his car.

11. (Man B)
 (A) The vehicles are stopping to pay a toll.
 (B) The cars have pulled in for repairs.
 (C) The new road is being opened.
 (D) The car has run into the truck.

12. (Man B)
 (A) The poor woman is standing in the cold.
 (B) The woman is making some copies.
 (C) The woman is pouring a cup of coffee.
 (D) The woman is fixing the machine.

13. (Woman)
 (A) Vegetation has covered everything.
 (B) The women are having their vegetables.
 (C) Vegetables are being sold at the stand.
 (D) The boxes of tomatoes are piled high.

14. (Man B)
 (A) The pharmacist is getting information.
 (B) The pills have spilled on the counter.
 (C) The woman is taking apart the computer.
 (D) The bottles have fallen from the shelves.

15. (Man B)
 (A) The ringing could be heard far away.
 (B) The jeweler is reaching into the case.
 (C) The rings were too high to reach.
 (D) The woman is running from the store.

16. (Woman)
 (A) The man and boy are reading together.
 (B) The couple are sitting in a chair.
 (C) The man is showing the boy the lawn.
 (D) The boy is looking at the man.

17. (Woman)
(A) The cats are standing in the window.
(B) The camera is being set up.
(C) The men are both in the film.
(D) The actors are watching the video.

18. (Man B)
(A) Many people are fishing from the pier.
(B) The fishermen are coming up to the dock.
(C) A load of fish is being brought on board.
(D) Fishing from the pier is prohibited.

19. (Woman)
(A) The goats are running at the men.
(B) The man's hand is on the goat.
(C) The men are putting on their coats.
(D) The animals are hiding from the man.

20. (Man B)
(A) The woman is picking up her hat.
(B) The women are looking for a bakery.
(C) Bread is being passed out.
(D) The woman is working in a bakery.

Part II

21. (Woman) Who's calling, please?
(Man B)
(A) Yes, we received the equipment yesterday.
(B) Jack Smith, from Indianapolis.
(C) I'd like to go along, if it's all right.

22. (Man B) Open your mouth ... let's have a look ... say ahh.... How are you feeling today?
(Woman)
(A) Much better, thank you.
(B) I've been on vacation this week.
(C) No, I still can't see it.

23. (Man B) When can we expect delivery of our order?
(Woman)
(A) I'm sorry. I finished it.
(B) We expect big profits.
(C) In three days, if all goes well.

24. (Man A) How long will the meeting last?
(Man B)
(A) Only about an hour.
(B) Around two meters, I'd say.
(C) Three kilos, exactly.

25. (Woman) Which do you like best?
    (Man A)
    (A) I still don't have any.
    (B) I'm sorry, I wasn't there.
    (C) I like the blue ones.

26. (Man A) Can you tell me how to complete this form?
    (Woman)
    (A) You should keep it in your file.
    (B) Just leave it at the next window.
    (C) Yes, I'll help you. I know it's confusing.

27. (Woman) Have you ever been to Spain?
    (Man B)
    (A) No, it hurts only when I laugh.
    (B) I usually don't care for vegetables.
    (C) No, but I've always wanted to go there.

28. (Man B) What kind of work do you do?
    (Man A)
    (A) It took me a full eight hours.
    (B) I'm a bookkeeper for a small company.
    (C) Please, don't mention it. It was nothing.

29. (Man A) How did you like the show last night?
    (Woman)
    (A) I like winter more than other seasons.
    (B) It was very entertaining, but a little long.
    (C) We went by taxi, but we arrived late.

30. (Woman) What flight will we be on?
    (Man A)
    (A) Later, please.
    (B) I was afraid, too.
    (C) Flight 7-0-2.

31. (Man B) Have you seen my keys?
    (Woman)
    (A) It's a beautiful hotel.
    (B) I think you left them on your desk.
    (C) There's a bus stop out front.

32. (Man A) May I see your ID, please?
    (Man B)
    (A) Yes, here it is.
    (B) Several items were taken.
    (C) Yes, I'll be right there.

33. (Woman) How's your new assistant working out?
    (Man B)
    (A) She's great! A very good worker.
    (B) Yes, she does aerobics every day.
    (C) I don't think I can take the time.

34. (Woman) Are you still working at UNIVEX?
(Man B) (A) I should be finished with it soon.
(B) Yes, but I get off at eleven.
(C) Yes. I've been there almost a year now.

35. (Man A) Is there a dentist's office nearby?
(Woman) (A) Thank you. But if you don't mind, I'll wait here.
(B) I know. I have an appointment at two o'clock.
(C) Yes. There's one just over on Bain Boulevard.

36. (Woman) How could you lose your briefcase?
(Man B) (A) It was a gift from my family.
(B) I wasn't paying attention, and somebody picked it up.
(C) The meeting was last Friday.

37. (Woman) Will our building be open over the weekend?
(Man B) (A) I worked seven days last week.
(B) No, we close every night at ten.
(C) On Saturday, but not on Sunday.

38. (Man B) Have you seen any good movies lately?
(Man A) (A) It's playing at the Main Street Theater.
(B) No, I've been too busy working to go out.
(C) The video was released late last month.

39. (Man A) Do you mind if I close the blinds?
(Man B) (A) No. Go ahead. The sun's too bright.
(B) Gee, I'm sorry to hear that.
(C) That's all right. I've been trying to quit.

40. (Man B) Do you have any idea how the copying machine got broken?
(Man A) (A) Yes, I was trying to unjam it, and it began to give off sparks.
(B) I never would have thought that.
(C) That's too bad. I hope it's not serious.

41. (Man A) Where did all these boxes come from?
(Man B) (A) He says he's from Atlanta.
(B) They were dropped off this morning, from the mail room.
(C) They're waiting for us in the reception area.

42. (Man B) Did you cancel my flight to San Francisco?
(Woman) (A) I'm going to San Francisco, too.
(B) I don't think anybody's left yet.
(C) Yes, but it's still open, if you've changed your mind.

43. (Woman) Is your grandfather's memory still good?
(Man B)
(A) If we replace it, we'll be able to accomplish a lot more.
(B) Yes, he's very good with computers.
(C) No, he often forgets things.

44. (Man B) Have we heard from the chairman since he left?
(Man A)
(A) Yes. He called in yesterday from California.
(B) I can't hear it very well, either.
(C) Yes, I heard about it a week ago.

45. (Woman) Is my application being processed?
(Man B)
(A) Yes. Apply this pad where it hurts.
(B) It was reviewed yesterday, and you'll be notified of our decision later today.
(C) I'm sure we have a lot to learn from your experience.

46. (Man B) Who should get credit for this project?
(Man A)
(A) The entire staff, of course.
(B) We're currently a little short.
(C) They refuse to lend us the money.

47. (Man A) I'm sure Jim said he's working at Vibex Systems.
(Woman)
(A) Jim's dad is a very nice fellow.
(B) I know he's feeling much better now.
(C) He was, but that job lasted only one week.

48. (Woman) Have the revised sales figures been posted?
(Man A)
(A) Yes, they went up this morning.
(B) It started just yesterday.
(C) I'm sorry, we're all out.

49. (Man A) What's the status of the proposal for O-BAN?
(Man B)
(A) It'll be ready for your review by noon.
(B) I'm not sure. I think they're in either California or New York.
(C) You should probably see a doctor as soon as possible.

50. (Man A) Do you think you'll ever again want to use Ajax Delivery Service?
(Man B)
(A) No, it's already used.
(B) No, they can never do anything right.
(C) No, I don't think they delivered it.

Part III

51. (Man B) I'm worried. We're just about out of gas.
(Woman) This map says there's a gas station a few miles up the road.
(Man B) That's luck. I don't think we can get much farther.

52. (Woman) Did you hear? We're getting a new director.
(Man B) No. Did Carter resign?
(Woman) Yes, yesterday after news broke about the missing donations.

53. (Woman) Our legal office says that these people have infringed our patents and that we should take action.
(Man A) What are our chances of winning?
(Woman) The outcome would be clear, in our favor. I say go after them.

54. (Man B) I'd like to schedule an appointment with the doctor for next Monday, if possible.
(Woman) I'm sorry, but Monday is completely booked. When would you next be available?
(Man B) Can you get me in on Tuesday?

55. (Woman) How much is this beef, here ... in front?
(Man A) Let's see ... that one? That's three-forty a pound.
(Woman) Fine. Give me two pounds of it, and can you please cut it from the other end?

56. (Man A) I'm on my way to the office.
(Woman) Can you drop these books off at the library for me on your way?
(Man A) Sure. I'd be glad to.

57. (Woman) You seem very anxious about this trip.
(Man A) I am. You know, I really don't like to fly.
(Woman) Take along a good book. Try to stay calm and think about something pleasant.

58. (Man B) For what benefit are they holding the concert?
(Woman) It's to raise money for the homeless and is being sponsored by some major corporations.
(Man B) It sounds worth going to. Where can we get tickets?

59. (Man B) I won't be able to attend this week's staff meeting.
(Woman) Is there anything you'd like me to report on for you?
(Man B) Yes. Could you please update everyone on developments in setting up our sales network in Mexico?

60. (Woman) Do you plan to sign up for that management course that starts next week?
(Man B) I tried, but they told me it's full and they can't take any more.
(Woman) It's given every six months. Let's get your name at the top of the list for next time.

61. (Man B) This postage meter is broken again.
(Woman) I know. We've already called the repairman.
(Man B) I think we need a new machine. This one is always breaking down.

62. (Man B) Miss, what kind of perfume do you recommend for a woman who is very, let's say, outgoing?
(Woman) Perhaps Red Fire. It's one of our most popular brands.
(Man B) If other people like it, it must be good. Please give me one of those large bottles.

63. (Man B) Do you have any rowboats to rent?
(Man A) Yes, and you'll need life vests. How many people will be going out?
(Man B) Only the two of us, my son and I.

64. (Woman) I need some lettuce and carrots. Is there a grocery store nearby?
(Man A) Yes. There's one just around the corner, if it's still open.
(Woman) Thanks. I hope it is.

65. (Man B) You know, I have no idea where we are.
(Man A) Did you bring a map?
(Man B) No. I thought we could find our way. After all, we've been here before.

66. (Woman) Do you like to ski?
(Man B) No. I don't like feeling there's nothing under my feet, especially if I'm sailing down a hill.
(Woman) I do cross-country, but downhill is just too frightening.

67. (Woman) That's a lovely mirror in your entryway.
(Man A) I'm glad you like it. It was an anniversary gift from our son.
(Woman) Well, it's beautiful. Your son has very good taste.

68. (Man B) How would you rate your English ability?
(Man A) I do all right in everyday conversation, but I often get lost in technical discussions.
(Man B) That's my problem too. I wish I understood more.

69. (Woman) How did the Anderson charity dinner go?
(Man B) There weren't as many guests as everyone expected, but those who came were from the highest levels in some major companies.
(Woman) Well, that's good news. They're the most influential.

70. (Man A) We should move now on our investments in the Republic of Suriland. They've just lifted trade restrictions.
(Man B) That's good news, but do you think it's a good idea to go in so early?
(Man A) I'd say that what it lacks in security, it more than makes up for in potential.

71. (Woman) I'm so angry! I thought I'd get a pay raise but I didn't.
(Man B) I was disappointed, too.
(Woman) Well, at least we got a bonus we weren't expecting.

72. (Man B) Mark, you have a call on line 2.
(Man A) I'm on my way out the door. Can I get back to them?
(Man B) I'll ask, but don't leave yet. It may be long distance.

73. (Man A) I hear that you're now expanding your operations to Africa and the Middle East.
(Woman) That's right. We're setting up offices in Cairo, Dubai, and Lagos.
(Man A) Can you tell me how you plan to go about it?

74. (Man A) What route do you take to get to work?
(Man B) I take Main Street across the Fourteenth Street Bridge, to Columbus Street.
(Man A) You might get here faster if you were to go back to using the McHenry Bridge, now that they've finished construction on it.

75. (Man A) This letter is so poorly written that I can hardly understand it.
(Woman) Shall I do it over?
(Man A) I wish you would, but be sure it makes sense before you give it to me.

76. (Man A) Do you think these union demands are fair?
(Man B) They're outrageous, especially considering the poor shape the company's in.
(Man A) That may be, but given the situation, we may have to give in anyway.

77. (Man B) What time did you tell Sue we'd pick her up?
(Woman) I told her we'd leave right after breakfast, and would be at her place a few minutes later, probably at around six-thirty.
(Man B) I'd like to get on the road. I hope she's ready when we get there. We always seem to have to wait for her.

78. (Man B) Did you hear that Art won an award for his reporting?
(Woman) No. What was it?
(Man B) It's the Press Institute Award for clear writing in journalism. It goes to reporters who are good writers.

79. (Man A) Can you buy some flowers today for the house?
(Woman) Yes. I'd planned to. It's spring and I feel like having flowers around.
(Man A) The days are so nice. I wish I didn't have to work.

80. (Man A) Jake is something of a maverick in the field. He's strange, but he's done very well and has left his mark on how we do business.
(Man B) Maybe in business, caution isn't always best.
(Man A) In Jake's case, you're right, but I wouldn't want to generalize.

Part IV

(Man A) Questions 81 and 82 refer to the following talk.

(Man B) Although violent crime is on the rise, it is still not nearly as common as the crime of fraud, in which an innocent victim may at any time lose an entire life's savings. If you think you may have been a victim of fraud or of any other crime arising from a business transaction, report the matter to the Legitimate Business Office at (toll-free) 1-800-555-6875. Remember, the first line of defense against fraud is with the victim. Practice good business sense. Avoid becoming that victim.

(Man A) Now read question 81 in your test book and answer it.

(Man A) Now read question 82 in your test book and answer it.

(Man A) Questions 83 and 84 refer to the following report.

(Man B) On Monday, the Dow Jones Industrials gained six points in light trading. Volume was only 120 million shares. Stock analysts believe that many investors are waiting for Tuesday's announcement of leading economic indicators before they buy and that trading will increase substantially on Wednesday.

(Man A) Now read question 83 in your test book and answer it.

(Man A) Now read question 84 in your test book and answer it.

(Man A) Questions 85 through 87 refer to the following notice.

(Woman) Shoppers are reminded that this week is specials week at Foodtown, celebrating our first anniversary. All fruits and vegetables are reduced by at least 10 percent, and meat products are reduced by at least 20 percent. We have special buys on steak for the grill and imported leg of lamb. We regret that our fresh seafood is in short supply, due to continuing storms off the coast, but frozen seafood is available at bargain prices. While you shop at Foodtown, please enjoy a free cup of coffee in the bakery department, where you are invited to sample our many delicious pastries. Thank you for shopping at Foodtown.

(Man A) Now read question 85 in your test book and answer it.

(Man A) Now read question 86 in your test book and answer it.

(Man A) Now read question 87 in your test book and answer it.

(Man A) Questions 88 through 90 refer to the following announcement.

(Man A) This is D.J. Mickey Dee, at WICM, bringing you lots of rock in Little Rock. You'll find us here all evening, starting at eight o'clock. We invite you to party along with our weekly classical rock n' roll show. Later, you won't want to miss a live interview with heavy-metal rocker Stevie Finger. As you know, Stevie is in town for his sold-out concert at the Arena Stage tomorrow night. Stay with WICM for all the rock in Little Rock!

(Man A) Now read question 88 in your test book and answer it.

(Man A) Now read question 89 in your test book and answer it.

(Man A) Now read question 90 in your test book and answer it.

(Man A) Questions 91 and 92 refer to the following statement.

(Woman) I'm afraid that on weekends here, it's always necessary to make reservations. We do have a few unreserved tables, but at the moment they're taken. If you would like to wait, I would be pleased to put you on our list for the next available table or for a cancelation. Of course, if you like, you may make a reservation now for next week.

(Man A) Now read Question 91 in your test book and answer it.

(Man A) Now read Question 92 in your test book and answer it.

(Man A) Questions 93 and 94 refer to the following recorded message.

(Woman) You have reached international information for France. If you know the number of the area in France for which you want information, please indicate the number now. If you do not know the area, please indicate the number twelve and an operator will come on the line. If you remain on the line, this recording will play again.

(Man A) Now read question 93 in your test book and answer it.

(Man A) Now read question 94 in your test book and answer it.

(Man A) Questions 95 through 97 refer to the following announcement.

(Man B) Good evening, ladies and gentlemen! Welcome again to the Bevo Bill Show. Tonight we have a great program with three guests who are very much in demand. First, we'll be talking with the unpredictable, exciting, and peripatetic author Charles Fagan about his latest travel book. Then you will meet actress and singer Millicent Beatty, who will talk about her new movie, to be released later this week. And finally, we will talk with a special guest, Mr. John Wilson, the former U.S. Ambassador to Russia, about the difficulties in attempting to jump-start a free-market economy in the former Soviet Union. Now, take a minute to listen to this message from our sponsor. We'll get right back to you.

(Man A) Now read question 95 in your test book and answer it.

(Man A) Now read question 96 in your test book and answer it.

(Man A) Now read question 97 in your test book and answer it.

(Man A) Questions 98 through 100 refer to the following announcement.

(Man A) Welcome to a tour of the Tidal Basin Nuclear Generating Facility. During the tour, we will pass through a restricted area. While you are in that area, we ask that you remain within the yellow lines painted on the walkway. Children 12 years and under must remain with their parents at all times. You may take photographs. We do ask, however, that you disconnect your flash; you will not need it because there is plenty of light. Food, drink, and smoking are prohibited at any point on the tour. Visitors are advised that anyone not obeying these rules will be escorted to a waiting area, where they will rejoin the group as it exits. Shall we begin?

(Man A) Now read question 98 in your test book and answer it.

(Man A) Now read question 99 in your test book and answer it.

(Man A) Now read question 100 in your test book and answer it.

This is the end of the Listening Comprehension portion of the test. Turn to Part V in your test book.

TEST 2 COMPARISON SCORES

The score range for the TOEIC is 10 to 990, 5 to 495 for listening and 5 to 495 for reading. This is a converted score, otherwise known as a scaled score, arrived at by converting an examinee's raw score by a formula that changes with every test. The raw score is merely the number of questions answered correctly. On the TOEIC, there is no penalty for answering a question incorrectly.

Converted scores are reported, rather than raw scores, because the developers of the TOEIC make a statistical adjustment for the relative ease or difficulty of each test. This procedure ensures that scores are equivalent over time and do not fluctuate because one or another test may be easier or more difficult than others.

The raw scores that appear below, for this test and for this test only, correspond to a total mean converted TOEIC score of 500, 250 for listening and 250 for reading. Other tests in this book have mean scores calculated on different formulas.

These scores are provided so, if they like, students can compare their performance on this test with a performance that would produce a total converted score of 500. Raw part scores of above the scores provided here would convert to a score of above 500, while raw part scores of below the scores provided here would convert to a score of below 500.

Part	**Mean Raw Score**
I	15
II	21
III	19
IV	11
Mean Listening	66
V	27
VI	11
VII	27
Mean Reading	65
Mean Total	131

Converted Scores for Above Mean Scores

Mean Listening	250
Mean Reading	250
Mean Total	500

ANSWER KEY FOR TEST 2—LISTENING

Key: Part I

1. (C) The benches are unoccupied.
2. (C) The girl is flying a kite.
3. (B) The women are looking in the file drawer.
4. (D) People are boarding the bus.
5. (C) The sky is overcast.
6. (D) The man is working on the wheels.
7. (A) The water has been turned off.
8. (D) The doctor is examining the patient.
9. (D) The men are standing outside the door.
10. (B) The policeman is next to his car.
11. (A) The vehicles are stopping to pay a toll.
12. (C) The woman is pouring a cup of coffee.
13. (C) Vegetables are being sold at the stand.
14. (A) The pharmacist is getting information.
15. (B) The jeweler is reaching into the case.
16. (A) The man and boy are reading together.
17. (B) The camera is being set up.
18. (A) Many people are fishing from the pier.
19. (B) The man's hand is on the goat.
20. (D) The woman is working in a bakery.

Key: Part II

21. (B) Jack Smith, from Indianapolis.
22. (A) Much better, thank you.
23. (C) In three days, if all goes well.
24. (A) Only about an hour.
25. (C) I like the blue ones.
26. (C) Yes, I'll help you. I know it's confusing.
27. (C) No, but I've always wanted to go there.
28. (B) I'm a bookkeeper for a small company.
29. (B) It was very entertaining, but a little long.
30. (C) Flight 7-0-2.
31. (B) I think you left them on your desk.
32. (A) Yes, here it is.
33. (A) She's great! A very good worker.
34. (C) Yes. I've been there almost a year now.
35. (C) Yes. There's one just over on Bain Boulevard.
36. (B) I wasn't paying attention, and somebody picked it up.
37. (C) On Saturday, but not on Sunday.
38. (B) No, I've been too busy working to go out.
39. (A) No. Go ahead. The sun's too bright.
40. (A) Yes, I was trying to unjam it, and and it began to give off sparks.
41. (B) They were dropped off this morning, from the mail room.
42. (C) Yes, but it's still open, if you've changed your mind.
43. (C) No, he often forgets things.
44. (A) Yes. He called in yesterday from California.
45. (B) It was reviewed yesterday, and you'll be notified of our decision later today.
46. (A) The entire staff, of course.
47. (C) He was, but that job lasted only one week.
48. (A) Yes, they went up this morning.
49. (A) It'll be ready for your review by noon.
50. (B) No, they can never do anything right.

Key: Part III

51. (D) A gas station
52. (B) He resigned.
53. (C) Sue a company for infringing patents
54. (D) Scheduling an appointment
55. (A) Meat
56. (B) Return some books to the library
57. (D) Nervous
58. (A) Attend a concert
59. (C) Report on a project in Mexico
60. (B) Take a management course
61. (D) Office equipment
62. (C) Popularity
63. (A) Take his son for a boat ride
64. (D) Buy vegetables
65. (A) They are lost.
66. (D) Downhill skiing
67. (A) A gift
68. (B) Adequate for simple conversation
69. (B) They were important.
70. (B) Foreign investment
71. (C) Her salary was not increased.
72. (B) He is about to leave the office.
73. (C) A company's overseas expansion
74. (C) The routes they take to get to work
75. (C) He wants a letter to be rewritten.
76. (A) Worker demands
77. (D) Being able to leave early
78. (A) For his writing
79. (A) People are feeling good because of the weather.
80. (D) Unconventional

Key: Part IV

81. (D) Business crime
82. (C) Potential victims
83. (C) 120 million shares
84. (D) Leading economic indicators will be announced.
85. (B) Temporary low prices
86. (A) Brewed coffee
87. (C) A limited supply of fresh seafood
88. (A) Rock
89. (B) A live interview
90. (B) No more tickets are available.
91. (B) It is very busy on weekends.
92. (A) They may wait for a while.
93. (D) From a country other than France.
94. (A) Press a number
95. (C) Three
96. (C) Charles Fagan
97. (B) There will be an advertisement.
98. (D) Thirteen
99. (D) They will have to leave the tour and wait for the others to finish.
100. (A) On a marked pathway

ANSWER KEY FOR TEST 2—READING

Key: Part V

101. (C) According
102. (A) kept
103. (D) tallest
104. (C) specific
105. (D) interruption
106. (D) responsible
107. (D) influenced
108. (A) drove
109. (D) improve
110. (C) after
111. (A) denser
112. (B) arrested
113. (D) are forbidden
114. (C) was founded
115. (C) prevented
116. (C) self-confident
117. (D) be prepared
118. (A) buying
119. (D) informed
120. (D) under
121. (C) precision
122. (B) reason to
123. (B) accept
124. (A) candid
125. (C) relocate
126. (C) rarely
127. (B) penalized
128. (B) in advance
129. (C) wishes
130. (D) distribution
131. (C) retired
132. (D) escalate
133. (C) hardly
134. (A) rose
135. (D) went on
136. (A) moved
137. (D) absenteeism
138. (B) motivated
139. (B) imposed
140. (B) submission

Key: Part VI

141. (B) have
142. (D) before it went out
143. (B) under control
144. (B) scheduled
145. (C) and forced, forcing
146. (A) that
147. (C) him to return
148. (D) being elected
149. (C) including
150. (C) hit, was hit by
151. (C) forecasting
152. (A) I would like
153. (A) how, where
154. (B) some time
155. (D) with extreme care
156. (D) customs inspections
157. (A) certain
158. (D) of participating
159. (A) production schedule
160. (B) every Frenchman

Key: Part VII

161. (C) Sales tax and shipping costs
162. (B) Read the fine print and get an order number
163. (B) Contact a HELP organization
164. (C) Business travelers
165. (A) Making doing business more convenient
166. (A) Low price and reliability
167. (B) Office
168. (A) The root system must not be damaged.
169. (D) Deep enough for the earth ball to be below ground level
170. (C) Two times per year
171. (A) Pack the soil and water the plant
172. (A) At the end of the fiscal year
173. (C) Employees at salary grade 7 and below
174. (B) Two weeks' pay
175. (D) Commercial property
176. (C) Future short supply
177. (A) They will be part of an experiment.
178. (C) They are asked to discuss the program with them.
179. (A) The program will be evaluated.
180. (B) desired.
181. (D) made convertible.
182. (A) As private property
183. (B) Invite investment
184. (B) New York
185. (D) Television sets
186. (B) Ability to work with people
187. (D) Conservative
188. (A) Change it completely
189. (C) Their inventories were too expensive.
190. (C) Certain commercial customers only
191. (A) Disposal
192. (C) In April
193. (B) Certain parts should be washed.
194. (D) have a protective coating in the cooking bin.
195. (C) Print responses rather than write longhand
196. (D) Millie K. Friedman
197. (C) One week
198. (C) October 12
199. (C) Staff knowledge
200. (A) As building on old resources

TOEIC®
TEST 3

LISTENING COMPREHENSION

In this section of the test, you will have the chance to show how well you understand spoken English. There are four parts to this section, with special directions for each part.

Part I

Directions: For each question, you will see a picture in your test book and you will hear four short statements. The statements will be spoken just one time. They will not be printed in your test book, so you must listen carefully to understand what the speaker says.

When you hear the four statements, look at the picture in your test book and choose the statement that best describes what you see in the picture. Then, on your answer sheet, find the number of the question and mark your answer.

Look at the sample below.

Now listen to the four statements.

Sample Answer

Ⓐ   Ⓒ Ⓓ

Statement (B), "They're having a meeting," best describes what you see in the picture. Therefore, you should choose answer (B).

1. 

2. 

GO ON TO THE NEXT PAGE

3.

4.

5.

6.

7. 

8. 

9.

10.

GO ON TO THE NEXT PAGE

11.

12.

13. 

14. 

15.

16.

17. 

18. 

GO ON TO THE NEXT PAGE

19.

20.

Part II

Directions: In this part of the test you will hear a question spoken in English, followed by three responses, also spoken in English. The question and the responses will be spoken just one time. They will not be printed in your test book, so you must listen carefully to understand what the speakers say. You are to choose the best response to each question.

Now listen to a sample question:

You will hear:

You will also hear:

Sample Answer

● Ⓑ Ⓒ

The best response to the question "How are you?" is choice (A) "I am fine, thank you." Therefore, you should choose answer (A).

21. Mark your answer on your answer sheet.
22. Mark your answer on your answer sheet.
23. Mark your answer on your answer sheet.
24. Mark your answer on your answer sheet.
25. Mark your answer on your answer sheet.
26. Mark your answer on your answer sheet.
27. Mark your answer on your answer sheet.
28. Mark your answer on your answer sheet.
29. Mark your answer on your answer sheet.
30. Mark your answer on your answer sheet.
31. Mark your answer on your answer sheet.
32. Mark your answer on your answer sheet.
33. Mark your answer on your answer sheet.
34. Mark your answer on your answer sheet.
35. Mark your answer on your answer sheet.
36. Mark your answer on your answer sheet.
37. Mark your answer on your answer sheet.
38. Mark your answer on your answer sheet.
39. Mark your answer on your answer sheet.
40. Mark your answer on your answer sheet.
41. Mark your answer on your answer sheet.
42. Mark your answer on your answer sheet.
43. Mark your answer on your answer sheet.
44. Mark your answer on your answer sheet.
45. Mark your answer on your answer sheet.
46. Mark your answer on your answer sheet.
47. Mark your answer on your answer sheet.
48. Mark your answer on your answer sheet.
49. Mark your answer on your answer sheet.
50. Mark your answer on your answer sheet.

GO ON TO THE NEXT PAGE

Part III

Directions: In this part of the test, you will hear 30 short conversations between two people. The conversations will not be printed in your test book. You will hear the conversations only once, so you must listen carefully to understand what the speakers say.

In your test book you will read a question about each conversation. The question will be followed by four answers. You are to choose the best answer to each question and mark it on your answer sheet.

51. What are the speakers going to do?

    (A) Go home
    (B) Have lunch
    (C) Plan a trip
    (D) Make a telephone call

52. What type of machine did the office have replaced?

    (A) A copier
    (B) A fax machine
    (C) A telephone system
    (D) A postage-issuing machine

53. What are the speakers discussing?

    (A) Where to shop
    (B) Directions to a museum
    (C) How to get out of the city
    (D) How to get to the train station

54. When will the man's bus leave?

    (A) In ten minutes
    (B) In fifteen minutes
    (C) In forty minutes
    (D) In fifty minutes

55. What is Mike doing?

    (A) Waiting in his car
    (B) Going to the airport
    (C) Phoning from far away
    (D) Leaving to go to lunch

56. What is the man's problem?

    (A) He has no money.
    (B) He does not have a ticket.
    (C) He does not know where he is going.
    (D) He does not think he should pay for his ride.

57. Why will the woman go to the library?

    (A) She has to return a book.
    (B) She works there.
    (C) She needs reference material.
    (D) She is supposed to meet a friend.

58. What did the supervisor tell the employees?

    (A) He was going to leave early.
    (B) He wanted them to work late.
    (C) They could leave when they finish their work.
    (D) They have to work together to finish the job.

59. Why is the man concerned about the weather?

    (A) He needs to repair his roof.
    (B) He is planning a day at the beach.
    (C) He becomes depressed when it rains.
    (D) He will go out of town for the weekend.

60. Why does the man need to go to the front desk?

(A) To get a new key
(B) To report a theft
(C) To meet a visitor
(D) To make a reservation

61. Why does the man prefer the Emperor Hotel?

(A) He likes the restaurant.
(B) The clients requested it.
(C) It is close to the airport.
(D) He is meeting important people.

62. What is the woman referring to?

(A) A trip abroad
(B) Some visitors
(C) A business deal
(D) Recent developments

63. What are the speakers discussing?

(A) A name for a restaurant
(B) Food at a new restaurant
(C) Restaurant decorations
(D) Where to go for dinner

64. Where is the stockholder's meeting going to be held?

(A) At the annex
(B) On the tenth floor
(C) In the president's office
(D) At the Tenth Street offices

65. What is the man looking for?

(A) A mall
(B) A hotel
(C) A restaurant
(D) A movie theater

66. What will the speakers do?

(A) Meet for lunch
(B) Ride to work together
(C) Hold regular meetings
(D) Go to work for the same company

67. What information is being sought?

(A) An address
(B) A person's name
(C) A telephone number
(D) A purchase order number

68. What are the speakers talking about?

(A) The opening of a factory
(B) Delivery of some plants
(C) Decorations in a house
(D) A change in the seasons

69. What has Marty been asked to do?

(A) Go somewhere
(B) Attend a meeting
(C) Read a document
(D) Make a phone call

70. What does the man want?

(A) A brochure
(B) Some money
(C) An address
(D) An account report

71. What does Mary's supervisor say about her work performance?

(A) She works very fast.
(B) She is often absent from work.
(C) She stays late to finish her work.
(D) She is punctual and never absent from work.

GO ON TO THE NEXT PAGE

72. What aspect of the port does the man ask about?

(A) Its size
(B) Its depth
(C) Its connections
(D) Its costs

73. What will happen to the accountant?

(A) He will be fired.
(B) He will receive a promotion.
(C) He will be sent to another department.
(D) He will be offered a permanent position.

74. What was the problem at the party?

(A) Nobody liked the pizza.
(B) There was not enough food.
(C) The neighbors complained.
(D) People stayed too late.

75. What was installed?

(A) A new machine
(B) New supervision
(C) A new product line
(D) New accounting procedures

76. Why is the meeting to be postponed?

(A) A necessary person is not available.
(B) It is too late in the day to start a meeting.
(C) Several people have not yet read the report.
(D) Construction in the building makes meeting difficult.

77. What problem do the speakers have?

(A) They lost some tickets.
(B) They are trying to bake a cake.
(C) They do not have a ride home.
(D) They cannot get a clear picture on their television.

78. What is the woman's problem?

(A) Window 3 is closed.
(B) The rate of exchange is not posted.
(C) The bank does not accept traveler's checks.
(D) Nobody seems to know where money can be exchanged.

79. What has the man done?

(A) He borrowed money to buy a car.
(B) He lent money to a friend to buy a car.
(C) He will lend the woman money to buy a car.
(D) He paid cash for his car to avoid paying interest.

80. What business are the speakers in?

(A) Entertainment
(B) Advertising
(C) Manufacturing
(D) Tourism and travel

Part IV

Directions: In this part of the test, you will hear several short talks. Each will be spoken just one time. They will not be printed in your test book, so you must listen carefully to understand and remember what is said.

In your test book you will read two or more questions about each short talk. The questions will be followed by four answers. You are to choose the best answer to each question and mark it on your answer sheet.

81. Where is the Esmeralda Resort?

 (A) In the Carolinas
 (B) In the Bahamas
 (C) In the Caribbean
 (D) In the Virgin Islands

82. How far is the Esmeralda Resort from the nearby town?

 (A) One mile
 (B) Two miles
 (C) Four miles
 (D) Ten miles

83. Where would this statement be heard?

 (A) On a ship
 (B) At a parking garage
 (C) In a school yard
 (D) On a public street

84. What does the speaker request?

 (A) A donation
 (B) Cooperation
 (C) Listeners' votes
 (D) Concern for personal safety

85. Why does the speaker praise Dr. Ramon?

 (A) He has taught a course.
 (B) He has provided research material.
 (C) He has given an interesting speech.
 (D) He has helped students with a project.

86. What subject are the students studying?

 (A) History
 (B) Science
 (C) English
 (D) Mathematics

87. During what season is the festival held?

 (A) Fall
 (B) Winter
 (C) Spring
 (D) Summer

88. How many people attended the event?

 (A) 40
 (B) 400
 (C) 4,000
 (D) 40,000

89. What is listed in the right-hand column of the Air Asia timetable?

 (A) Air Asia's flight times
 (B) Air Asia's flight mileage
 (C) Air Asia's flight numbers
 (D) Number of stops on Air Asia flights

90. Where can the timetable be found?

 (A) In the seat pocket.
 (B) At ticket counters.
 (C) In the flight magazine.
 (D) Passengers may ask for copies.

91. What does the city expect?

(A) A flood
(B) A hurricane
(C) An earthquake
(D) A snowstorm

92. What have people been instructed to do?

(A) Drive to high ground
(B) Prepare to remain indoors
(C) Evacuate to the nearest shelter
(D) Put boards and tape over windows

93. Who has been given special instructions?

(A) Pregnant women
(B) School children
(C) Hospital personnel
(D) Civil defense workers

94. Where is this announcement made?

(A) On an airplane
(B) Over the radio
(C) On board a ship
(D) In a department store

95. What does this announcement concern?

(A) A world event
(B) A serious problem
(C) Special opportunities
(D) Developments and expectations

96. In what does the company deal?

(A) Vehicles
(B) Electricity
(C) Investments
(D) Travel and tourism

97. What does the company say about the work it does?

(A) It is new.
(B) It is exciting.
(C) It is demanding.
(D) It is highly profitable.

98. What does the company say it wants to do?

(A) Pay off its debt
(B) Export its services
(C) Devise new products
(D) Attract new accounts

99. Who called the meeting?

(A) It happened by chance.
(B) The speaker called it.
(C) The president called it.
(D) It was regularly scheduled.

100. Why is the speaker leaving the company?

(A) He is ill.
(B) He is retiring.
(C) He does not say.
(D) He has been dismissed.

This is the end of the Listening Comprehension portion of the test. Turn to Part V in your test book.

YOU WILL HAVE ONE HOUR AND FIFTEEN MINUTES TO COMPLETE PARTS V, VI, AND VII OF THE TEST.

READING

In this section of the test, you will have a chance to show how well you understand written English. There are three parts to this section, with special directions for each part.

Part V

Directions: Questions 101–140 are incomplete sentences. Four words or phrases, marked (A), (B), (C), (D), are given beneath each sentence. You are to choose the one word or phrase that best completes the sentence. Then, on your answer sheet, find the number of the question and mark your answer.

Example

Because the equipment is very delicate, it must be handled with ———.

(A) caring
(B) careful
(C) care
(D) carefully

Sample Answer

The sentence should read, "Because the equipment is very delicate, it must be handled with care." Therefore, you should choose answer (C).

As soon as you understand the directions, begin work on the questions.

101. The two meetings were called for the ——— time.

(A) four
(B) only
(C) late
(D) same

102. Several trees were ——— over during the storm.

(A) blew
(B) blows
(C) blown
(D) blowing

103. Business property mortgage rates have ——— substantially.

(A) inserted
(B) incensed
(C) increased
(D) ineligible

104. While aspirin may not always be the ——— medicine for a headache, it usually helps.

(A) one
(B) best
(C) last
(D) using

105. Saturday was going to be a busy day, so everyone ——— retire early Friday night.

(A) decided
(B) decision
(C) decided to
(D) make a decision

106. Concert tickets ——— purchased by phone with a credit card.

(A) to be
(B) being
(C) can be
(D) has been

107. Trains on national schedules usually arrive ——— time.

(A) on
(B) at
(C) for
(D) over

108. With a rise in crime, prison overcrowding is ——— a serious problem in many developing countries.

(A) fast
(B) decide
(C) becoming
(D) enormous

109. The survey indicates that consumers find product A ——— to product B.

(A) like
(B) the same
(C) superior
(D) different

110. The engineer was asked to ——— the surface temperatures generated by the rocket's speed.

(A) advise
(B) function
(C) calculate
(D) determinate

111. Soon after the game began, the catcher fell and ——— an arm.

(A) held
(B) broke
(C) hurts
(D) turned

112. The automobile dealership plays soft music in its showroom to ——— a pleasant atmosphere.

(A) put
(B) help
(C) light
(D) create

113. There was no ——— to reach the stranded swimmers.

(A) way
(B) easy
(C) want
(D) times

114. Communication between the main office and the branch offices was ———.

(A) lately
(B) sometimes
(C) perfectly
(D) infrequent

115. The ladder was not ——— high enough to reach the third story.

(A) so
(B) only
(C) quite
(D) almost

116. A dinner for two at the Casablanca was the prize awarded to the couple ——— the winning ticket.

(A) to buy
(B) holding
(C) who arrived
(D) turning around

117. Studies ——— that physical health is closely linked to mental health.

(A) have
(B) show
(C) explains
(D) demonstrates

118. Tickets for the benefit ——— sold at the National Theater.

(A) to be
(B) is being
(C) has been
(D) are being

119. Fire ——— the east wing of the old hotel.

(A) down
(B) damage
(C) burning
(D) destroyed

120. The decision of the city planners ——— the opinion of the public.

(A) refers
(B) reflected
(C) interpret
(D) interfered

121. Before turning east and going out to sea, the hurricane left a path of ——— across the region.

(A) weather
(B) high wind
(C) insecurity
(D) destruction

122. They were so busy ——— the new house that they forgot to ask for water service.

(A) remover
(B) removing
(C) moving into
(D) moving about

123. The car gave out on the highway and ——— towed.

(A) had to be
(B) has to be
(C) needs to be
(D) was meant to be

124. Your receipt will serve as ——— of purchase.

(A) proof
(B) price
(C) offer
(D) place

GO ON TO THE NEXT PAGE

125. In addition to the application form, applicants need to ——— forms 290-A and 291-D, revised.

(A) apply
(B) submit
(C) script
(D) insert

126. The ——— sector was left to languish, while manufacturing and finance received strong support from the government.

(A) culture
(B) accurate
(C) accomplished
(D) agricultural

127. The accident ——— the road to eastbound traffic.

(A) hurt
(B) made
(C) closed
(D) detoured

128. The radio station began to ——— with its new antenna.

(A) transmit
(B) transfer
(C) transport
(D) transcribe

129. The office closes ——— at 6:00 P.M.

(A) almost
(B) evenly
(C) earliest
(D) promptly

130. The police set up a roadblock to ——— traffic.

(A) run
(B) stop
(C) keep
(D) drive

131. Many people are more ——— of their finances than of their health.

(A) prepared
(B) protective
(C) productive
(D) preoccupied

132. The president imposed an ——— program to curb unauthorized spending by the ministries.

(A) active
(B) efficient
(C) excessive
(D) austerity

133. The new process fast became ——— for assembly line workers.

(A) able
(B) routine
(C) gone on
(D) finished

134. The piece of equipment was ——— and could not cross the bridge without causing serious damage.

(A) oversize
(B) powerful
(C) magnified
(D) especially

135. Everyone was surprised to see the ——— made in the field of computer graphics software.

(A) progress
(B) technology
(C) appliances
(D) production

136. The man was ——— the hospital for tests.

(A) admitted to
(B) registered
(C) in for
(D) into

137. Three large trading blocs, all going their own way, appear to be ——— international markets.

(A) leaving
(B) adopting
(C) charging
(D) polarizing

138. The company refused to ——— on behalf of its employee.

(A) intervene
(B) implicate
(C) interview
(D) intercept

139. A breakthrough in technology gave the company ——— over the competition.

(A) a profit
(B) an interest
(C) an advantage
(D) an investment

140. Manufacturing processes require ——— power source.

(A) a needful
(B) an energetic
(C) a dependable
(D) an indeterminable

GO ON TO THE NEXT PAGE

Part VI

Directions: In Questions 141–160 each sentence has four words or phrases underlined. The four underlined parts of the sentence are marked (A), (B), (C), (D). You are to identify the one underlined word or phrase that should be corrected or rewritten. Then, on your answer sheet, find the number of the question and mark your answer.

Example

All employee (A) are required to wear (B) their identification (C) badges while (D) at work.

Sample Answer

● (B) (C) (D)

Choice (A), the underlined word "employee," is not correct in this sentence. This sentence should read, "All employees are required to wear their identification badges while at work." Therefore, you should choose answer (A).

As soon as you understand the directions, begin work on the questions.

141. Sky diving (A) have become (B) the (C) favorite sport of some (D) college students.

142. Although I have known him for many years, (A) there are times as (B) I feel as though (C) I do not know what he is really thinking (D).

143. Traditions (A) wooden (B) shoes have always (C) been made (D) in Holland.

144. The committee has met (A) yesterday, but Mr. Kim was (B) not ready to make (C) his presentation (D).

145. The woman said she is (A) happier than she had ever been, although she seemed to have little (B) to be (C) happy about (D).

146. Earlier approaches to management in the United States have been showing (A) to discourage worker concern for (B) involvement in (C) quality control and improvement of production processes (D).

147. It is necessary (A) to remove all unsatisfactory (B) machine parts from the delivery when receive, (C) and to inform (D) the supplier of any shortage in the order.

148. Please complete (A) the enclosed application and return (B) it us (C) in the envelope provided. (D)

149. Several business trips (A) were scheduled (B) during (C) the early part of the month, before the holidays break. (D)

150. Fewest (A) voters are eligible to vote in the next election, (B) compared with (C) the numbers (D) eligible to vote in previous elections.

151. Because of high overhead associates (A) with selling (B) through (C) retail outlets, many department store chains have (D) catalog-sales departments.

152. If I were (A) in his position, I would do (B) exactly a same (C) as he. (D)

153. Visits (A) to the United States complain that (B) the American system of weights and measures is both (C) confusing and irrational. (D)

154. Of (A) the two alternatives, (B) this (C) is the best (D) one.

155. For a variety of reasons, including (A) a better understanding (B) of its causes, skin cancer has become a major concern between (C) people who vacation (D) at the beach.

156. Television viewers cannot (A) see live (B) coverage of Olympic events until (C) after 11:00 P.M., because of the different (D) in time zones.

GO ON TO THE NEXT PAGE

157. Almost students in the advanced class
A
have been studying English for many
B
years, which is why their grades are
C
better than average.
D

158. The tour guide instructed everyone

to go back up to the bus after two
A B
hours, to ensure their arrival at the next
C
city before nightfall.
D

159. I quickly replied to your inquiry of

July 18, because I was afraid that if I
A
delayed, you were thinking I was not
B
concerned about the difficulties
C
you are experiencing.
D

160. Regardless of what the problem
A
may be, a team of experienced
B
technicians can usually handle
C
the problem.
D

Part VII

Directions: Questions 161–200 are based on a variety of reading material (for example, announcements, paragraphs, advertisements, and the like). You are to choose the one best answer, (A), (B), (C), or (D), to each question. Then, on your answer sheet, find the number of the question and mark your answer. Answer all questions following a passage on the basis of what is stated or implied in that passage.

Read the following example.

> The Museum of Technology is a "hands-on" museum, designed for people to experience science at work. Visitors are encouraged to use, test, and handle the objects on display. Special demonstrations are scheduled for the first and second Wednesdays of each month at 1:30 P.M. Open Tuesday–Friday, 2:30–4:30 P.M., Saturday 11:00 A.M.–4:30 P.M., and Sunday 1:00–4:30 P.M.
>
> When during the month can visitors see special demonstrations?
>
> (A) Every weekend
> (B) The first two Wednesdays
> (C) One afternoon a week
> (D) Every other Wednesday

Sample Answer

The passage says that the demonstrations are scheduled for the first and second Wednesdays of the month. Therefore, you should choose answer (B).

As soon as you understand the directions, begin work on the questions.

Questions 161 and 162 refer to the following health plan.

HEALTH INSURANCE COVERAGE

Medical Expenses: The plan pays the first $2,500 of any non-dental surgery and 85 percent of remaining surgical expenses. For all other medical care, including hospitalization, the plan will provide full coverage after the $60 deductible.

Vaccinations: The plan covers children under the age of 14.

Dental Expenses: The plan does not cover routine dental checkups. There is a $50 deductible. The plan will pay for 70 percent of any expenses for dental work or surgery after the deductible is paid.

161. How much is the deductible for hospitalization?

(A) $40
(B) $50
(C) $60
(D) $70

162. How does the plan treat dental checkups?

(A) It provides full coverage.
(B) It carries a $50 deductible.
(C) It pays for children under 14.
(D) It has no coverage.

Questions 163–165 refer to the following notice.

Voter Registration Information

To register to vote in Twin Buttes County, you must be a citizen of the United States, a resident of Twin Buttes, and at least 18 years of age by the date of the next election.

Registration is conducted weekdays from 8:00 A.M. to 4:30 P.M. at all county libraries. Call for voting information or for an absentee-voter application. Disabled persons may request a voter registrar to make a home visit.

163. Which of the following is a requirement for voting in Twin Buttes?

(A) The voter must live in Twin Buttes County.
(B) Ability to read the English language.
(C) Residency in Twin Buttes for minimum of six months.
(D) The voter must not have previously registered elsewhere.

164. Where can a person register to vote in Twin Buttes County?

(A) At any post office
(B) At any county library
(C) At the Registrar's Office
(D) At the Office of Elections

165. Who may register at home to vote?

(A) Voters who are physically impaired
(B) Rural voters without transportation
(C) Municipal, county, or state employees
(D) People who have registered at least once in the past

GO ON TO THE NEXT PAGE

Questions 166–168 refer to the following telephone listings.

Telephone Listings

Craig, Mary	1245 Grayson Ln.	541-0987
Craig, Samuel	1346 Bear Ct.	541-3211
Lambert, Wm.	4567 Center St.	654-9087
Layton, Tim	1235 Grayson Ln.	541-2345
McGrath, R.	1897 Lee Dr.	541-8765
Meyer, Walter	1346 Bear Ct.	541-3211
Ryan, Patrick	5678 Taylor St.	541-9087

166. Which two people are probably neighbors?

(A) Patrick Ryan and Wm. Lambert
(B) Walter Meyer and Tim Layton
(C) Mary Craig and Tim Layton
(D) Samuel Craig and Walter Meyer

167. What makes Wm. Lambert's listing different from the others?

(A) He is in a different telephone area.
(B) He is the only listing under L.
(C) He is the only one with 9087 in his phone number.
(D) He is married and his wife is also listed.

168. Which two people have the same address?

(A) Mary Craig and Patrick Ryan
(B) R. McGrath and Wm. Lambert
(C) Mary Craig and Tim Layton
(D) Samuel Craig and Walter Meyer

Questions 169–171 refer to the following letter.

Dear Mr. Jackson,

We were sorry to learn that no representative from your company will be able to accompany our group on its first fact-finding trip to Algeria.

During this trip, we plan to lay the groundwork for future business activities and had hoped the interest you expressed earlier still held.

As we discussed at the London conference, we are planning to go on to Tunisia and Morocco after leaving Algiers. We will provide ongoing communications to your office concerning our findings. Our invitation still stands. Feel free to have someone from your company join us at any point in the trip.

Sincerely,

Bob Miller
Chief Investment Officer
MedTech Securities

169. How does this letter begin?

(A) With an extension of credit
(B) With an expression of regret
(C) With a withdrawal of an offer
(D) With an accounting correction notice

170. What was the purpose of the proposed visit?

(A) To plan a conference
(B) To present a proposal
(C) To come to an agreement
(D) To prepare for the future

171. What does Mr. Miller offer Mr. Jackson?

(A) To meet Mr. Jackson in Morocco
(B) To take Mr. Jackson on his next trip
(C) To visit Mr. Jackson upon returning
(D) To welcome a visitor from Mr. Jackson's office while on the trip

GO ON TO THE NEXT PAGE

Questions 172 and 173 refer to the following advertisement.

GET AWAY

Would you like the vacation of a lifetime? Have you always thought of taking a romantic cruise but could never afford it? Now you can, with SUPER GETAWAY TOURS. For a limited time, we are offering a Caribbean cruise with stops in Caracas, Grenada, and San Juan for only $899.

Tour includes:

- o Round-trip airfare from Miami to Caracas
- o All meals and entertainment
- o Scuba diving and wind surfing
- o Special shopping discounts

Seven days/six nights. Each day a new adventure! Departures every Monday until September 15. Reservations needed two weeks in advance.

[Taxes not included. Price based on double occupancy. Service charges included.]

172. Which of the following is NOT included in the tour price?

(A) Taxes
(B) Meals
(C) Airfare
(D) Entertainment

173. According to the advertisement, which of the following statements is TRUE?

(A) Price is based on single occupancy.
(B) Tours begin departing on September 15.
(C) Service charges are not included in the price.
(D) Reservations must be made two weeks in advance.

Questions 174–176 refer to the following memorandum.

Memorandum for: John Kline
CFO, Harris Co.

From: Marty Upton
President

Date: December 12, 19—

Subject: Matrix Takeover

As you know, on November 16 Harris Company was purchased by the Matrix Corporation for the sum of five million dollars. Appropriately, Harris will be incorporated into Matrix's Aerospace Division. Because of the merged company's redundancy in operations and expertise, only the Harris main plant will remain operational. Seager Lake, Clearview, and Tipton 3 manufacturing facilities will be phased out over a twelve-month period. Please keep this information confidential until I notify the general manager at each location.

174. Which facility will NOT be closed?

(A) Tipton 3
(B) Clearview
(C) Seager Lake
(D) Harris main plant

175. What type of industry is Harris Company?

(A) Computer
(B) Aerospace
(C) Automobile
(D) Electronics

176. What has the finance officer been asked to do?

(A) Notify all affected employees
(B) Transfer to Matrix headquarters
(C) Not inform anyone of the changes
(D) Remit payment of five million dollars

GO ON TO THE NEXT PAGE

Questions 177 and 178 refer to the following article.

Local School Enrollment Soars

Local school enrollment hit a new high this fall, giving officials even more to worry about at a time of layoffs and diminishing classroom resources. The preliminary enrollment figure in local schools for the year is 135,626 students, the highest total since enrollment reached a peak of 135,166 two decades ago.

177. Which of the following statements about local school enrollment is true?

(A) It has increased.
(B) It has decreased.
(C) It has leveled off.
(D) It has not changed for several years.

178. At what point was local school enrollment about the same as it is currently?

(A) Five years before
(B) Ten years before
(C) Fifteen years before
(D) Twenty years before

Questions 179–181 refer to the following letter.

February 13, 19—

Dear Mr. Carlton:

On behalf of the Tiger Rowing Club, I would like to invite you and the Fan Dance Rowing Club to the 24th Annual Golden Wave Regatta, to be held October 2nd in Sambakan. The race will be held on the Dukon River and will be run over the same course as last year. Amateur teams from 11 countries will compete, promising that the Regatta will be the highlight of the international rowing competition circuit's activities.

As with all attending clubs and special guests, you are invited to sit with other club commissions in the Lotus Pavilion V.I.P. Observation Deck.

Lunch will be served at 12 noon, with events scheduled to get underway by 2 o'clock.

Do let me know if you and your club will be able to attend.

Sincerely,

Richard Philpot
Events Coordinator

179. To what is the invitation?

(A) A marathon
(B) A boat race
(C) Reserved seats
(D) An awards luncheon

180. Who sent the letter?

(A) Sambakan
(B) Tiger Rowing Club
(C) The Lotus Pavilion
(D) The Fan Dance Rowing Club

181. Who does Mr. Carlton represent?

(A) Advertisers
(B) A rowing club
(C) The Golden Wave Regatta
(D) An international circuit

GO ON TO THE NEXT PAGE

Questions 182 and 183 refer to the following faculty memorandum.

> A welcome coffee hour will be held on Wednesday, September 10, in the Wellington Room.
>
> Attire is informal.
> Refreshments will be served.
>
> All faculty are encouraged to attend, as this will be an opportunity for everybody to meet new lecturers in the department before the school year opens.

182. What is the purpose of the meeting?

    (A) To prepare future plans
    (B) To review policies
    (C) To debate a controversial topic
    (D) To greet new people

183. How does the letter say people are to dress?

    (A) Formally
    (B) Casually
    (C) Prepared to work
    (D) In academic robes

Questions 184 and 185 refer to the following advertisement.

ENTRY TO CANADA

Obtain Canadian residency and employment permission via investments, intra-company transfers, and the like. All matters personally handled by licensed Canadian attorney fluent in Mandarin and Japanese, a frequent traveler to Asia.

Contact: Alan P. Rice
P.O. Box 95DP3
Prairie City, Alberta
Canada
Tel: 301/555-3010

184. What is Mr. Rice's area of specialization?

(A) Investments
(B) Import licensing
(C) Immigration law
(D) Background investigations

185. Who would use Mr. Rice's services?

(A) Politicians
(B) Corporations
(C) Foreigners
(D) Financiers

GO ON TO THE NEXT PAGE

Questions 186–188 refer to the following article.

> Malaysia's ancient symbol of power and integrity, the kris, has long been a favorite of local collectors. But now the antique wavy-bladed dagger is beginning to fascinate European investors.
>
> Some historians say the weapon may have been imported from Java in the 15th century. Legend claims that it was developed indigenously. Whatever its origins, the kris has flourished for centuries as the chosen weapon of sultans and village fighters alike.
>
> Because of their enduring popularity, finely crafted krises have always been in short supply, a fact that has led to a sharp rise in their value in recent years. Today, the finest examples can command prices of more than $4,000.
>
> Dealers usually take krises to the National Museum to determine their age and authenticity. Asking prices, however, are anybody's guess, and a tour of antique shops will show them to be arbitrary. Investors would do well to consult a reputable appraiser before making a major investment in one.

186. Where is the kris said to have originated?

    (A) Java
    (B) Turkey
    (C) The Orient
    (D) Near East

187. Where do dealers take krises to have them authenticated?

    (A) To antique shops
    (B) To local craftsmen
    (C) To the National Museum
    (D) To the National Art Treasures Office

188. How old is the kris?

    (A) About two hundred years
    (B) More than four hundred years
    (C) One thousand years
    (D) Two thousand years

Questions 189–191 refer to the following advertisement.

Acquaint Millions of People with Your Products Fast by Promoting on Cable with Cable Promotions!

Cable television promotion is fast becoming one of the most widespread and effective mediums for advertising in the world. With an ability to access an international viewership of more than 120 million households in North America, Europe, and Asia, Cable Promotions is the world's retail outlet of the air. Cable viewers are affluent consumers and often impulsive buyers, and cable television advertising has far fewer regulations than regular broadcast television.

If you have a product that you want to promote, consider today's technology and the potential it holds for increasing your sales. Phone Cable Promotions today at 555-6000. Let us tell you how we can help you double, triple, or even quadruple your sales.

189. What does Cable Promotions say about the cable market?

(A) It is fast-growing.
(B) Specific locations can be targeted.
(C) There are a few licenses still available.
(D) Viewers in cable households are younger than viewers in regular television households.

190. What is an advantage of cable television advertising over regular broadcast television?

(A) It is less regulated.
(B) It accesses more households.
(C) It is available around the clock.
(D) It requires less lead time to arrange.

191. What does Cable Promotions say it can do for advertisers?

(A) Increase sales by more than 100 percent
(B) Put them ahead of the competition
(C) Put them in touch with retail outlets
(D) Increase profits by reducing advertising costs

GO ON TO THE NEXT PAGE

Questions 192–194 refer to the following letter.

Battelle Insurance Company
Chicago, Illinois

William P. Mervin
23 Dribble Drive
Hobart, IL 33456

Policy Number:
A987 8907 E08

Car Description:
1993 Ford Escort

Enclosed is your latest dividend check. Since Battelle's claim costs continue to be less than anticipated, our Board of Directors has authorized payment of this dividend on your auto insurance policy.

If you have any questions about your auto policy, or about insurance for your home, life, or health, please call me.

We are pleased to send you this dividend and to take this opportunity to thank you for selecting Battelle as your insurer.

Sincerely,

Joe Mullee
Battelle Insurance Agent

192. For what insurance is the coverage on the above policy?

(A) Home
(B) Life
(C) Health
(D) Automobile

193. What has William Mervin received from his insurance company?

(A) A payment on a claim
(B) A rebate on his payment
(C) A bill for insurance coverage
(D) A notice of cancelation of his policy

194. Why was this notification made?

(A) To settle an outstanding claim
(B) To enable Battelle to balance its accounts
(C) Because coverage was originally overpriced
(D) Because claim costs were not as high as expected

Questions 195 and 196 refer to the following statement.

Advertising and the Public Perception

Companies often seek the services of well-known sports or entertainment personalities to promote their products. Although this is a good practice when the person embodies wholesome qualities, it can backfire when the person engages in scandalous or otherwise reprehensible behavior. In such cases, the public comes to associate antisocial behavior with the product, and will avoid buying it. It is advisable that before retaining a famous person for endorsement, a complete background check be made. If a person has exhibited undesirable behavior in the past, he will probably exhibit undesirable behavior in the future. Also, the contract should cancel automatically, should the personality bring discredit to the product advertised.

195. Who would be interested in the advice given?

(A) Famous people who want to endorse products
(B) The public who buy products endorsed by famous people
(C) Companies that hire famous people to endorse products
(D) People who do background checks on public personalities

196. What is said to be a problem in using personalities to advertise products?

(A) They are very expensive.
(B) They may not like the product.
(C) They can bring discredit to the product.
(D) They may endorse a competitor's product as well.

GO ON TO THE NEXT PAGE

Questions 197 and 198 refer to the following advertisement.

IT'S NO SECRET—OR IS IT?

Ask any businessman: the mid-size business jet fleets of 80 percent of the world's largest corporations are made up of only two models of aircraft, Chevon Corporation's Pegasus and Polestar's White Eagle.

It's no secret that of the two, our competition, the Chevon Pegasus, currently holds the lead in sales. What might be a secret to some people, however, is that since it was introduced only six years ago, our White Eagle has been steadily gaining ground and is now running a very close second. Watch out, Pegasus, the Eagle is hot on your tail!

197. What does the advertisement say about mid-size business jet fleets?

(A) They are upgrading their aircraft.
(B) They like to keep their aircraft a secret.
(C) Most are composed of two models of aircraft.
(D) Corporations are selling their fleets.

198. What does the Polestar company imply about the White Eagle?

(A) It will soon outsell the Pegasus.
(B) It is a faster aircraft than the Pegasus.
(C) It will soon be available in a new model.
(D) It is the most popular aircraft with businessmen.

Questions 199 and 200 refer to the following notice.

PLEASE DON'T LOSE ME!

I'm the only ORBIS catalog you will receive.

To help the solid waste crisis and to conserve our forests, this is the only copy you will receive of this year's Orbis catalog.

So, help us—by not losing us!

Call toll free, 24 hours a day, 7 days a week, 1-800-789-2345, and use your credit card.

199. What is the purpose of this notice?
   (A) To save on postage costs
   (B) To give customers a new phone number
   (C) To inform people about the waste crisis
   (D) To tell customers they will receive just one catalog

200. What is implied that people do with the catalog?
   (A) Show it to friends
   (B) Keep it in a safe place
   (C) Dispose of it appropriately
   (D) Photocopy pages they want to keep

Stop! This is the end of the test. If you finish before time is called, you can go back to Parts V, VI, and VII and check your work.

TEST 3—SCRIPT

Part I

1. (Man B)
(A) They are planting trees close together.
(B) People are playing in the park.
(C) The couple are sitting alone.
(D) The children are going for a walk.

2. (Woman)
(A) They are looking for the dog.
(B) His watch does not give good time.
(C) He is waiting for his dog.
(D) The dog is sitting.

3. (Man B)
(A) It is hard to walk in the street.
(B) People are holding hands.
(C) The man is standing on his hands.
(D) He is handing over the shoes.

4. (Woman)
(A) The cup of water is sitting on the sink.
(B) The woman is filling the cup with water.
(C) The chickens are running from the woman.
(D) The woman is drinking from a cup.

5. (Woman)
(A) People are having their meal.
(B) The restaurant is about to open.
(C) Books are on the shelves.
(D) They are lifting the tables.

6. (Woman)
(A) The ocean is still far away.
(B) Waves have washed away part of the beach.
(C) The surf is too high to allow for swimming.
(D) People are playing in the surf.

7. (Man B)
(A) The truck is towing the car.
(B) A car has run into the truck.
(C) The car is racing the truck.
(D) A truck is turning in front of the car.

8. (Woman)
(A) The police cars are waiting at the light.
(B) The police are looking into the car.
(C) The officer is talking on the radio.
(D) The man is taking the radio to the car.

9. (Woman)
(A) The women are looking at the sailor.
(B) The sailors are walking in the park.
(C) The sailors are lost in the dark.
(D) The women have spoken to the sailors.

10. (Man B)
(A) The workers are cutting the trees.
(B) The trees are going to fall.
(C) The men have fallen down.
(D) A man is standing on the rim.

11. (Man B)
(A) The seats in the room are all vacant.
(B) The girl has long, straight hair.
(C) The people are watching the glass.
(D) They're looking for their jackets.

12. (Man B)
(A) The three are standing in the stream.
(B) The team is running through the park.
(C) Trees are reflected in the water.
(D) People are at the edge of the stream.

13. (Man B)
(A) The man threw a brick in the well.
(B) Stones were piled against the wall.
(C) A wall encloses the small yard.
(D) The worker is repairing the wall.

14. (Man B)
(A) The market has a great variety of fruit.
(B) The fruit is being taken to market.
(C) The market will begin to sell fruit.
(D) The fruit has come from the market.

15. (Woman)
(A) The girls are moving the table.
(B) The girls are writing at the table.
(C) The girls are playing a game on the table.
(D) The girls are eating at the table.

16. (Woman)
(A) The plant is being watered.
(B) The woman is drinking water.
(C) The plants are in water.
(D) The woman is getting some water.

17. (Woman)
(A) It's been nearly seven hours.
(B) It took us seven hours.
(C) It's a little after seven.
(D) This one is the seventh.

18. (Man B)
(A) The building has fallen in the water.
(B) Some fish washed up on the beach.
(C) People are fishing on a sunny day.
(D) Fishermen are coming in from the sea.

19. (Woman)
(A) Office employees are standing around.
(B) The staff have all left the office.
(C) The men are working at computers.
(D) The office has been vacated.

20. (Man B)
(A) People have left town for the country.
(B) Trees have fallen across the road.
(C) Traffic has pulled off the road.
(D) No one is on the quiet country road.

Part II

21. (Man B) When is Mike coming?
(Woman)
(A) I think he's alone.
(B) He'll get in on Friday.
(C) He's driving his car.

22. (Woman) Whose coat is this?
(Man B)
(A) It's a size ten.
(B) It's made of wool.
(C) It's mine.

23. (Woman) Have you seen my notebook anywhere?
(Man B)
(A) I always take notes.
(B) Yes, you left it on your desk.
(C) I think it's black.

24. (Man A) Can you help me connect these cables on my new computer?
(Man B) (A) Yes, but these are the wrong ones. We'll need to get some others.
(B) No, I've already had my lunch, thanks.
(C) Yes, I think that monitor is better.

25. (Man A) What would you say is the major reason for their success?
(Man B) (A) We are very competitive.
(B) They work harder than anyone else.
(C) Yes, but I've sacrificed a lot.

26. (Man B) Where does this tool belong?
(Man A) (A) Thank you. I was sitting on it.
(B) No, it's too short.
(C) Put it in the top drawer of my tool chest.

27. (Man B) Do you know what time we're supposed to get in?
(Woman) (A) I thought it was my turn.
(B) Yes, I expect all three of them.
(C) At around six o'clock, local time.

28. (Woman) What did he say he wanted?
(Man B) (A) He said he'd like to talk to you.
(B) He has to go abroad for a while.
(C) His company's not doing well.

29. (Man A) Can I talk to you for a minute?
(Man B) (A) No, he hasn't arrived yet.
(B) You should get here quickly.
(C) Yes, please come in and sit down.

30. (Man B) How do you like your new car?
(Man A) (A) I'd like it well-done, please.
(B) I like it a lot. It's the first new car I've ever owned.
(C) They said they'll be here by two.

31. (Man B) What time is the flight?
(Woman) (A) It departs at ten-ten.
(B) We were all very afraid.
(C) It's now five-thirty.

32. (Woman) Where is the new office?
(Man A) (A) On the sixth floor.
(B) Captain John Belmont.
(C) He's in the cafeteria.

33. (Woman) Could you send a bellhop to help me with my bags?
(Man A)
(A) Of course. I'll page him.
(B) We send everything by air cargo.
(C) The bells ring every day at noon.

34. (Man B) How often does the group meet?
(Man A)
(A) We meet at the community center.
(B) Only once a month, for about two hours.
(C) He'll do it two or three times a day.

35. (Man B) Do you have a phone number for the library?
(Woman)
(A) It closed about an hour ago.
(B) No. You'll have to look it up in the directory.
(C) Sure, use the phone on my desk.

36. (Man B) Do you need some help?
(Woman)
(A) No, I'm not finished yet.
(B) I don't understand why he did it.
(C) No, I think I can manage it.

37. (Man A) Have there been many burglaries in this neighborhood?
(Woman)
(A) No. Isn't that a shame?
(B) I believe it's a residential area.
(C) Very few, and not as many as last year.

38. (Man A) Can you show me the way to Redmond Square?
(Woman)
(A) Come with me; I'm going right past it.
(B) Yes, I made it just this morning.
(C) I believe he's waiting in the other room.

39. (Man A) Do you think she'll come back soon?
(Man B)
(A) No, I won't be back until tomorrow.
(B) I'm sure she will.
(C) Yes. It's right there.

40. (Man A) Are you ready to go over those sales figures?
(Woman)
(A) No. I can't find our tickets anywhere.
(B) I've tried, but they're still very low.
(C) Not yet. I still need to get the inventory lists.

41. (Man B) Why do they say they haven't shipped our order?
(Man A)
(A) They'll be here by the tenth.
(B) They're out of stock, but have reordered.
(C) They didn't receive the invitation.

42. (Man A) We lost at trial level, but can't we take it up on appeal?
    (Man B) (A) Our lawyers are already working on it.
    (B) No, I don't care for the way it looks.
    (C) I hope we find it soon.

43. (Man B) How much longer before you can begin production?
    (Man A) (A) I was, but I feel a lot stronger now.
    (B) It was three weeks ago this Friday.
    (C) We'll be ready in ten days, at the latest.

44. (Man B) They're from London, aren't they?
    (Man A) (A) Yes, but they've lived here a long time.
    (B) I think they leave tomorrow.
    (C) Only a few days, but we really enjoyed it.

45. (Woman) When do you think you'll be done with that report?
    (Man B) (A) I didn't like the way it was done.
    (B) It'll be finished by the first.
    (C) I expect it to arrive later today.

46. (Woman) Have the contest winners been announced yet?
    (Man A) (A) Yes. Notification went out yesterday by registered mail.
    (B) Lunch service will start at noon.
    (C) I think they were put in the closet for the weekend.

47. (Man B) I'll have to see some identification.
    (Woman) (A) I'm new in the neighborhood.
    (B) Will my driver's license do?
    (C) I'd like to see the manager, please.

48. (Woman) Is their company really that big?
    (Man B) (A) They are based in Scotland.
    (B) We're small, but growing.
    (C) Yes, they have over 8,000 employees.

49. (Woman) Please let me know when our printing shipment arrives.
    (Man B) (A) I've asked Receiving to call as soon as it comes in.
    (B) We print only on high-quality paper.
    (C) All of our trucks are on the road.

50. (Woman) Did you hear that next season we're discontinuing the Happy Time line of children's clothing?
    (Man B) (A) Yes, it's very good business right now.
    (B) Of course, everybody likes to see happy children.
    (C) I knew that sales were bad the past few seasons.

Part III

51. (Man B) I'm getting hungry.
(Woman) So am I. Do you want to break for lunch?
(Man B) Yes, I think we should. Let's try that new Mexican place on the corner.

52. (Woman) I see we got a new postage meter.
(Man B) Yes. It was installed yesterday.
(Woman) Great. The old one was always breaking down. It must have cost us a fortune in unused stamps.

53. (Man A) Excuse me. Can you direct us to the Museum of Natural History?
(Man B) It's on the corner of Roosevelt and Bokimbo. Go down the boulevard and turn right at the second light.
(Man A) Thank you. I'm sure we'll find it.

54. (Man B) When does the next bus for Garrison leave?
(Woman) Let's see ... There's one leaving in fifteen minutes, and another one in an hour. Both will leave from Gate 4.
(Man B) I'd like two tickets on the earlier bus.

55. (Woman) Al! Mike is on line two. Can you pick up?
(Man A) Tell him I'll be right with him!
(Woman) O.k, but please try to hurry. He's calling long distance.

56. (Man B) May I see everybody's ticket, please?
(Man A) I don't have one. Can I buy one from you?
(Man B) No. You have to get your ticket at a ticket counter. We can't sell them on board. You'll have to get off at the next stop.

57. (Woman) Do you know when the library closes?
(Man A) At seven o'clock, I think.
(Woman) I'd better hurry, then. I've only 20 minutes to return this book or I pay a fine.

58. (Man A) The supervisor said we can leave as soon as we finish our work.
(Man B) Good; I'm almost through here.
(Man A) Can you help me with mine? I'd like to go home early, too.

59. (Man B) Have you heard what the weather's supposed to be like?
(Woman) Yes. It's supposed to be beautiful.
(Man B) I'm glad for that. I'm taking my family to the mountains this weekend.

60. (Woman) May I help you, sir?
(Man B) Yes. I seem to have lost my room key.
(Woman) You'll need to go to the front desk to get another one.

61. (Woman) Do you have to entertain these people at the Emperor Hotel? We don't have an unlimited expense account, you know.
(Man A) I know it's expensive, but these are important people we're dealing with. I don't want anything to go wrong.
(Woman) Well, I guess you're right, but please try to keep the cost down.

62. (Woman) Have you been reading the news this week?
(Man A) No. I've been working on some reports and haven't had time.
(Woman) Be sure to see the Sunday paper. You'll be interested in what's happening in China.

63. (Woman) While we're planning, what do you think would be a good name for the restaurant?
(Man B) I don't know. Maybe something like "The Garden" ... or ... "A Garden Place"?
(Woman) I like the idea of the word "garden." It's green, and it certainly would let everyone know we'll be decorating with plants.

64. (Man B) Where is the stockholder's meeting being held?
(Man A) In the executive suite on the tenth floor.
(Man B) How convenient! I thought I was going to have to take a taxi over to the annex.

65. (Man A) Isn't there a Greek restaurant around here somewhere?
(Woman) No, but there's one in the Village Mall. It's too far to walk. If you want to go there, you'll have to take a taxi.
(Man A) Oh, I thought there was one just around the block. I'm too hungry to wait.

66. (Man B) Would you all like to get together once a week to go over our sales figures? I think the information would be helpful.
(Man A) I agree, but I think twice a week would be better. Things change very quickly around here.
(Man B) O.k. Twice a week, then. Let's say Wednesday and Friday, at eleven o'clock.

67. (Man A) You'll need to ask Jenny for the phone number of the machine shop. It should be in her file.
(Woman) I already asked her. She doesn't have it.
(Man A) Then check the directory. I know it's listed.

68. (Man B) Did you notice that all of the plants are starting to bud?
(Woman) Yes. I guess that means spring is finally here.
(Man B) And not a day too soon! This winter has been too long and too cold.

69. (Man A) Marty, I'd like you to go over this proposal and make corrections and suggestions. It's only thirty pages. Can you do it?
(Man B) I suppose so. When do you need it?
(Man A) As soon as possible. Maybe by next Wednesday?

70. (Man B) Do you know if my brochure is ready to go to the printer?
(Woman) I only wrote the copy. You'll have to check with Judy. She's handling production.
(Man B) I would, but she's out today. I was hoping somebody could give me an answer as to when I could expect it back.

71. (Woman) Mary works only half time, but I'm always surprised at the amount of work she gets done.
(Man B) I know. I don't know what we'd do without her.
(Woman) Do you realize that we used to have two full-timers doing the same work? What did they ever do with their time?

72. (Woman) This port is one of the nation's largest.
(Man B) I read that, but how do goods get moved inland from here?
(Woman) A lot of highways and railroads link up here and carry anything we bring in.

73. (Man A) How's that accountant I sent over working out?
(Man B) He's very bright. I think he already understands our entire financial picture—good and bad. I'm trying to hire him permanently.
(Man A) I'm glad. I thought you'd like him.

74. (Woman) How was your party last night? My neighbor said it lasted until after midnight.
(Man B) It was fine until about eleven, when we ran out of food. By the time we sent out for pizza, many people had gone home.
(Woman) That's too bad. Now I suppose you'll be eating pizza for a month!

75. (Man A) How is the new equipment working out?
(Man B) Fine. We've had no line shutdowns since we installed it six weeks ago.
(Man A) It's a quality piece of equipment. It should give you no trouble.

76. (Man A) I suggest we postpone until Monday the meeting on the project accounting. It won't be an easy meeting.
(Man B) Why postpone it? Everyone but Ralph is here.
(Man A) Yes, but Ralph is the only person who understands how the accounting was arrived at.

77. (Woman) I thought a new antenna would give us better reception.
(Man B) It doesn't seem to, does it? Maybe it's not hooked up right.
(Woman) We did just as it says on the box, so I doubt that that's the problem.

78. (Woman) Can I exchange traveler's checks at this window?
(Man B) No, I'm sorry. You have to go to Window 3.
(Woman) Someone is confused. I went to Window 3, and the clerk there sent me here.

79. (Woman) Did you pay cash for your car, or is it financed?
(Man A) I financed it. The interest rate is down to only 11 percent.
(Woman) Only 11 percent, you say. That's a lot of money you're going to have to pay over the life of the loan.

80. (Woman) The visitors from Tokyo will arrive any minute. Are we ready?
(Man A) Yes. I'll take them to meet the president first. Then they'll meet the art and production staff, and finally my concept team.
(Woman) You've worked hard on this. I'm sure we'll get their account.

Part IV

(Man A) Questions 81 and 82 refer to the following advertisement.

(Woman) The Esmeralda Resort Hotel, situated outside the popular resort town of Hakulu on the Carolina island of Yolo, is now open. Esmeralda Resort offers you fine food, elegant rooms, superb service, luxurious grounds, and a view of the ocean from every room. We are only two miles from the center of Hakulu, a town famous for its history, water activities, and shopping. Call today for an Esmeralda Resort brochure at our toll-free number: 800-555-9876.

(Man A) Now read question 81 in your test book and answer it.

(Man A) Now read question 82 in your test book and answer it.

(Man A) Questions 83 and 84 refer to the following statement.

(Man B) Attention, motorists! Attention, motorists! Please pull to the right to let emergency vehicles pass. I repeat: Please do not block traffic. Make way. Pull to the right to let emergency vehicles pass.

(Man A) Now read question 83 in your test book and answer it.

(Man A) Now read question 84 in your test book and answer it.

(Man A) Questions 85 and 86 refer to the following message.

(Man B) Thank you, Dr. Ramon, for your presentation to our class today. I'm sure I speak for all of us when I say that your talk was not only informative but entertaining as well. As we've learned, comedy, as a form of entertainment in the 1800s, is a very interesting subject, and until today not one that any of us has given much thought to. Your unusual perspective helps us understand life in America a hundred and fifty years ago, during a period of tremendous industrial growth in our nation's history. Everyone, let's give Dr. Ramon a big round of applause!

(Man A) Now read question 85 in your test book and answer it.

(Man A) Now read question 86 in your test book and answer it.

(Man A) Questions 87 and 88 refer to the following report.

(Woman) In Wipit this week, hundreds of tourists flocked to Blini Park to see young and old alike compete in the annual Frisbee Festival. With winter over and summer just around the corner, people were out in full force. Park officials estimate that nearly four thousand people packed the park to see and to take part in this annual ritual.

(Man A) Now read question 87 in your test book and answer it.

(Man A) Now read question 88 in your test book and answer it.

(Man A) Questions 89 and 90 refer to the following announcement.

(Woman) You will find a copy of Air Asia's frequent flyer timetable, as well as the Air Asia flight magazine, in the seat pocket in front of you. The right-hand column of the timetable lists the approximate mileage for each Air Asia flight. This information is provided so our frequent flyer passengers can keep track of their mileage account. For more information, visit our ticket counter at any airport terminal. Thank you for flying Air Asia.

(Man A) Now read question 89 in your test book and answer it.

(Man A) Now read question 90 in your test book and answer it.

(Man A) Questions 91 through 93 refer to the following news report.

(Man A) We interrupt regular programming for this special bulletin. We have been informed by the National Weather Bureau that a major cold front is moving in, bringing high winds and heavy snow. City officials have been advised to close down all public buildings, including schools, and ensure that everyone is prepared for an accumulation of at least two meters of snow. The storm will last three days and will require at least three more to dig out from under, so do not expect to resume your regular schedule for a minimum of six days, perhaps longer, beginning at midnight tonight.

Everyone should have on hand plenty of food and fuel. Expectant women within ten days of predicted delivery date should go now to the hospital. Anyone else requiring special medical attention, including prescriptions, should contact the hospital for instructions. Stay tuned to this station for further instructions. We now return to our regular programming.

(Man A) Now read question 91 in your test book and answer it.

(Man A) Now read question 92 in your test book and answer it.

(Man A) Now read question 93 in your test book and answer it.

(Man A) Questions 94 and 95 refer to the following announcement.

(Man B) During the past twenty-four hours we have traveled a total of 438 nautical miles, at an average speed of eighteen point two knots. We will experience some storms during the next twenty-four-hour period, so we expect to be slowed somewhat. Nevertheless, we see no reason why we should not reach port on schedule, Thursday morning at 0800 hours.

(Man A) Now read question 94 in your test book and answer it.

(Man A) Now read question 95 in your test book and answer it.

(Man A) Questions 96 through 98 refer to the following advertisement.

(Woman) Every minute of the day, Japan's Kudo Power Company needs to know exactly where the demand for energy is and exactly how to get it there. That is not easy. Japan is the most competitive trade economy in Asia, and our economic health depends upon a continuous flow of electricity. In Japan, Kudo Power does not shrink from its responsibility. We perform it with pride and excellence. Now, as we seek overseas clients, we want to bring that same pride and excellence to the world.

(Man A) Now read question 96 in your test book and answer it.

(Man A) Now read question 97 in your test book and answer it.

(Man A) Now read question 98 in your test book and answer it.

(Man A) Questions 99 and 100 refer to the following statement.

(Man B) And now, finally, I want to take advantage of everybody's presence at our annual board meeting to inform you that, due to circumstances beyond my control, I must resign my position, effective the first of August. I cannot now explain the nature of these circumstances, but they will become clear as time passes. Please understand that I cannot take an alternative course because I have no choice in the matter. It has been a pleasure working with you these past five years. I ask for your patience and understanding. Thank you.

(Man A) Now read question 99 in your test book and answer it.

(Man A) Now read question 100 in your test book and answer it.

This is the end of the Listening Comprehension portion of the test. Turn to Part V in your test book.

TEST 3 COMPARISON SCORES

The score range for the TOEIC is 10 to 990, 5 to 495 for listening and 5 to 495 for reading. This is a converted score, otherwise known as a scaled score, arrived at by converting an examinee's raw score by a formula that changes with every test. The raw score is merely the number of questions answered correctly. On the TOEIC, there is no penalty for answering a question incorrectly.

Converted scores are reported, rather than raw scores, because the developers of the TOEIC make a statistical adjustment for the relative ease or difficulty of each test. This procedure ensures that scores are equivalent over time and do not fluctuate because one or another test may be easier or more difficult than others.

The raw scores that appear below, for this test and for this test only, correspond to a total mean converted TOEIC score of 500, 250 for listening and 250 for reading. Other tests in this book have mean scores calculated on different formulas.

These scores are provided so, if they like, students can compare their performance on this test with a performance that would produce a total converted score of 500. Raw part scores of above the scores provided here would convert to a score of above 500, while raw part scores of below the scores provided here would convert to a score of below 500.

Part	**Mean Raw Score**
I	16
II	20
III	19
IV	10
Mean Listening	65
V	27
VI	11
VII	28
Mean Reading	66
Mean Total	131

Converted Scores for Above Mean Scores

Mean Listening	250
Mean Reading	250
Mean Total	500

ANSWER KEY FOR TEST 3—LISTENING

Key: Part I

1. (B) People are playing in the park.
2. (D) The dog is sitting.
3. (C) The man is standing on his hands.
4. (D) The woman is drinking from a cup.
5. (A) People are having their meal.
6. (D) People are playing in the surf.
7. (A) The truck is towing the car.
8. (C) The officer is talking on the radio.
9. (B) The sailors are walking in the park.
10. (A) The workers are cutting the trees.
11. (B) The girl has long, straight hair.
12. (C) Trees are reflected in the water.
13. (D) The worker is repairing the wall.
14. (A) The market has a great variety of fruit.
15. (B) The girls are writing at the table.
16. (A) The plant is being watered.
17. (C) It's a little after seven.
18. (C) People are fishing on a sunny day.
19. (B) The staff have all left the office.
20. (D) No one is on the quiet country road.

Key: Part II

21. (B) He'll get in on Friday.
22. (C) It's mine.
23. (B) Yes, you left it on your desk.
24. (A) Yes, but these are the wrong ones. We'll need to get some others.
25. (B) They work harder than anyone else.
26. (C) Put it in the top drawer of my tool chest.
27. (C) At around six o'clock, local time.
28. (A) He said he'd like to talk to you.
29. (C) Yes, please come in and sit down.
30. (B) I like it a lot. It's the first new car I've ever owned.
31. (A) It departs at ten-ten.
32. (A) On the sixth floor.
33. (A) Of course. I'll page him.
34. (B) Only once a month, for about two hours.
35. (B) No. You'll have to look it up in the directory.
36. (C) No, I think I can manage it.
37. (C) Very few, and not as many as last year.
38. (A) Come with me; I'm going right past it.
39. (B) I'm sure she will.
40. (C) Not yet. I still need to get the inventory lists.
41. (B) They're out of stock, but have reordered.
42. (A) Our lawyers are already working on it.
43. (C) We'll be ready in ten days, at the latest.
44. (A) Yes, but they've lived here a long time.
45. (B) It'll be finished by the first.
46. (A) Yes. Notification went out yesterday by registered mail.
47. (B) Will my driver's license do?
48. (C) Yes, they have over 8,000 employees.
49. (A) I've asked Receiving to call as soon as it comes in.
50. (C) I knew that sales were bad the past few seasons.

Key: Part III

51. (B) Have lunch
52. (D) A postage-issuing machine
53. (B) Directions to a museum
54. (B) In fifteen minutes
55. (C) Phoning from far away
56. (B) He does not have a ticket.
57. (A) She has to return a book.
58. (C) They could leave when they finish their work.
59. (D) He will go out of town for the weekend.
60. (A) To get a new key
61. (D) He is meeting important people.
62. (D) Recent developments
63. (A) A name for a restaurant
64. (B) On the tenth floor
65. (C) A restaurant
66. (C) Hold regular meetings
67. (C) A telephone number
68. (D) A change in the seasons
69. (C) Read a document
70. (A) A brochure
71. (A) She works very fast.
72. (C) Its connections
73. (D) He will be offered a permanent position.
74. (B) There was not enough food.
75. (A) A new machine
76. (A) A necessary person is not available.
77. (D) They cannot get a clear picture on their television.
78. (D) Nobody seems to know where money can be exchanged.
79. (A) He borrowed money to buy a car.
80. (B) Advertising

Key: Part IV

81. (A) In the Carolinas
82. (B) Two miles
83. (D) On a public street
84. (B) Cooperation
85. (C) He has given an interesting speech.
86. (A) History
87. (C) Spring
88. (C) 4,000
89. (B) Air Asia's flight mileage
90. (A) In the seat pocket
91. (D) A snowstorm
92. (B) Prepare to remain indoors
93. (A) Pregnant women
94. (C) On board a ship
95. (D) Developments and expectations
96. (B) Electricity
97. (C) It is demanding.
98. (B) Export its services
99. (D) It was regularly scheduled.
100. (C) He does not say.

ANSWER KEY FOR TEST 3—READING

Key: Part V

101. (D) same
102. (C) blown
103. (C) increased
104. (B) best
105. (C) decided to
106. (C) can be
107. (A) on
108. (C) becoming
109. (C) superior
110. (C) calculate
111. (B) broke
112. (D) create
113. (A) way
114. (D) infrequent
115. (C) quite
116. (B) holding
117. (B) show
118. (D) are being
119. (D) destroyed
120. (B) reflected
121. (D) destruction
122. (C) moving into
123. (A) had to be
124. (A) proof
125. (B) submit
126. (D) agricultural
127. (C) closed
128. (A) transmit
129. (D) promptly
130. (B) stop
131. (B) protective
132. (D) austerity
133. (B) routine
134. (A) oversize
135. (A) progress
136. (A) admitted to
137. (D) polarizing
138. (A) intervene
139. (C) an advantage
140. (C) a dependable

Key: Part VI

141. (B) has become, had become
142. (B) when
143. (A) Traditional
144. (A) met
145. (A) was
146. (A) shown
147. (C) received
148. (C) it to us
149. (D) holiday break
150. (A) Fewer
151. (A) associated
152. (C) the same
153. (A) Visitors
154. (D) better
155. (C) among
156. (D) difference
157. (A) Most students
158. (A) to return to, to go back to
159. (B) would think
160. (D) it

Key: Part VII

161. (C) $60
162. (D) It has no coverage.
163. (A) The voter must live in Twin Buttes County.
164. (B) At any county library
165. (A) Voters who are physically impaired
166. (C) Mary Craig and Tim Layton
167. (A) He is in a different telephone area.
168. (D) Samuel Craig and Walter Meyer
169. (B) With an expression of regret
170. (D) To prepare for the future
171. (D) To welcome a visitor from Mr. Jackson's office while on the trip
172. (A) Taxes
173. (D) Reservations must be made two weeks in advance.
174. (D) Harris main plant
175. (B) Aerospace
176. (C) Not inform anyone of the changes
177. (A) It has increased.
178. (D) Twenty years before
179. (B) A boat race
180. (B) Tiger Rowing Club
181. (B) A rowing club
182. (D) To greet new people
183. (B) Casually
184. (C) Immigration law
185. (C) Foreigners
186. (A) Java
187. (C) To the National Museum
188. (B) More than four hundred years
189. (A) It is fast-growing.
190. (A) It is less regulated.
191. (A) Increase sales by more than 100 percent
192. (D) Automobile
193. (B) A rebate on his payment
194. (D) Because claim costs were not as high as expected
195. (C) Companies that hire famous people to endorse products
196. (C) They can bring discredit to the product.
197. (C) Most are composed of two models of aircraft.
198. (A) It will soon outsell the Pegasus.
199. (D) To tell customers they will receive just one catalog
200. (B) Keep it in a safe place

TOEIC®
TEST 4

LISTENING COMPREHENSION

In this section of the test, you will have the chance to show how well you understand spoken English. There are four parts to this section, with special directions for each part.

Part I

Directions: For each question, you will see a picture in your test book and you will hear four short statements. The statements will be spoken just one time. They will not be printed in your test book, so you must listen carefully to understand what the speaker says.

When you hear the four statements, look at the picture in your test book and choose the statement that best describes what you see in the picture. Then, on your answer sheet, find the number of the question and mark your answer.

Look at the sample below.

Now listen to the four statements.

Sample Answer

Statement (B), "They're having a meeting," best describes what you see in the picture. Therefore, you should choose answer (B).

1. 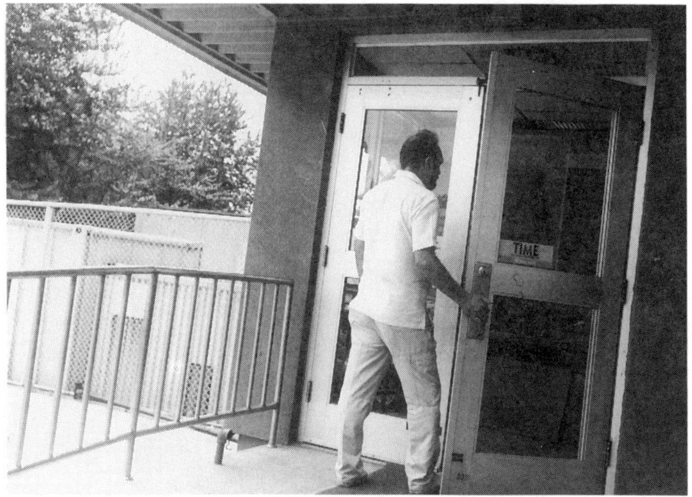

2. 

GO ON TO THE NEXT PAGE

3.

4.

5. 

6. 

7. 

8. 

9.

10.

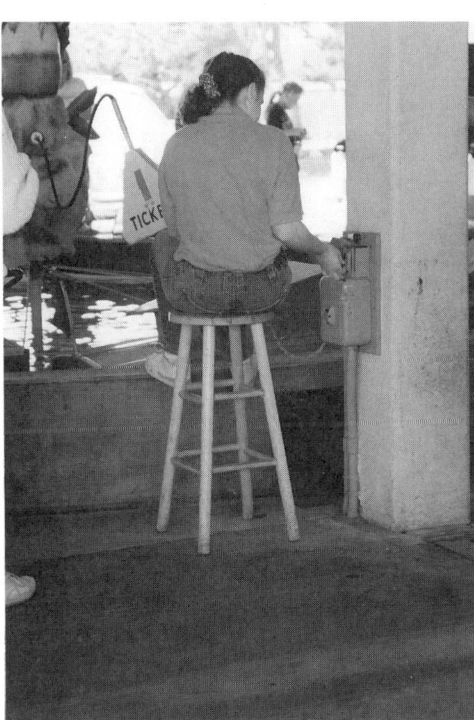

GO ON TO THE NEXT PAGE

11.

12.

13.

14.

GO ON TO THE NEXT PAGE

15.

16.

17.

18.

GO ON TO THE NEXT PAGE

19.

20.

Part II

Directions: In this part of the test you will hear a question spoken in English, followed by three responses, also spoken in English. The question and the responses will be spoken just one time. They will not be printed in your test book, so you must listen carefully to understand what the speakers say. You are to choose the best response to each question.

Now listen to a sample question:

You will hear:

You will also hear:

Sample Answer

● (B) (C)

The best response to the question "How are you?" is choice (A) "I am fine, thank you." Therefore, you should choose answer (A).

21. Mark your answer on your answer sheet.
22. Mark your answer on your answer sheet.
23. Mark your answer on your answer sheet.
24. Mark your answer on your answer sheet.
25. Mark your answer on your answer sheet.
26. Mark your answer on your answer sheet.
27. Mark your answer on your answer sheet.
28. Mark your answer on your answer sheet.
29. Mark your answer on your answer sheet.
30. Mark your answer on your answer sheet.
31. Mark your answer on your answer sheet.
32. Mark your answer on your answer sheet.
33. Mark your answer on your answer sheet.
34. Mark your answer on your answer sheet.
35. Mark your answer on your answer sheet.
36. Mark your answer on your answer sheet.
37. Mark your answer on your answer sheet.
38. Mark your answer on your answer sheet.
39. Mark your answer on your answer sheet.
40. Mark your answer on your answer sheet.
41. Mark your answer on your answer sheet.
42. Mark your answer on your answer sheet.
43. Mark your answer on your answer sheet.
44. Mark your answer on your answer sheet.
45. Mark your answer on your answer sheet.
46. Mark your answer on your answer sheet.
47. Mark your answer on your answer sheet.
48. Mark your answer on your answer sheet.
49. Mark your answer on your answer sheet.
50. Mark your answer on your answer sheet.

GO ON TO THE NEXT PAGE

Part III

Directions: In this part of the test, you will hear 30 short conversations between two people. The conversations will not be printed in your test book. You will hear the conversations only once, so you must listen carefully to understand what the speakers say.

In your test book you will read a question about each conversation. The question will be followed by four answers. You are to choose the best answer to each question and mark it on your answer sheet.

51. What will John do?

    (A) He will quit his job.
    (B) He will go on vacation.
    (C) He will substitute for the man.
    (D) He will come to work for the company.

52. What did the woman offer the man?

    (A) Lunch
    (B) A ride
    (C) A place to sleep
    (D) Something to drink

53. What is said about the staff meeting?

    (A) It will finish on time.
    (B) It has been rescheduled.
    (C) It has been canceled.
    (D) It will go on longer than planned.

54. How do the man and Joel know one another?

    (A) They are neighbors.
    (B) They are relatives.
    (C) They are co-workers.
    (D) They are classmates.

55. What does the man say he will take on his visit?

    (A) A camera
    (B) Some books
    (C) A house gift
    (D) Warm clothing

56. Where does the woman feel closed in?

    (A) In elevators
    (B) In dark theaters
    (C) In phone booths
    (D) In airplanes

57. What is the situation?

    (A) The woman has no more coffee.
    (B) The man is turning down a cup of coffee.
    (C) The man will have coffee without cream.
    (D) The man would like another cup of coffee.

58. What is the man's problem?

    (A) His car has had a flat tire.
    (B) He left his wallet in a taxi.
    (C) He needs to go to the bus station.
    (D) He is meeting a friend at the airport.

59. What does the man say?

(A) He thinks study is not important.
(B) He is anxious to begin his studies.
(C) He regrets that he was not a serious student.
(D) He was not admitted to the university he wanted.

60. What are the people discussing?

(A) A health regimen
(B) A new movie
(C) The price of a product
(D) The location of a company

61. What happened to Joe's car?

(A) It was in an accident.
(B) It was stolen.
(C) It was sent to the shop for repairs.
(D) It had a flat tire.

62. About what is the man concerned?

(A) He is supposed to meet a friend at the bus stop.
(B) He finds changes in the schedule inconvenient.
(C) He is worried about missing the bus that takes him home.
(D) He is not pleased with the quality of the bus service.

63. What does the man want to do?

(A) Reserve a flight
(B) Go to the theater
(C) Have a picnic in a park
(D) Meet a friend for dinner

64. How did Molly break her leg?

(A) While skiing
(B) Mountain climbing
(C) In a bicycle accident
(D) In an automobile accident

65. Why does the man ask about another hotel?

(A) His room is too noisy.
(B) The hotel has no rooms available.
(C) His hotel does not give good service.
(D) The hotel does not have any non-smoking areas.

66. Why is the man anxious for the plane plane to land?

(A) He does not feel well.
(B) He does not like to fly.
(C) He is late for a meeting.
(D) He has another plane to catch.

67. What does the woman recommend?

(A) That the man take a vacation
(B) That the man read a book on travel
(C) That the man go to the bookstore
(D) That the man read about places he will visit

68. What is the woman's problem?

(A) She gets lost in the building.
(B) She is looking for a rest room.
(C) She wants to buy a ticket.
(D) She has something in her throat and wants something to drink.

GO ON TO THE NEXT PAGE

69. What are the speakers discussing?

(A) Borrowing money
(B) Paying off debts
(C) Investment opportunities
(D) Hiring additional personnel

70. What does the man agree to?

(A) Exchange his typewriter
(B) Buy another typewriter
(C) Accept a refund
(D) Have his typewriter repaired

71. What is the topic of this interview?

(A) An experience in China
(B) Qualifications for a job
(C) Educational opportunity
(D) A teaching position

72. Why is the man going to buy a new car?

(A) His car is not reliable.
(B) His wife wants a new car.
(C) He needs a bigger car.
(D) His car was in an accident and cannot be repaired.

73. What does the woman say about Mary?

(A) She should wear longer dresses.
(B) Her clothes are not in fashion.
(C) She wears her clothes until they wear out.
(D) She always dresses well in the latest fashions.

74. Where are the speakers?

(A) At home
(B) In a clothing store
(C) In a restaurant
(D) In a library

75. What are the couple discussing?

(A) The weather
(B) The man's work
(C) Going for a visit
(D) Going out in the evening

76. Why will the man be charged extra?

(A) He wants room service.
(B) He wants the penthouse.
(C) He wants a room with a view.
(D) He wants flowers and fruit in his room.

77. What has the man done?

(A) He missed his bus stop.
(B) He wants to take a taxi.
(C) He has taken the wrong bus.
(D) He told the driver where to let him off.

78. When will the meeting take place?

(A) In the afternoon.
(B) That evening.
(C) The next morning.
(D) It has not been rescheduled.

79. What do the speakers think about Alice?

(A) She will win the competition.
(B) She should practice more.
(C) She will not be able to participate.
(D) She will lose the competition.

80. What does the woman say has to be done with the system?

(A) New software is needed.
(B) It should be upgraded.
(C) It should be replaced.
(D) It should be expanded upon.

Part IV

Directions: In this part of the test, you will hear several short talks. Each will be spoken just one time. They will not be printed in your test book, so you must listen carefully to understand and remember what is said.

In your test book you will read two or more questions about each short talk. The questions will be followed by four answers. You are to choose the best answer to each question and mark it on your answer sheet.

81. What is required in the restricted area?

    (A) Rubber boots and jackets
    (B) Hard hats and steel-toed shoes
    (C) Flashlights and gloves
    (D) Protective eyewear

82. Who must wait until the group returns?

    (A) Sick people
    (B) The elderly
    (C) The handicapped
    (D) Children under 12

83. Why must people be escorted on the tour?

    (A) It is private property.
    (B) It is a restricted area.
    (C) It is a national landmark.
    (D) It is a military facility.

84. According to the speaker, how is broccoli often characterized?

    (A) Tasteless
    (B) Expensive
    (C) Not good in salads
    (D) Lacking in nutritional value

85. What does the speaker say goes well with broccoli?

    (A) Rice
    (B) Soups
    (C) Sauces
    (D) Breads

86. What does this advertisement concern?

    (A) Early retirement
    (B) High interest rates
    (C) Personal savings
    (D) Real estate investments

87. What minimum investment period is required?

    (A) 5 years
    (B) 10 years
    (C) 12 years
    (D) 15 years

88. What are listeners urged to do?

    (A) Send money
    (B) Sell to friends
    (C) Speak with their broker
    (D) Request more information

89. For what office are Tom Brady and Kermit Wilton running?

    (A) Mayor of the city
    (B) President of the club
    (C) Governor of the state
    (D) Chairman of the city council

90. Why has this meeting been called?

    (A) For a public debate
    (B) To make campaign speeches
    (C) To discuss election procedures
    (D) To answer questions from voters

91. Where are people asked to stand?

(A) At a designated location
(B) At the far end of the terminal
(C) At one of several taxi stations
(D) At a meeting point inside the terminal

92. What will people do if they follow the rules?

(A) Avoid a fine
(B) Arrive faster
(C) Avoid paying too much
(D) Receive better service

93. Why have some firms not invested?

(A) To return a profit to shareholders
(B) Because of political instability
(C) To comply with government regulations
(D) Because credit is unavailable

94. What does the speaker want to do?

(A) Sell unproductive assets
(B) Merge with one of two companies
(C) Invest company profits
(D) Form a joint venture

95. What is the speaker discussing?

(A) An ad campaign
(B) Company profits
(C) A business competitor
(D) Plans for a new product

96. In what field does the speaker's company work?

(A) Food
(B) Finance
(C) Textiles
(D) Electronics

97. What is the purpose of the talk?

(A) To explain elevator operation
(B) To explain building safety
(C) To announce a building closing
(D) To explain parking regulations

98. What requires that this announcement be made?

(A) Local laws
(B) Common sense
(C) Contracts with tenants
(D) Complaints from the public

99. Where do people get off the Rotogyro?

(A) Across the park from where they begin
(B) Opposite Hannaland Park
(C) Near the parking lot
(D) Where they got on

100. What is the Outer Space Castle?

(A) The newest ride at Hannaland
(B) A ride close to the Rotogyro
(C) An attraction that is designed for older children
(D) A ride that takes people rapidly in circles

This is the end of the Listening Comprehension portion of the test. Turn to Part V in your test book.

YOU WILL HAVE ONE HOUR AND FIFTEEN MINUTES TO COMPLETE PARTS V, VI, AND VII OF THE TEST.

READING

In this section of the test, you will have a chance to show how well you understand written English. There are three parts to this section, with special directions for each part.

Part V

Directions: Questions 101–140 are incomplete sentences. Four words or phrases, marked (A), (B), (C), (D), are given beneath each sentence. You are to choose the one word or phrase that best completes the sentence. Then, on your answer sheet, find the number of the question and mark your answer.

Example

Because the equipment is very delicate, it must be handled with ———.

(A) caring
(B) careful
(C) care
(D) carefully

Sample Answer

Ⓐ Ⓑ ● Ⓓ

The sentence should read, "Because the equipment is very delicate, it must be handled with care." Therefore, you should choose answer (C).

As soon as you understand the directions, begin work on the questions.

101. The project results were ——— than people expected.

(A) best
(B) good
(C) better
(D) the best

102. Grain production increased by ——— 20 percent over the previous year.

(A) nearly
(B) somewhat
(C) eventual
(D) including

103. Because of the author's lecture schedule, progress on his next book was ———.

(A) error
(B) erred
(C) errand
(D) erratic

104. The supervisor was asked ——— with his employees.

(A) met
(B) to meet
(C) meeting
(D) will meet

GO ON TO THE NEXT PAGE

105. For their spring sale, the computer store will offer their finest equipment at a large ———.

(A) recount
(B) account
(C) counting
(D) discount

106. Miami to Key West flights depart ——— daily.

(A) two
(B) pair
(C) twice
(D) double

107. It is now possible to manufacture small computer chips that are ——— powerful.

(A) as
(B) very
(C) too
(D) extreme

108. There is a pharmacy ——— the corner from the office.

(A) about
(B) around
(C) above
(D) along

109. The retailer ——— the mislabeled goods to the manufacturer.

(A) left
(B) ordered
(C) returned
(D) repeated

110. If people are ———, they are bound to have accidents.

(A) careless
(B) useless
(C) careful
(D) helpless

111. The letter said that the company was to be ——— from the plan.

(A) excluded
(B) discussed
(C) considerate
(D) interesting

112. Mice had chewed the wires and were ——— to have caused a short in the electrical system.

(A) knew
(B) thinking
(C) establish
(D) suspected

113. Medical teams were ——— to the war-torn region.

(A) pushed
(B) delighted
(C) displaced
(D) transported

114. The heating unit ——— to pass inspection and had to be rebuilt.

(A) often
(B) failed
(C) heated
(D) broken

115. The building won ——— awards for architectural design.

(A) any
(B) several
(C) eventful
(D) multiply

116. The doctors could not ——— the patient's pain.

(A) relieve
(B) appeal
(C) detail
(D) retire

117. After the board turned down the proposal, it refused to ——— its decision.

(A) decide
(B) sponsor
(C) underwrite
(D) reconsider

118. Several swans swam ——— the pond.

(A) on
(B) at
(C) by
(D) as

119. Trash was left in the parking lot and ——— to be removed.

(A) had
(B) has
(C) are
(D) want

120. Last year, the managing director ——— cellular phones for all of his salesmen.

(A) buys
(B) called
(C) ordered
(D) employs

121. The unit was established to find new ——— for old technologies.

(A) applications
(B) associations
(C) recreations
(D) estimations

122. They were going to meet in Australia the ——— summer.

(A) this
(B) follow
(C) next time
(D) following

123. A number of business meetings were scheduled to be held ——— the exposition.

(A) into
(B) during
(C) through
(D) between

124. She had already ——— her mind.

(A) making
(B) made up
(C) finished
(D) fixed up

GO ON TO THE NEXT PAGE

125. The postal clerk ——— that the package be sent express, to guarantee arrival on time.

(A) request
(B) advocate
(C) insisting
(D) suggested

126. To communicate ——— with its customers, a company has to know who they are.

(A) lately
(B) exactly
(C) effectively
(D) sufficiently

127. The training session ——— last four hours each day for two weeks.

(A) is
(B) be
(C) will
(D) that

128. The new schedule called for the cafeteria ——— close at 2:00 P.M.

(A) to
(B) is
(C) was
(D) will

129. Telemarketing, or telephone sales, is the planned use of the telephone as a sales ———.

(A) rate
(B) medium
(C) middle
(D) company

130. The librarian told the student ——— to find the book.

(A) who
(B) what
(C) which
(D) where

131. Indecisiveness in business can lead to serious ———.

(A) occurs
(B) applications
(C) consequences
(D) misappropriations

132. As interest rates ———, stock prices fell.

(A) ran
(B) held
(C) moved
(D) climbed

133. The bottle contained a poison for which there was no known ———.

(A) autopsy
(B) antidote
(C) antibiotic
(D) antiseptic

134. They accepted the consequences, ——— the responsibility.

(A) but not
(B) but also
(C) with also
(D) with only

135. The company achieved ——— savings with their new supplier agreement.

(A) far
(B) much
(C) mostly
(D) substantial

136. His success ——— that of an earlier generation of entrepreneurs.

(A) liked
(B) reduced
(C) rivaled
(D) relieved

137. The ——— report was not issued until eight months after the incident.

(A) offer
(B) office
(C) official
(D) officious

138. The last chapter ——— as a summary of the entire book.

(A) shows
(B) plays
(C) serves
(D) explains

139. The man's family claimed it was his strength of ——— that helped him survive his ordeal at sea.

(A) money
(B) number
(C) patience
(D) character

140. The name Giannini is well known in banking ———.

(A) homes
(B) circles
(C) districts
(D) officials

GO ON TO THE NEXT PAGE

Part VI

<u>Directions</u>: In <u>Questions 141–160</u> each sentence has four words or phrases underlined. The four underlined parts of the sentence are marked (A), (B), (C), (D). You are to identify the <u>one</u> underlined word or phrase that should be corrected or rewritten. Then, on your answer sheet, find the number of the question and mark your answer.

Example

All <u>employee</u> (A) are required <u>to wear</u> (B) their <u>identification</u> (C) badges <u>while</u> (D) at work.

<u>Sample Answer</u>

● Ⓑ Ⓒ Ⓓ

Choice (A), the underlined word "employee," is not correct in this sentence. This sentence should read, "All employees are required to wear their identification badges while at work." Therefore, you should choose answer (A).

As soon as you understand the directions, begin work on the questions.

141. He <u>was sure could</u> (A) <u>get</u> (B) a better job <u>if</u> (C) he <u>tried.</u> (D)

142. The building <u>of which</u> (A) he <u>lived</u> (B) was <u>one</u> (C) of the <u>tallest</u> (D) in the city.

143. Although he <u>had suspected it</u> (A) for a long time, it <u>still</u> (B) came as a <u>shock he heard</u> (C) that his son was <u>about to</u> (D) abandon his studies.

144. Two Italian <u>dish,</u> (A) <u>which</u> (B) Americans <u>enjoy greatly,</u> (C) <u>are</u> (D) pizza and spaghetti.

145. The investigation cleared <u>he and his</u> (A) company of any <u>wrongdoing,</u> (B) but all of the defendants were <u>still</u> (C) <u>liable</u> (D) for civil penalties.

146. <u>Strong management</u> (A) can <u>carry</u> (B) a company <u>through</u> (C) <u>financial difficulty</u> (D) times.

147. They <u>will</u> (A) <u>work on the</u> (B) project with the <u>new crew</u> (C) for <u>more three</u> (D) months.

148. The manager's administrative assistant
A
was known around the office for her
B C
speed type.
D

149. Two senior officers were chosing
A
to represent the company in its contract
B C
negotiations with the government.
D

150. I am like to show you our company's
A B C
newest product, if you have time on
D
Friday.

151. We have made many attempts to locate
A
the problem in the wiring, but
B
as of date have met with no success.
C D

152. Most scientists agree that the earth's
A
climate will change greatly in the future
B C
dues to industrial pollution.
D

153. Modern theories of worker motivation

speak to the universal needing for time
A B
away from the job, when the employee

involves himself in activities wholly
C D
unrelated to his employment.

154. The president was busy planning his
A
re-election campaigning strategy,
B
realizing that by the following January,
C
he could be out of office.
D

155. The microwave oven were introduced to
A
the public in the 1970s, but did not
B
receive general acceptance until many
C
years later.
D

156. Employees were told to stay home from
A
work on the day the storm

was expected, which was good advise
B C
because the city was later snowed in for
D
three days.

157. Company officials were asked to trip to
A
Jakarta to inspect production facilities
B
there, before recommending
C
construction of additional production

capacity.
D

GO ON TO THE NEXT PAGE

158. Television, which was <u>formerly</u> (A) a luxury, for most people <u>has become</u> (B) a necessity as <u>their major</u> (C) source of information on local, national, and international <u>topic</u> (D).

159. The role of the jury <u>is to hear</u> (A) the facts, judge the <u>credibility</u> (B) of witnesses, weigh the evidence, and <u>render a verdict</u> (C) <u>of</u> (D) the applicable law.

160. <u>To serve</u> (A) the public, <u>communication system</u> (B) must be reliable <u>and</u> (C) inexpensive, and must be accessible <u>to</u> (D) everyone.

Part VII

Directions: Questions 161–200 are based on a variety of reading material (for example, announcements, paragraphs, advertisements, and the like). You are to choose the one best answer, (A), (B), (C), or (D), to each question. Then, on your answer sheet, find the number of the question and mark your answer. Answer all questions following a passage on the basis of what is stated or implied in that passage.

Read the following example.

> The Museum of Technology is a "hands-on" museum, designed for people to experience science at work. Visitors are encouraged to use, test, and handle the objects on display. Special demonstrations are scheduled for the first and second Wednesdays of each month at 1:30 P.M. Open Tuesday–Friday, 2:30–4:30 P.M., Saturday 11:00 A.M.–4:30 P.M., and Sunday 1:00–4:30 P.M.
>
> When during the month can visitors see special demonstrations?
>
> (A) Every weekend
> (B) The first two Wednesdays
> (C) One afternoon a week
> (D) Every other Wednesday

Sample Answer

The passage says that the demonstrations are scheduled for the first and second Wednesdays of the month. Therefore, you should choose answer (B).

As soon as you understand the directions, begin work on the questions.

GO ON TO THE NEXT PAGE

Questions 161–163 refer to the following notice.

School Board Sets Next Meeting Date

The school board meeting is scheduled for Monday, Nov. 17, at 7:30 P.M. in the high school cafeteria. Agenda items include funding for new buses, construction of a new sports stadium, and the purchase of books for the library. All parents and area residents are welcome. If you would like to speak at the meeting, please contact the office of Superintendent of Schools Glenn A. Martin, 865-5432, before Friday, Nov. 14.

161. Where will the school board meet?

(A) In the school library
(B) In the school cafeteria
(C) In the city council chamber
(D) In the Superintendent's office

162. Who may attend the meeting?

(A) Parents only
(B) Board members only
(C) All area residents
(D) Students and their parents

163. Who should be contacted about speaking at the meeting?

(A) The librarian
(B) The superintendent
(C) The school principal
(D) The chairman of the school board

Questions 164 and 165 refer to the following advertisement.

> NEW LIFE CATALOG: Our famous catalog features highlights from our collection of classic fashion, including swimwear and sportswear, leather goods, gifts, and accessories.
>
> You will find exceptional style and quality in these catalogs, which you will receive quarterly, one for each season of the year, for only $7.00 annually, plus postage and handling. Order today for a full year of style!

164. How many times per year is this catalog sent out?

   (A) One
   (B) Four
   (C) Six
   (D) Twelve

165. What sort of catalog is this?

   (A) Books
   (B) Music
   (C) Fashion
   (D) Theater

GO ON TO THE NEXT PAGE

Questions 166–168 refer to the following menu.

LES FAIRES
Rive Gauche

Appetizers:

Smoked salmon	$ 4.95
Brie and crackers	$ 3.15

Entrees:

Beef tips *au jus*	$14.95
Chicken Kiev	$12.95
Grilled swordfish	$16.95

Includes salad and vegetable

Beverages:

Coffee	$ 1.50
Tea	$ 1.50
Soft drinks	$ .75

Desserts:

Ice cream	$ 1.00
Chocolate cake	$ 1.50
Fruit w/cream (in season)	$ 2.50

Tax and tip not included.

166. What is the least expensive item on the Les Faires menu?

   (A) Ice cream
   (B) Swordfish
   (C) Soft drinks
   (D) Brie and crackers

167. What item is available only at certain times of the year?

   (A) Fish
   (B) Salad
   (C) Fruit
   (D) Cheese

168. What menu items are NOT charged separately?

   (A) Tax and tip
   (B) Coffee and tea
   (C) Bread and butter
   (D) Salad and vegetable

Questions 169 and 170 refer to the following advertisement.

Save $15.00
On Your Next Eye Exam

Submit This Coupon

Only $39.00*
Complete Eye Examination

Not valid with other offers
Good Aug. 30 through Oct. 30

**With coupon*

169. What is the regular price of an eye exam?

(A) $15.00
(B) $24.00
(C) $39.00
(D) $54.00

170. What is the maximum period during which this coupon may be used?

(A) Two weeks
(B) Two months
(C) Three months
(D) Four months

GO ON TO THE NEXT PAGE

Questions 171 and 172 refer to the following announcement.

APPEARING TONIGHT

Fernando Alcuaz
Famed International Pianist

Recently arrived from the Philippines

Jazz, modern, and classical pieces

Surrey Room, 8 P.M. to 10 P.M.

Admission gratis for hotel guests

171. Who is Mr. Alcuaz?

(A) A poet
(B) A singer
(C) A comedian
(D) A musician

172. Where is Mr. Alcuaz performing?

(A) In Surrey
(B) At a hotel
(C) In the Philippines
(D) At a jazz festival

Questions 173–175 refer to the following notice.

Attention, Park Visitors

Visitors planning to camp in the park must obtain permits and be assigned campsites. This is necessary to facilitate control of camper services, as well as to reduce the danger of forest fires. Campers and other visitors who fail to comply with park regulations are subject to expulsion from the park. Do not feed park animals. If you want to participate in animal feeding, look for feeding schedules posted near feeding sites.

This is your park. Protect it by reporting any violation of park regulations. Enjoy your visit.

173. Why must campers obtain permits?

(A) To ensure payment of required fees
(B) To avoid camping in dangerous areas
(C) To allow for counting of all campers
(D) To reduce possibility of forest fires

174. What will happen to visitors who do not follow rules?

(A) They will have to pay a fine.
(B) They will be asked to leave the park.
(C) They will not be allowed to camp in the park.
(D) They will be charged a higher fee for a permit.

175. How may park visitors feed the animals?

(A) If they ask a park guard to help them.
(B) If they agree to feed them only certain foods.
(C) If they join in the park animal-feeding program.
(D) Under no circumstance may visitors feed the animals.

GO ON TO THE NEXT PAGE

Questions 176–178 refer to the following notice.

Society of Food Marketers
Corporate Sponsorship Structure and Dues

Dues are $800 per year for companies with gross annual sales under $50,000,000. Dues provide for an individual membership for the Corporate Representative, plus two additional memberships.

Dues are $1,200 per year for companies with gross annual sales over $50,000,000. Dues provide for an individual membership for the Corporate Representative, plus four others.

Each Corporate Sponsor company must designate a named individual, who ex officio is a member, to serve as the Corporate Representative.

176. What are the gross annual sales of Corporate members paying $800 annual dues?

(A) Over 5 thousand dollars
(B) Over 50 million dollars
(C) Under 50 million dollars
(D) Over 5 billion dollars

177. How many memberships in the Food Marketing Society will a Corporate Sponsor paying annual dues of $1,200 receive?

(A) Two
(B) Three
(C) Four
(D) Five

178. What are Corporate Sponsors required to do?

(A) Designate a corporate representative
(B) Pay their dues by the first of the year
(C) Encourage employees to become members in the society
(D) Increase sales within the first year of membership

Questions 179–181 refer to the following memorandum.

CALL REPORT

For: Howard Brever
Date: 9/8 Time: 10:30
Call taken by: Emma
From: Travel agent/Alice

All flights scheduled to arrive in Hong Kong on September 12 are full. The first available flight leaves here on the 12th and arrives in H.K. at 11:30 P.M., September 13. You are booked in economy on that flight. Please confirm before 5:00 P.M. today. Unless you inform her otherwise, Alice will make a reservation for you at the Kowloon Princess Hotel for three nights.

179. On which day is Mr. Brever booked to depart for Hong Kong?

(A) September 8
(B) September 11
(C) September 12
(D) September 13

180. What must Mr. Brever do?

(A) Call a hotel to make reservations
(B) Confirm the flight with his travel agent
(C) Let his agent know which hotel he wants to stay at
(D) Let his agent know the number of nights he will be staying in Hong Kong

181. When was this message received?

(A) At 8:00 A.M.
(B) At 10:30 A.M.
(C) At 5:00 P.M.
(D) At 11:30 P.M.

GO ON TO THE NEXT PAGE

Questions 182 and 183 refer to the following advertisement.

Beware of Unscrupulous Insurance Salesmen!

A recent national survey revealed that, of fifteen major professions, insurance salespeople are regarded by the public as those most likely to sell a customer a product that is not in the customer's best interests, rather than a product that is, for the sole purpose of making a higher profit. Our company tells you this because we want your trust. We sell insurance, and we are out to change the public perception of our industry. For all your insurance needs, call us today. Let us show you what we have. We welcome the challenge.

182. Who placed this advertisement?

    (A) An insurance company
    (B) An angry insurance salesman
    (C) A company that surveys public opinion
    (D) Consumers who fight insurance companies

183. What does the advertisement say the public believes insurance salespeople do?

    (A) Sell a product only to make a high profit
    (B) Charge too much for their services
    (C) Misrepresent their products to the public
    (D) Avoid the client after making a sale

Questions 184–186 refer to the following invoice.

INVOICE

Meyer & Ramsey Publications
1987 Juniper Court, Suite A
Hunting, NY 12330

Bill to:	Ship to:	Date: 10-09-94
John Forrest	Mary Forrest	
18 Ayr Hill Rd.	45 Bekin Lane	
Pace, NY 14567	Baltimore, MD 34789	

Qty.	Item		
1	Book: Greek Art and Sculpture	Price	$68.95
		Discount 10%	6.90
		Subtotal	62.05
		Tax @ 6%	3.73
		Shipping	3.20
		Total	$68.98

Questions about your bill? Call 1-800-555-0900

184. Who placed the order with Meyer & Ramsey?

(A) Bill Forrest.
(B) Mary Forrest.
(C) John Forrest.
(D) It is not known.

185. Where is the book to be sent?

(A) Pace
(B) Hunting
(C) New York
(D) Baltimore

186. What is the retail price of the book?

(A) $6.90
(B) $62.05
(C) $68.95
(D) $68.98

GO ON TO THE NEXT PAGE

Questions 187–189 refer to the following memorandum.

To: All managers working on the Branston account

From: Keith Pocard, Chief Executive Officer

Next Monday, May 5, at 10:00 A.M., there will be a meeting in my office concerning unusually heavy losses incurred by the Branston Trust account in the four months since the first of the year, this contrary to market trend for the period. Mr. Branston, whose family has traded with our company for many years, has discontinued his association with this firm.

All account managers with access to Branston Trust's investments should be prepared to submit detailed reports on their transactions involving the account for the period in question. I have also asked for all relevant computer records.

187. What does the above memorandum concern?

(A) Results of a meeting
(B) Heavy investment losses
(C) Bringing in a new investor
(D) Withdrawal from unstable markets

188. What does the above memorandum say about Mr. Branston?

(A) He manages many accounts.
(B) He has requested a detailed report.
(C) He is considering joining the company.
(D) He will no longer use the firm for investment.

189. What should the company's managers be prepared to explain?

(A) Their plans for expansion
(B) An amount of stolen money
(C) Recent transactions on an account
(D) Discrepancies in a computer record

Questions 190 and 191 refer to the following notice.

Discovery Academy Tuition Policy

Tuition for all students for the month of enrollment is due on the first of each month and must be paid by close of business on the tenth day of the month. Payments not received on or before the tenth will be considered late and will incur a five-dollar daily late fee.

190. On which of the following dates would a payment incur a late fee?

(A) The first of the month
(B) The fifth of the month
(C) The tenth of the month
(D) The eleventh of the month

191. What service is provided for which people are required to pay?

(A) Library
(B) Banking
(C) Education
(D) Transportation

GO ON TO THE NEXT PAGE

Questions 192–194 refer to the following statement.

On the Trade Union Front

Latip's trade unions are pushing for pay raises of 9 percent and shorter working hours, beginning April 1. If union demands are met in full, pay raises would be much higher than the 5.9 percent pay boost granted last year, and roughly double the rate of inflation. Negotiations are being carried on with individual employers by national labor groups, such as the Latipese Confederation of Trade Unions, or LACTU.

Although pay awards are likely to fall far short of the levels sought, analysts believe cuts in working hours are likely. LACTU says Latipese workers in the central district put in 68 hours a year more than their counterparts in the South, and 73 hours more than those in the North.

192. What is the approximate inflation rate in Latip?

 (A) 4.5 percent
 (B) 5.9 percent
 (C) 6.5 percent
 (D) 9.0 percent

193. With whom do Latipese labor groups negotiate?

 (A) Worker committees
 (B) Individual employers
 (C) Government arbitrators
 (D) Groups of employer representatives

194. According to the article, what will be a likely result of the negotiations?

 (A) A shorter workweek
 (B) Sharply higher wages
 (C) More paid vacation time
 (D) Better working conditions

Questions 195–198 refer to the following advertisement.

Need CD-ROM Information?

What is available? Where? Price? New developments?

Then you should be reading the most informative magazine dedicated to CD-ROM publishers and users ...

CD-ROM Professional

Until July 31, save more than 50 percent! New subscribers only. You pay $39.95, not the regular subscription price of $86.00. Here's the deal: Now, *CD-ROM Professional* is available to new subscribers at tremendous savings over the newsstand and regular subscription price. After ordering, if at any time you are not satisfied with your subscription, call 1-800-987-3456 for a FULL refund. You have nothing to lose; simply fill out and return the attached card today! But hurry, because this offer expires July 31. (If card is missing, call 1-800-345-9000.)

195. What information is contained in *CD-ROM Professional*?

(A) CD-ROM advertising
(B) Technical specifications
(C) Standards for the profession
(D) A listing of professional organizations

196. How much will a subscriber pay when renewing a subscription?

(A) $29.95
(B) $39.95
(C) $43.00
(D) $86.00

197. When may subscribers request a refund on their subscription?

(A) Any time during the year
(B) At the end of a subscription year
(C) Any time before receiving the fourth issue
(D) Not until they have accepted delivery of the first four issues

198. To order without a subscription card, what should a person do?

(A) Call 1-800-345-9000
(B) Call 1-800-987-3456
(C) Buy a magazine at a newsstand
(D) Write and send an order letter

GO ON TO THE NEXT PAGE

Questions 199 and 200 refer to the following report.

> The Asian air travel market is currently in a downturn, but Japanese airlines continue to prosper because the Japanese economy has not been as hard hit as other economies and, traditionally, most of their passengers have been Japanese. It is safe to assume that in the coming months, other flag carriers should expect redoubled competition from Japanese rivals in the larger Asian market, and that once the market regains its momentum, the Japanese airlines will emerge with a considerably larger market share than previously.

199. How does the writer describe the Asian air travel market?

(A) As weak
(B) As normal
(C) As prosperous
(D) As expanding rapidly

200. In the future, what will happen to Japanese airlines?

(A) They will become smaller.
(B) They will hold an advantage.
(C) They will look for new markets.
(D) They will face strong competition.

Stop! This is the end of the test. If you finish before time is called, you can go back to Parts V, VI, and VII and check your work.

TEST 4—SCRIPT

Part I

1. (Man B)
(A) The door has been left open.
(B) The man is opening the door.
(C) People have come out the door.
(D) The doors are about to open.

2. (Man B)
(A) A building is in the park.
(B) Several spaces are for rent.
(C) Cars are parked near the building.
(D) They are going down the street.

3. (Woman)
(A) The man is at the photocopier.
(B) The coffee machine is broken.
(C) The copies are in the box.
(D) The man has gone after coffee.

4. (Man B)
(A) The woman is on a bicycle.
(B) The women are outside talking.
(C) People are handing in their work.
(D) Shoppers take their bags into the store.

5. (Woman)
(A) He's eighteen.
(B) There're eight or ten of them.
(C) It's ten to eight.
(D) It's eight-ten.

6. (Woman)
(A) The girl is blowing out candles on the cake.
(B) The girl has dropped the cake on the floor.
(C) The children are eating the birthday cake.
(D) The cake is being served at a party.

7. (Man B)
(A) Swimmers are racing to the pool.
(B) Bathers are walking into the water.
(C) The water is undisturbed by swimmers.
(D) Rain has forced bathers from the pool.

8. (Man B)
(A) The taxi is dropping off a passenger.
(B) He is working on a new case.
(C) Nobody is allowed to walk here.
(D) The man is carrying his suitcase.

9. (Man B)
(A) The bridge is on fire.
(B) Water is coming off the bridge.
(C) The bridge is lighted up at night.
(D) The lights are moving to the right.

10. (Woman)
(A) The woman is holding her breath.
(B) The woman is seeking her fortune.
(C) The woman is looking out the window.
(D) The woman is sitting on a stool.

11. (Woman)
(A) The man is walking past the tree.
(B) The picker is going up the tree.
(C) The man is reaching for fruit on the tree.
(D) The trees have lost all their fruit.

12. (Man B)
(A) The men have been arrested.
(B) The boys are sitting with their heads down.
(C) The class is interested in the lesson.
(D) The books are standing on the desk.

13. (Woman)
(A) People are coming up the walk.
(B) Vehicles are parked along the street.
(C) Horses are walking along the sidewalk.
(D) The stores are crowded with shoppers.

14. (Man B)
(A) The window is under a tree.
(B) The washers are on the window sill.
(C) The washer is in the room next to the window.
(D) The window washer is high up on the building.

15. (Woman)
(A) The car is crossing the tracks.
(B) Cars are standing at the crossing.
(C) A car has stalled near the tracks.
(D) Cars are approaching the tracks.

16. (Man B)
(A) A lot of wires lead to the poles.
(B) They are holding two sticks.
(C) He wants to buy some electrical wires.
(D) They are standing in the woods.

17. (Woman) (A) The table is against the kitchen wall.
(B) The chicken is going to the light.
(C) A light is on in the kitchen.
(D) The refrigerator door is open.

18. (Man B) (A) The man is stopping the woman.
(B) People are walking in the aisles.
(C) The young people are buying a store.
(D) The couple are doing their shopping.

19. (Woman) (A) The technician is laughing at the film.
(B) The worker is looking at the screen.
(C) The men are leaving for work.
(D) The man has turned to the right.

20. (Man B) (A) The batter is watching for the ball.
(B) A baseball is on the ground.
(C) The team is leaving the diamond.
(D) Players are going onto the field.

Part II

21. (Man B) May I borrow your pen?
(Woman) (A) Yes, I'll be there in the morning.
(B) Yes, here it is.
(C) No, it opens at nine.

22. (Man B) How can we attract better applicants for these jobs?
(Man A) (A) We may have to offer more money.
(B) I've already applied. Have you?
(C) Yes, I find them very attractive.

23. (Man A) What time is the flight to New York?
(Man B) (A) No, I'm afraid that flight's full.
(B) It leaves from gate one.
(C) At two-o-five.

24. (Man A) Do you know anything about computers?
(Man B) (A) I read about it in a magazine.
(B) Yes, in my work, I've always had a computer.
(C) I believe it has a 40-megabyte hard drive.

25. (Woman) Does this winter seem colder to you than last winter?
(Man B)
(A) No, I never get sick.
(B) No, I thought the other fellow won.
(C) Yes, but that may be because it has snowed so much.

26. (Man B) When should we schedule a follow-up meeting?
(Man A)
(A) Would everyone be available Thursday, at nine o'clock?
(B) He called in an hour ago to say he'd be late.
(C) It's in Conference Room C, on the second floor.

27. (Man A) What time does the bus leave?
(Man B)
(A) At three o'clock, sharp.
(B) Fall is my favorite season.
(C) It should be here soon.

28. (Woman) Is it very far to the new warehouse?
(Man B)
(A) It shouldn't cost very much.
(B) It took me only 30 minutes to get there yesterday.
(C) It will work better if we cut it off.

29. (Woman) Are they serious professionals, or do they only dabble?
(Man A)
(A) No, they're professionals.
(B) They're getting smaller.
(C) I can't persuade them.

30. (Woman) What are the requirements for this job?
(Man A)
(A) No, I'm not very skilled.
(B) We may transfer you to another division.
(C) An engineering degree and fluency in English.

31. (Man B) Are you still thinking about buying a new house?
(Man A)
(A) I visited them just last week.
(B) Yes. We've decided ours is too small for us.
(C) Yes. I'll pick it up tomorrow when I go shopping.

32. (Man A) Did you say that you're taking Monday off?
(Man B)
(A) Yes, I have some personal business to take care of.
(B) Thank you. I'll hang it in the closet.
(C) No. The plane is still waiting on the runway.

33. (Man B) Do you have any idea why Mike left the reception early?
(Woman)
(A) No, right now I have no ideas at all.
(B) He said he was exhausted from his trip.
(C) I talked with him for only a short time.

34. (Man A) In what currency should we make payment?
(Man B) (A) In about a month.
(B) In either U.S. dollars or Japanese yen.
(C) To all salaried employees.

35. (Woman) When did Bill get promoted?
(Man B) (A) He's been working here for eight years now.
(B) I think he's probably in his office.
(C) On July 1st, when all of the promotions were announced.

36. (Man B) How does your daughter like medical school?
(Man A) (A) We expect her to be out of the hospital soon.
(B) Just fine. She's getting very good grades.
(C) The doctor said to keep her out of school until Monday.

37. (Man A) What sort of growth are we looking at in the long run?
(Man B) (A) We can safely predict a 10 percent annual increase.
(B) Yes, he's bound to grow up sometime.
(C) They must get very tired.

38. (Woman) Exactly what kind of car are you in the market for?
(Man B) (A) Actually, I'd rather get a truck than a car.
(B) I went to get some vegetables.
(C) I usually go by bus, but I had a lot to carry.

39. (Man A) How on earth did they find you?
(Man B) (A) My sister gave them my address.
(B) Yes, we all are.
(C) It isn't time yet.

40. (Woman) Are you going to have to cancel your dental appointment?
(Man A) (A) I'm sorry. I'll be ready in a minute.
(B) Yes, but I've already taken care of it.
(C) It's for ten o'clock tomorrow morning.

41. (Man B) If you don't think you're being paid enough, why not ask for a raise?
(Woman) (A) I paid him a month ago, when he asked me.
(B) I really don't mind working on weekends.
(C) I should, but I don't like to talk about money.

42. (Man B) What does your father do?
(Woman) (A) She's not working just now.
(B) The farther you go, the more it costs.
(C) He's a freight forwarder.

43. (Man B) What can we do to increase sales?
(Woman)
(A) Hire more salespeople and advertise.
(B) Somewhere between 10 and 15 percent.
(C) Show them your financial statements.

44. (Man A) Do your parents want you to go home?
(Woman)
(A) There are many opportunities.
(B) That's very important.
(C) Of course. They always want me to.

45. (Woman) Does he have a lot of influence with the government?
(Man A)
(A) Yes, he always recommends their stock.
(B) Yes, but only because of his family's connections.
(C) No, I don't think he'd do a very good job.

46. (Woman) Has the snow made it difficult to drive?
(Man B)
(A) Not really. I went to truck-driving school.
(B) He now says he agrees with us.
(C) No. The roads are clean, and there's no ice.

47. (Man B) Do you think we should raise our prices?
(Man A)
(A) I paid nearly one hundred dollars.
(B) No, I wouldn't say anything about it.
(C) Yes, considering how production costs have gone up.

48. (Man A) Which gate will the passengers come out of?
(Woman)
(A) It should get to my hotel before I do.
(B) Yes, I have a ticket for that flight.
(C) The arrivals board said Gate One.

49. (Woman) Will your mother be going with you?
(Man B)
(A) Yes, she spends a lot of time working in her garden.
(B) No, she hasn't been feeling well lately.
(C) I'm sure she's going to be here.

50. (Man B) How did they decide on a name like "Snappy" for a car?
(Woman)
(A) They polled people in the target market.
(B) Because it made a snapping sound.
(C) I guess they like the way it looks.

Part III

51. (Man B) Did I tell you, I'll be taking my vacation next week?
(Woman) I heard it somewhere. Who'll cover for you while you're gone?
(Man B) John will. He's been here a long time and can probably do a better job than I can. Don't be afraid to call on him if you need anything.

52. (Man A) It's awfully hot out today! I'm thirsty.
(Woman) Would you like something to drink?
(Man A) Yes, thanks. A glass of water would be fine.

53. (Man A) When will the staff meeting be over?
(Man B) It's supposed to end at 3 o'clock, but it'll probably run over.
(Man A) I thought it might. There's a lot to discuss.

54. (Woman) I didn't know that you know Joel.
(Man A) Yes. We've lived in the same apartment building for the past five years.
(Woman) That's nice. It's good that you have a friend who lives so close.

55. (Man B) What's the weather there been like?
(Woman) It's been cold and rainy lately, and we expect it to continue that way.
(Man B) Well, I'll be sure to dress for it, although I wish it were warm and sunny.

56. (Man B) Don't you like to fly?
(Woman) Not really. I don't like to feel so closed in.
(Man B) That's too bad. It sure cuts down on travel time, if you have to go very far.

57. (Man B) May I please have a cup of coffee?
(Woman) Yes, but we're out of both milk and cream. You'll have to take it black.
(Man B) That's o.k. It won't hurt me to have one cup of black coffee.

58. (Man B) I'm supposed to meet someone at the bus station. What's the fastest way to get there from here?
(Man A) Take a taxi. There's a stand just around the corner.
(Man B) Thanks! ... have to go!

59. (Man B) I wish I had studied harder when I was at the university.
(Woman) You always said you didn't think study was that important.
(Man B) Yes, I know, but now I realize I was wrong, and now it's too late.

60. (Woman) Are you able to get any exercise in your free time?
(Man A) Yes. I manage to get out and jog five miles a day.
(Woman) You must be in very good shape.

61. (Man B) Did you hear about Joe's auto accident?
(Woman) No. What happened?
(Man B) He was hit by a truck as he was pulling out of his driveway.

62. (Man B) Has this month's shuttle schedule been posted yet?
(Woman) Yes, they put it up this afternoon, but it's the same as last month's. No changes.
(Man B) Good. Lately, it seems that whenever they change it, it becomes less convenient for me.

63. (Man A) Are there any seats left for the five o'clock show?
(Woman) Yes. We still have a lot of tickets. There must be something else going on today.
(Man A) For us, that's good news. We've been looking forward to this all week.

64. (Man A) I heard that Molly broke her leg in a bad fall.
(Woman) That's right. She had a skiing accident.
(Man A) That's too bad. She'll be on crutches for the rest of the winter.

65. (Man A) I'd like a no-smoking room, please. Is one available?
(Woman) I'm sorry, sir. Ordinarily one would be, but we have no rooms of any kind available tonight.
(Man A) Oh, that's too bad. Can you refer me to another hotel?

66. (Man B) When will the plane land?
(Woman) The captain says we'll land as soon as we get clearance from the tower.
(Man B) I hope that's soon. I have to catch a connecting flight.

67. (Man B) Have you read any good books lately?
(Woman) I read a travel book that, although it doesn't sound very interesting, was really quite good. Perhaps you'd like to borrow it?
(Man B) I have nothing against travel books, except that they make me want to go places.

68. (Woman) I always get lost in this building. It's so big, I never know where I am. Can you tell me how to get out on the north side?
(Man B) Yes, it's over that way, but if you go down that corridor, near the water fountain you'll find a diagram telling you where everything is.
(Woman) Thank you. Now I'll know for the future.

69. (Man B) I hope we can soon climb out from under these debts. They're keeping us from making the investments we need to make to expand.
(Man A) Look, in two and a half years, everything'll be paid up and we can do what we want.
(Man B) For me, those two and a half years can't pass fast enough.

70. (Man B) This typewriter doesn't work, and I'd like a refund.
(Woman) We can't give refunds on equipment, sir, but we can exchange it and give you a new one.
(Man B) That's fine. I just want a machine that works.

71. (Man B) We're based in Malaysia, but we do a lot of business with China. Do you speak either Mandarin or Cantonese?
(Man A) I speak fluent Cantonese, but only a little Mandarin.
(Man B) To work here, you'll have to get up to speed on your Mandarin.

72. (Man A) I'm going to buy a new car.
(Man B) Why? Is there something wrong with your old one?
(Man A) Yes. I've always had trouble with it, and I don't want to fight with it any longer.

73. (Woman) Mary is a pretty girl, but her clothes are so out-of-date!
(Man B) What do you mean "out-of-date"? I think she looks very fashionable.
(Woman) No, nobody wears those long dresses any more.

74. (Man A) What would you like?
(Woman) I don't know. What would you recommend?
(Man A) The broiled salmon is very good. It's the specialty of the house.

75. (Woman) Let's go for a walk this evening, before it gets too late.
(Man B) O.k. I should be able to finish my work by seven.
(Woman) That would be a good time to go, after it cools off a little.

76. (Man A) If you have one available, we'd like an ocean-view room above the 10th floor.
(Woman) We have a very nice one. Of course, there's an extra charge for ocean-view rooms, sir.
(Man A) That's o.k. We're on our honeymoon and we want the best.

77. (Man B) I'm sorry. I have no idea where I am. Can you tell me when we get to Avalon Boulevard?
(Woman) It was two stops back. Tell the driver and he'll give you a pass for a ride in the other direction.
(Man B) It's not that far. I can walk it. Thanks for your help.

78. (Man A) The afternoon meeting has been canceled.
(Woman) Has it been rescheduled?
(Man A) Yes. For tomorrow at 9 A.M. in the Lotus Meeting Room.

79. (Man A) Do you think Alice'll win the singing competition? From the way she talks, she's sure working hard at it.
(Woman) I don't think she stands a chance, regardless of how hard she works.
(Man A) I have to agree with you. Sometimes she tries too hard.

80. (Woman) I'm afraid we have to scrap the H24 Computer System.
(Man B) Alan said that for now we might be able to get by with an upgrade. That sure would be a lot cheaper.
(Woman) It might appear that way, but the way I see it, in the long run it would work out to be more expensive.

Part IV

(Man A) Questions 81 through 83 refer to the following announcement.

(Man B) May I have your attention, please? We are about to enter a restricted area. Hard hats and steel-toed shoes are required beyond this point. If you go through the doorway on the right, you will be provided with hats and shoes. I see some children in the group. I'm sorry, but for safety reasons no children under 12 are allowed in this area. They should go to the exit waiting area. Cameras are not permitted. If you have a heart condition or are claustrophobic, you should consider waiting here until the rest of the tour group returns. We will be entering the underground facility in approximately 15 minutes, which will allow you time to get your equipment. Thank you.

(Man A) Now read question 81 in your test book and answer it.

(Man A) Now read question 82 in your test book and answer it.

(Man A) Now read question 83 in your test book and answer it.

(Man A) Questions 84 and 85 refer to the following health report.

(Woman) Broccoli is a great source of nutrition and doesn't deserve the reputation of "tastelessness," of which it is often accused. It's good alone, with butter, with sauces, or in a salad. Broccoli is rich in potassium and Vitamin A, low in calories, tasty, and nutritious. Make broccoli a part of your next meal and every meal. This message is brought to you by the New Jersey Broccoli Growers Association.

(Man A) Now read Question 84 in your test book and answer it.

(Man A) Now read Question 85 in your test book and answer it.

(Man A) Questions 86 through 88 refer to the following advertisement.

(Woman) Are you planning for your financial future? Do you take your personal finances seriously? If so, enroll now in our "Twilight Years in Wealth" program. There your savings will earn maximum interest in a secure combination of IRAs, CDs, and treasury bills. Investment is for a minimum 15-year period, but by the end of that time your account is guaranteed to be greatly increased. This may be the program for you. It's new. It's innovative. It's secure. Write today for more information. Your announcer will give you the address. Act now!

(Man A) Now read Question 86 in your test book and answer it.

(Man A) Now read Question 87 in your test book and answer it.

(Man A) Now read Question 88 in your test book and answer it.

(Man A) Questions 89 and 90 refer to the following introduction.

(Man A) Good afternoon! We have with us today two very important people: our mayor, Tom Brady, and his opponent, Kermit Wilton. Both candidates for the mayoral office have agreed to debate the issues here today. We hope this debate and the discussion that will follow will help you, the voters, to decide who is the better candidate to serve as your mayor.

(Man A) Now read question 89 in your test book and answer it.

(Man A) Now read question 90 in your test book and answer it.

(Man A) Questions 91 and 92 refer to the following notice.

(Man B) Taxi customers are asked to go to the front of the terminal and stand between the yellow lines on the sidewalk. This is the only location where passengers are allowed to board taxis. It is important that all passengers abide by the rules. By doing so, you will arrive at your destination faster than by attempting to avoid the wait. The terminal management thanks you for your cooperation.

(Man A) Now read question 91 in your test book and answer it.

(Man A) Now read question 92 in your test book and answer it.

(Man A) Questions 93 and 94 refer to the following report.

(Woman) Lately, many public companies have held back from making new investments because of shareholder demands for short-term profits. Others, including heavyweights such as Raymond and Bintech, have moved quickly to make the most of their current liquidity. My suggestion is that we join them, and the sooner the better.

(Man A) Now read Question 93 in your test book and answer it.

(Man A) Now read Question 94 in your test book and answer it.

(Man A) Questions 95 and 96 refer to the following presentation.

(Man B) Today we're going to be looking at Migo Electronics, our biggest rival. Migo, as you can see from this chart, has holdings of more than 4 billion dollars, is a leader in many high-tech fields, and is squeezing us out of even the North American market for consumer products. They're a serious competitor, but we can beat them. And that's why we're here.

(Man A) Now read question 95 in your test book and answer it.

(Man A) Now read question 96 in your test book and answer it.

(Man A) Questions 97 and 98 refer to the following announcement.

(Woman) A reminder to all building visitors and occupants about building safety. There are two exits from this building. One is alongside the rest rooms on every floor. The other is at the end of the main hall. Please remember where these exits are in case of an emergency. We are required by city fire regulations to make this announcement during working hours once every thirty days.

(Man A) Now read question 97 in your test book and answer it.

(Man A) Now read question 98 in your test book and answer it.

(Man A) Questions 99 and 100 refer to the following announcement.

(Man B) We welcome you to the Rotogyro, the newest addition to our growing family of attractions here at the Hannaland complex. No child under the height of one hundred twenty-five centimeters is allowed on the Rotogyro, for safety reasons. You will whirl at speeds of up to 60 kilometers per hour, feeling the sensation of speed, but without going anywhere. At the end of your ride, you will get off at the same place where you began. And when you get off, be sure to visit the Rotogyro's sister attraction directly opposite, the Outer Space Castle, where even infants can enjoy the beauty of outer space, recreated for your pleasure.

(Man A) Now read question 99 in your test book and answer it.

(Man A) Now read question 100 in your test book and answer it.

This is the end of the Listening Comprehension portion of the test. Turn to Part V in your test book.

TEST 4 COMPARISON SCORES

The score range for the TOEIC is 10 to 990, 5 to 495 for listening and 5 to 495 for reading. This is a converted score, otherwise known as a scaled score, arrived at by converting an examinee's raw score by a formula that changes with every test. The raw score is merely the number of questions answered correctly. On the TOEIC, there is no penalty for answering a question incorrectly.

Converted scores are reported, rather than raw scores, because the developers of the TOEIC make a statistical adjustment for the relative ease or difficulty of each test. This procedure ensures that scores are equivalent over time and do not fluctuate because one or another test may be easier or more difficult than others.

The raw scores that appear below, for this test and for this test only, correspond to a total mean converted TOEIC score of 500, 250 for listening and 250 for reading. Other tests in this book have mean scores calculated on different formulas.

These scores are provided so, if they like, students can compare their performance on this test with a performance that would produce a total converted score of 500. Raw part scores of above the scores provided here would convert to a score of above 500, while raw part scores of below the scores provided here would convert to a score of below 500.

Part	Mean Raw Score
I	15
II	19
III	19
IV	12
Mean Listening	65
V	25
VI	11
VII	28
Mean Reading	64
Mean Total	129

Converted Scores for Above Mean Scores

Mean Listening	250
Mean Reading	250
Mean Total	500

ANSWER KEY FOR TEST 4—LISTENING

Key: Part I

1. (B) The man is opening the door.
2. (C) Cars are parked near the building.
3. (A) The man is at the photocopier.
4. (B) The women are outside talking.
5. (D) It's eight-ten.
6. (A) The girl is blowing out candles on the cake.
7. (C) The water is undisturbed by swimmers.
8. (D) The man is carrying his suitcase.
9. (C) The bridge is lighted up at night.
10. (D) The woman is sitting on a stool.
11. (C) The man is reaching for fruit on the tree.
12. (B) The boys are sitting with their heads down.
13. (B) Vehicles are parked along the street.
14. (D) The window washer is high up on the building.
15. (A) The car is crossing the tracks.
16. (A) A lot of wires lead to the poles.
17. (C) A light is on in the kitchen.
18. (D) The couple are doing their shopping.
19. (B) The worker is looking at the screen.
20. (A) The batter is watching for the ball.

Key: Part II

21. (B) Yes, here it is.
22. (A) We may have to offer more money.
23. (C) At two-o-five.
24. (B) Yes, in my work, I've always had a computer.
25. (C) Yes, but that may be because it has snowed so much.
26. (A) Would everyone be available Thursday, at nine o'clock?
27. (A) At three o'clock, sharp.
28. (B) It took me only 30 minutes to get there yesterday.
29. (A) No, they're professionals.
30. (C) An engineering degree and fluency in English.
31. (B) Yes. We've decided ours is too small for us.
32. (A) Yes, I have some personal business to take care of.
33. (B) He said he was exhausted from his trip.
34. (B) In either U.S. dollars or Japanese yen.
35. (C) On July 1st, when all of the promotions were announced.
36. (B) Just fine. She's getting very good grades.
37. (A) We can safely predict a 10 percent annual increase.
38. (A) Actually, I'd rather get a truck than a car.
39. (A) My sister gave them my address.
40. (B) Yes, but I've already taken care of it.
41. (C) I should, but I don't like to talk about money.
42. (C) He's a freight forwarder.
43. (A) Hire more salespeople and advertise.
44. (C) Of course. They always want me to.
45. (B) Yes, but only because of his family's connections.
46. (C) No. The roads are clean, and there's no ice.
47. (C) Yes, considering how production costs have gone up.
48. (C) The arrivals board said Gate One.
49. (B) No, she hasn't been feeling well lately.
50. (A) They polled people in the target market.

Key: Part III

51. (C) He will substitute for the man.
52. (D) Something to drink
53. (D) It will go on longer than planned.
54. (A) They are neighbors.
55. (D) Warm clothing
56. (D) In airplanes
57. (C) The man will have coffee without cream.
58. (C) He needs to go to the bus station.
59. (C) He regrets that he was not a serious student.
60. (A) A health regimen
61. (A) It was in an accident.
62. (B) He finds changes in the schedule inconvenient.
63. (B) Go to the theater
64. (A) While skiing
65. (B) The hotel has no rooms available.
66. (D) He has another plane to catch.
67. (B) That the man read a book on travel
68. (A) She gets lost in the building.
69. (B) Paying off debts
70. (A) Exchange his typewriter
71. (B) Qualifications for a job
72. (A) His car is not reliable.
73. (B) Her clothes are not in fashion.
74. (C) In a restaurant
75. (D) Going out in the evening
76. (C) He wants a room with a view.
77. (A) He missed his bus stop.
78. (C) The next morning.
79. (D) She will lose the competition.
80. (C) It should be replaced.

Key: Part IV

81. (B) Hard hats and steel-toed shoes
82. (D) Children under 12
83. (B) It is a restricted area.
84. (A) Tasteless
85. (C) Sauces
86. (C) Personal savings
87. (D) 15 years
88. (D) Request more information
89. (A) Mayor of the city
90. (A) For a public debate
91. (A) At a designated location
92. (B) Arrive faster
93. (A) To return a profit to shareholders
94. (C) Invest company profits
95. (C) A business competitor
96. (D) Electronics
97. (B) To explain building safety
98. (A) Local laws
99. (D) Where they got on
100. (B) A ride close to the Rotogyro

ANSWER KEY FOR TEST 4—READING

Key: Part V

101. (C) better
102. (A) nearly
103. (D) erratic
104. (B) to meet
105. (D) discount
106. (C) twice
107. (B) very
108. (B) around
109. (C) returned
110. (A) careless
111. (A) excluded
112. (D) suspected
113. (D) transported
114. (B) failed
115. (B) several
116. (A) relieve
117. (D) reconsider
118. (A) on
119. (A) had
120. (C) ordered
121. (A) applications
122. (D) following
123. (B) during
124. (B) made up
125. (D) suggested
126. (C) effectively
127. (C) will
128. (A) to
129. (B) medium
130. (D) where
131. (C) consequences
132. (D) climbed
133. (B) antidote
134. (A) but not
135. (D) substantial
136. (C) rivaled
137. (C) official
138. (C) serves
139. (D) character
140. (B) circles

Key: Part VI

141. (A) was sure he could
142. (A) in which
143. (C) shock when he heard
144. (A) dishes
145. (A) him and his
146. (D) financially difficult
147. (D) three more
148. (D) typing speed, speedy typing
149. (A) were chosen
150. (A) would
151. (C) to date, as of yet, as of this date
152. (D) due to
153. (B) need
154. (B) campaign
155. (A) was introduced
156. (C) good advice
157. (A) to travel
158. (D) topics
159. (D) on
160. (B) communication systems, a communication system

Key: Part VII

161. (B) In the school cafeteria
162. (C) All area residents
163. (B) The superintendent
164. (B) Four
165. (C) Fashion
166. (C) Soft drinks
167. (C) Fruit
168. (D) Salad and vegetable
169. (D) $54.00
170. (B) Two months
171. (D) A musician
172. (B) At a hotel
173. (D) To reduce possibility of forest fires
174. (B) They will be asked to leave the park.
175. (C) If they join in the park animal-feeding program
176. (C) Under 50 million dollars
177. (D) Five
178. (A) Designate a corporate representative
179. (C) September 12
180. (B) Confirm the flight with his travel agent
181. (B) At 10:30 A.M.
182. (A) An insurance company
183. (A) Sell a product only to make a high profit
184. (C) John Forrest
185. (D) Baltimore
186. (C) $68.95
187. (B) Heavy investment losses
188. (D) He will no longer use the firm for investment.
189. (C) Recent transactions on an account
190. (D) The eleventh of the month
191. (C) Education
192. (A) 4.5 percent
193. (B) Individual employers
194. (A) A shorter workweek
195. (A) CD-ROM advertising
196. (D) $86.00
197. (A) Any time during the year
198. (A) Call 1-800-345-9000
199. (A) As weak
200. (B) They will hold an advantage.

TOEIC®
TEST 5

LISTENING COMPREHENSION

In this section of the test, you will have the chance to show how well you understand spoken English. There are four parts to this section, with special directions for each part.

Part I

Directions: For each question, you will see a picture in your test book and you will hear four short statements. The statements will be spoken just one time. They will not be printed in your test book, so you must listen carefully to understand what the speaker says.

When you hear the four statements, look at the picture in your test book and choose the statement that best describes what you see in the picture. Then, on your answer sheet, find the number of the question and mark your answer.

Look at the sample below.

Now listen to the four statements.

Sample Answer

Statement (B), "They're having a meeting," best describes what you see in the picture. Therefore, you should choose answer (B).

1. 

2. 

3. 

4. 

5.

6.

GO ON TO THE NEXT PAGE

7.

8.

9.

10.

GO ON TO THE NEXT PAGE

11.

12.

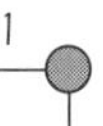

13.

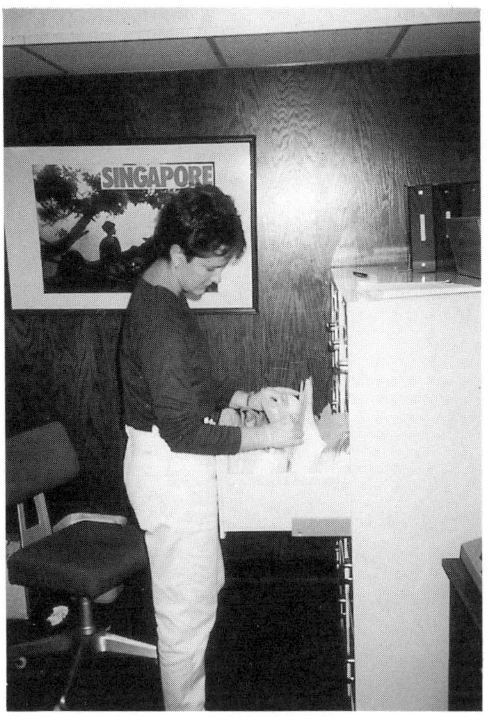

14.

GO ON TO THE NEXT PAGE

15.

16.

17.

18.

GO ON TO THE NEXT PAGE

19.

20.

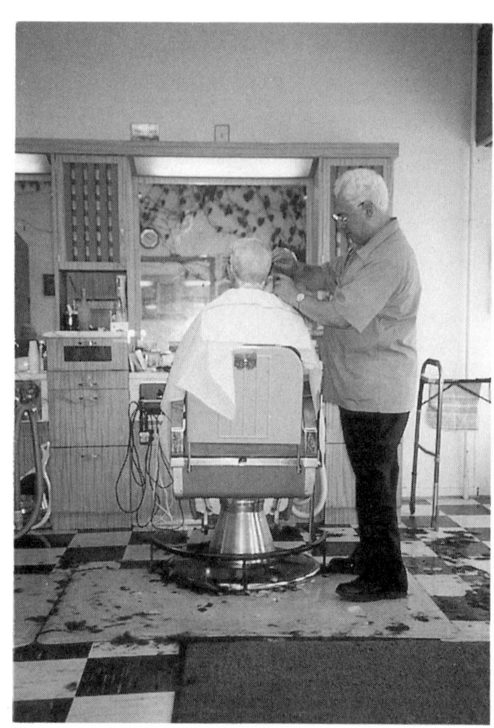

Part II

Directions: In this part of the test you will hear a question spoken in English, followed by three responses, also spoken in English. The question and the responses will be spoken just one time. They will not be printed in your test book, so you must listen carefully to understand what the speakers say. You are to choose the best response to each question.

Now listen to a sample question:

You will hear:

You will also hear:

Sample Answer

● Ⓑ Ⓒ

The best response to the question "How are you?" is choice (A) "I am fine, thank you." Therefore, you should choose answer (A).

21. Mark your answer on your answer sheet.
22. Mark your answer on your answer sheet.
23. Mark your answer on your answer sheet.
24. Mark your answer on your answer sheet.
25. Mark your answer on your answer sheet.
26. Mark your answer on your answer sheet.
27. Mark your answer on your answer sheet.
28. Mark your answer on your answer sheet.
29. Mark your answer on your answer sheet.
30. Mark your answer on your answer sheet.
31. Mark your answer on your answer sheet.
32. Mark your answer on your answer sheet.
33. Mark your answer on your answer sheet.
34. Mark your answer on your answer sheet.
35. Mark your answer on your answer sheet.
36. Mark your answer on your answer sheet.
37. Mark your answer on your answer sheet.
38. Mark your answer on your answer sheet.
39. Mark your answer on your answer sheet.
40. Mark your answer on your answer sheet.
41. Mark your answer on your answer sheet.
42. Mark your answer on your answer sheet.
43. Mark your answer on your answer sheet.
44. Mark your answer on your answer sheet.
45. Mark your answer on your answer sheet.
46. Mark your answer on your answer sheet.
47. Mark your answer on your answer sheet.
48. Mark your answer on your answer sheet.
49. Mark your answer on your answer sheet.
50. Mark your answer on your answer sheet.

GO ON TO THE NEXT PAGE

Part III

Directions: In this part of the test, you will hear 30 short conversations between two people. The conversations will not be printed in your test book. You will hear the conversations only once, so you must listen carefully to understand what the speakers say.

In your test book you will read a question about each conversation. The question will be followed by four answers. You are to choose the best answer to each question and mark it on your answer sheet.

51. Why will the man go to the lobby?

    (A) To pay his hotel bill
    (B) To get a cup of coffee
    (C) To meet a business associate
    (D) To go to the business center

52. What are the men discussing?

    (A) Education
    (B) Housing
    (C) Automobiles
    (D) Politics

53. What is said about Bill?

    (A) He does not want to be appointed.
    (B) He does not know he has an appointment.
    (C) He is usually on time.
    (D) He is always late for meetings.

54. How will the woman get to the housewares department?

    (A) By the stairs
    (B) By taking the elevator
    (C) By riding the escalator
    (D) By going to the rear of the store

55. How far is the new building from the woman's office?

    (A) One block
    (B) Several blocks
    (C) One kilometer
    (D) Two kilometers

56. Why were the men late?

    (A) They overslept.
    (B) Their car broke down.
    (C) They were in meetings.
    (D) They were stopped in traffic.

57. Why is the woman upset?

    (A) Her work has not been satisfactory.
    (B) A close friend has died.
    (C) She did not get promoted.
    (D) She is out of work.

58. What is the woman trying to do?

    (A) Buy a gift
    (B) Find a friend
    (C) Buy a dress
    (D) Find a store

59. What will happen at ten o'clock?

    (A) A sale will begin.
    (B) The office will open.
    (C) Paul will leave the office.
    (D) The men will discuss a sales report.

60. What can be said about the woman's package?

    (A) It did not arrive.
    (B) The contents broke.
    (C) It was returned to her.
    (D) She is about to send it.

61. Who worked on the room?

(A) A contractor
(B) An architect
(C) A carpenter
(D) The speaker

62. What are the speakers discussing?

(A) Post Office hours
(B) An increase in postal rates
(C) A postal employee employment contract
(D) The need for more space at the Post Office

63. Why might the neighbors move?

(A) They found new jobs.
(B) They want a bigger house.
(C) They do not like the neighborhood.
(D) They want to be near their family.

64. Where does this conversation take place?

(A) In a police station
(B) In a hotel
(C) In a post office
(D) In a bank

65. Where will the people eat their pizza?

(A) At home
(B) At work
(C) In their car
(D) At the restaurant

66. What is the woman's concern?

(A) Repairs
(B) Product quality
(C) High price
(D) Delivery date

67. Why did the woman NOT go any farther?

(A) Her son asked her not to.
(B) Her plane had already left.
(C) She did not have a boarding pass.
(D) She was carrying too much luggage.

68. Who will give the patient the results?

(A) The nurse
(B) The family doctor
(C) The head of surgery
(D) The testing clinic

69. What is the man trying to do?

(A) Place an order
(B) Explain an accident
(C) Find something he lost
(D) Report something stolen

70. When will the woman go to Manila?

(A) Right away.
(B) She does not know.
(C) When she is called to go.
(D) When she feels it is necessary.

71. What does the woman want to do?

(A) Sell
(B) Buy
(C) Open
(D) Close

72. For what does the man express concern?

(A) Protecting the environment
(B) An increase in crime
(C) Whether the bank is safe
(D) His financial future

GO ON TO THE NEXT PAGE

73. What do the men want to do?

(A) Take a tour
(B) Find employment
(C) Buy new equipment
(D) Start the machine

74. What has the woman been asked to do?

(A) Type a document
(B) Make photocopies
(C) Make some changes
(D) Get some information

75. What has happened to the company?

(A) It has made new contacts.
(B) It fears being taken over.
(C) It no longer enjoys a good reputation.
(D) It signed up an important new account.

76. What is the subject of this conversation?

(A) A corporate relationship
(B) A difficult business problem
(C) German finance laws
(D) Breaking up a partnership

77. What will the man do?

(A) Buy a new television
(B) Make a telephone call
(C) Help his mother-in-law
(D) Take his mother to dinner

78. What does the woman want to do?

(A) Open an account
(B) Borrow some money
(C) Close out her account
(D) Complete an application form

79. What are the speakers discussing?

(A) Television programs
(B) Japanese factories
(C) A new and growing company
(D) Investment trading techniques

80. What does the woman need to do?

(A) Write a letter to Bill
(B) Send General Affairs a letter
(C) Send a bill to General Affairs
(D) Speak with someone in General Affairs

Part IV

Directions: In this part of the test, you will hear several short talks. Each will be spoken just one time. They will not be printed in your test book, so you must listen carefully to understand and remember what is said.

In your test book you will read two or more questions about each short talk. The questions will be followed by four answers. You are to choose the best answer to each question and mark it on your answer sheet.

81. Where is the speaker?

(A) At an auto show
(B) At an airport
(C) At a shipyard
(D) At an amusement park

82. How large is the place?

(A) Very large
(B) Average size
(C) Below average
(D) Small

83. How long will the visitors remain at the site?

(A) Two hours
(B) One and a half hours
(C) One hour
(D) A half hour

84. What has been found?

(A) Gloves
(B) A wallet
(C) A package
(D) A briefcase

85. Where can the owner claim the item?

(A) At the security office
(B) At the manager's office
(C) At the checkout counter
(D) In the Electronics Department

86. What group does Mr. Allison represent?

(A) The medical center
(B) The Wildlife Foundation
(C) An environmental group
(D) The fire department

87. What is Mr. Allison asking for?

(A) Food
(B) Votes
(C) Money
(D) Clothes

88. Where do the airline's expansion routes take it?

(A) To Asia
(B) To Europe
(C) To the South Pacific
(D) To Latin America

89. What is a benefit of the new service?

(A) Reduced airfares
(B) Special tickets
(C) Fast aircraft
(D) Daily departures

90. What is Dr. Elizabeth Tuttle's position?

(A) Information officer
(B) Executive director
(C) Company president
(D) Company analyst

GO ON TO THE NEXT PAGE

91. What is Dr. Tuttle's major interest?

(A) Medical research
(B) Cost of medical services
(C) Laws governing health care
(D) Investment opportunities in medicine

92. What is the audience asked to do?

(A) Take their seats and be quiet
(B) Read some information about the speaker
(C) Direct all questions to the speaker
(D) Welcome Dr. Tuttle

93. Why will the drill take place?

(A) To test evacuation procedures
(B) To comply with government requirements
(C) To ensure that alarms function properly
(D) To demonstrate efficiency for visiting officials

94. What have employees been instructed to do?

(A) Meet in the downstairs lobby
(B) Report to their area supervisor
(C) Gather valuable computer files
(D) Shut doors as they leave

95. How is *Trekkie* said to be different from previous shuttle craft?

(A) It is lighter.
(B) It is smaller.
(C) It is faster.
(D) It carries more weight.

96. What covering does *Trekkie* have on its underside to avoid damage on reentry?

(A) Metal
(B) Fabric
(C) Ceramic
(D) Special paints

97. What role does *Trekkie* have in future space programs?

(A) It will travel to Mars.
(B) It will travel to the moon.
(C) It will be used to establish space stations.
(D) It will carry vehicles into space to be launched to distant bodies.

98. Who won the election for district supervisor?

(A) Mary Keller
(B) Mark Prowse
(C) Lester Burl
(D) H. Harry Kaplan

99. What happened at the Tenth Street overpass?

(A) It has been opened to traffic.
(B) It will be temporarily closed.
(C) It was the scene of an accident.
(D) It was flooded by a broken water main.

100. What weather is expected during the night?

(A) Rain
(B) A snowstorm
(C) Clear skies
(D) Cold temperatures

This is the end of the Listening Comprehension portion of the test. Turn to Part V in your test book.

YOU WILL HAVE ONE HOUR AND FIFTEEN MINUTES TO COMPLETE PARTS V, VI, AND VII OF THE TEST.

READING

In this section of the test, you will have a chance to show how well you understand written English. There are three parts to this section, with special directions for each part.

Part V

Directions: Questions 101–140 are incomplete sentences. Four words or phrases, marked (A), (B), (C), (D), are given beneath each sentence. You are to choose the one word or phrase that best completes the sentence. Then, on your answer sheet, find the number of the question and mark your answer.

Example

Because the equipment is very delicate, it must be handled with ———.

(A) caring
(B) careful
(C) care
(D) carefully

Sample Answer

The sentence should read, "Because the equipment is very delicate, it must be handled with care." Therefore, you should choose answer (C).

As soon as you understand the directions, begin work on the questions.

101. Forming a joint ——— company is a common practice among related businesses.

(A) mobile
(B) action
(C) venture
(D) adventure

102. The order was shipped on time, but ——— a day late.

(A) out
(B) sent
(C) returned
(D) delivered

103. Around the world, coffee is a ——— year-round beverage.

(A) enjoy
(B) today
(C) popular
(D) likened

104. The company ——— having polluted the river.

(A) sorry
(B) sorry for
(C) apologize
(D) apologized for

105. Unemployment in California is relatively high, ——— the national average.

(A) like as not
(B) just as much
(C) on looking to
(D) compared with

106. He had no selection from which to choose, as he had been ——— by only one university.

(A) studied
(B) accepted
(C) rejected
(D) interested

107. His father ——— one of the most important men in the government.

(A) thinking
(B) deciding
(C) considered to
(D) was considered

108. After letting the phone ring ——— times, the receptionist finally answered it.

(A) few
(B) some
(C) couple
(D) several

109. An annual report is issued the first of ——— year.

(A) day
(B) one
(C) every
(D) January

110. The document that we were ——— for was in the bottom drawer of the filing cabinet.

(A) digging
(B) looking
(C) working
(D) seeking

111. All product designs must be ——— before production begins.

(A) removed
(B) approved
(C) recessed
(D) appealed

112. After an unsuccessful ——— to reach the climbers by air, the rescuers decided to go overland.

(A) visit
(B) trying
(C) attempt
(D) decision

113. The Customs Office works hard to ——— counterfeit goods.

(A) keep out
(B) tune out
(C) give away
(D) throw away

114. Camping equipment can be ——— on the second floor.

(A) buy
(B) have
(C) sell
(D) found

115. The play ——— nearly three hours, but few people left the theater early.

(A) over
(B) ended
(C) lasted
(D) actors

116. The currency exchange laws must be strictly ———.

(A) enjoyed
(B) enforced
(C) enrolled
(D) encouraged

117. Political leaders often ask their people to ——— unnecessary hardship.

(A) invest
(B) endure
(C) become
(D) require

118. He ——— for a grant to study quantum mechanics.

(A) applied
(B) entered
(C) was applied
(D) application

119. The speaker was ——— by the audience's response.

(A) please
(B) taken up
(C) impressing
(D) overwhelmed

120. Professional boxers ——— very poorly paid, but now can do quite well.

(A) were once
(B) are always
(C) have to be
(D) used before

121. The accident occurred when the supervisor was ——— to leave the area.

(A) upon
(B) about
(C) lately
(D) telling

122. The company invested in employee health programs to reduce ———.

(A) budgets
(B) overhead
(C) absenteeism
(D) unemployment

123. People attending the meeting were asked to keep the auditor's report ———.

(A) safely
(B) important
(C) influential
(D) confidential

124. The witness claimed to be unable to ——— what he had said about the matter.

(A) recall
(B) detain
(C) remind
(D) decide

GO ON TO THE NEXT PAGE

125. ——— reconsidering their position, the bankers decided to refinance the loan.

(A) On
(B) As
(C) From
(D) Near

126. Road crews ——— the snow-covered roads within hours of the storm.

(A) moved
(B) washed
(C) shoved
(D) cleared

127. The argument took ——— in public, which embarrassed everyone.

(A) part
(B) over
(C) place
(D) charge

128. The department ——— to invest heavily in research and development.

(A) lost time
(B) made mistakes
(C) found resources
(D) investment capital

129. ——— the passengers realized there was a famous actor on board the plane.

(A) Few of
(B) Nearly
(C) Although
(D) Somewhat

130. The building's roof ——— under the winter snows.

(A) collapsed
(B) was built
(C) falling down
(D) had been designed

131. The restaurant served homemade bread with every ———.

(A) eat
(B) meal
(C) food
(D) table

132. The judge was convinced that he had been ——— misled by the plaintiff's attorney.

(A) overly
(B) informed
(C) listening
(D) deliberately

133. Rainy weather, ——— with traffic tie-ups, made the commute to work much longer than usual.

(A) having
(B) combined
(C) resulting
(D) additionally

134. On his ——— from the company, the director went from department to department to say good-bye.

(A) left
(B) retire
(C) departure
(D) terminate

135. The discussion turned into a ———, in which neither side would concede defeat.

(A) argue
(B) debate
(C) fighting
(D) decision

136. Only seven people ——— the presentation.

(A) arrived
(B) here for
(C) attend to
(D) showed up for

137. Any discussion at this time of the causes of the accident would be purely ———.

(A) special
(B) stipulate
(C) speculate
(D) speculative

138. After the scandal, the former prime minister thought it best to take up ——— abroad.

(A) place
(B) vacation
(C) residence
(D) information

139. The men maintained their school ———, even after entering business, and all benefited from their contacts.

(A) ties
(B) talk
(C) notes
(D) class

140. The economist traveled ——— the country to speak at a conference on the currency crisis.

(A) near
(B) over
(C) across
(D) around

GO ON TO THE NEXT PAGE

Part VI

Directions: In Questions 141–160 each sentence has four words or phrases underlined. The four underlined parts of the sentence are marked (A), (B), (C), (D). You are to identify the one underlined word or phrase that should be corrected or rewritten. Then, on your answer sheet, find the number of the question and mark your answer.

Example

All employee (A) are required to wear (B) their identification (C) badges while (D) at work.

Sample Answer

● (B) (C) (D)

Choice (A), the underlined word "employee," is not correct in this sentence. This sentence should read, "All employees are required to wear their identification badges while at work." Therefore, you should choose answer (A).

As soon as you understand the directions, begin work on the questions.

141. It was (A) the country's (B) free enterprise policy that attracted foreign investment and led (C) to its rapid developing (D).

142. The degree of government involvement in private affairs became (A) an embarrassment to the nation when (B) it was revealed (C) that directors being contacted (D) regarding their decisions.

143. Without proper treatment, even (A) a small cut can develop (B) an infection and became (C) a medical (D) emergency.

144. For each of (A) the past three quarters (B), the subscription renewal rate dropping (C) by a minimum of 6.2 percent over (D) the previous year.

145. As a cost-saving measure, it is
not uncommonly that several students
A
join to share a large house while
B C
studying at the university.
D

146. The designers had some troubling
A B
assessing the extent of the damage.
C D

147. I cannot find fault with their
A B
intentions, yet I am not agree with
C
their actions.
D

148. Several sheets of high-quality paper are
A B C
need to print the brochures.
D

149. The recommendation that he will be
A
promoted to vice president met with a
B C
a great deal of resistance from the
D
board.

150. Several people stood in line for over a
A B
hour, waiting to get inside.
C D

151. The workload was so backed up in the
A
office that several temporary employees
are brought in early in the week to
B C D
help everyone catch up.

152. After the Civil War in America, many
men had nothing to go home to and
A B
were become used to a life of hardship
C D
and violence.

153. Because of heavy traffic,
A
commuters enter the city in the
B
morning usually take at least
C
45 minutes to get across the bridge.
D

GO ON TO THE NEXT PAGE

154. Radio was the primary
means of communication to warn city
A B
and surrounding area residents of the
potentials for heavy flooding.
C D

155. As profits went down, interest rates
A
rose, making it extremely difficult for
B
newly companies to finance programs
C
to develop new products.
D

156. Management has asked for a complete
A
report on the results of the last survey,
B
having into account the cost of
C
increasing the response rate.
D

157. Evaluation criteria was developed by
A
the quality control staff, but
implemented by all production workers.
B C D

158. There were more than 50,000
steelworkers lived in the small
A
community, most of whom
B C
had been born there.
D

159. An inability to identify potential
A
high-volume customers is a major
failing of the marketing department,
B
but the lacks of credit in general has
C D
contributed to the company's poor
performance.

160. The fast serving of the restaurant
A
made it a favorite with business people,
B C
who regularly went there for lunch.
D

Part VII

Directions: Questions 161–200 are based on a variety of reading material (for example, announcements, paragraphs, advertisements, and the like). You are to choose the one best answer, (A), (B), (C), or (D), to each question. Then, on your answer sheet, find the number of the question and mark your answer. Answer all questions following a passage on the basis of what is stated or implied in that passage.

Read the following example.

> The Museum of Technology is a "hands-on" museum, designed for people to experience science at work. Visitors are encouraged to use, test, and handle the objects on display. Special demonstrations are scheduled for the first and second Wednesdays of each month at 1:30 P.M. Open Tuesday–Friday, 2:30–4:30 P.M., Saturday 11:00 A.M.–4:30 P.M., and Sunday 1:00–4:30 P.M.
>
> When during the month can visitors see special demonstrations?
>
> (A) Every weekend
> (B) The first two Wednesdays
> (C) One afternoon a week
> (D) Every other Wednesday

Sample Answer

The passage says that the demonstrations are scheduled for the first and second Wednesdays of the month. Therefore, you should choose answer (B).

As soon as you understand the directions, begin work on the questions.

GO ON TO THE NEXT PAGE

Questions 161–164 refer to the following announcement.

An Arts Open House

The Maybury Center for the Arts celebrates the cultures of the world at its eighth annual open house, Sunday, August 30, from noon to 6 P.M. There will be performances by the National String Quartet, the Brass Ensemble, soloists from the Maybury Opera Company, and more than forty other entertainers and troupes, on all the stages and open areas of the center. For a schedule of performances, call the center. Admission is free, but donations will be gratefully accepted.

161. How many times in the past has the Maybury Center held an open house?

(A) 2
(B) 6
(C) 7
(D) 8

162. How long will the Maybury Center open house last?

(A) For six hours
(B) For eight hours
(C) For two days
(D) For one week

163. How many groups and entertainers will perform during the open house?

(A) Four
(B) Ten
(C) Thirty
(D) More than forty

164. What is the Maybury Center's policy concerning admission and payment?

(A) Admission is free.
(B) Admission price is not stated.
(C) A five-dollar donation is required.
(D) Only subscribing members are admitted.

Questions 165 and 166 refer to the following advertisement.

> The Tulace Peoples Service (TPS) offers fax service to anywhere in the world.
>
> It's faster than mail and guaranteed to arrive, or no fee. The service is speedy, and the price is right! TPS offices are located worldwide.
>
> Call 842-0133 for details.

165. To where can TPS transmit?

    (A) Anywhere in the world
    (B) To Tulace and the surrounding area
    (C) To a few countries
    (D) To other TPS facilities

166. What happens if a transmission does not arrive at its destination?

    (A) It is sent to another number.
    (B) No fee is charged.
    (C) It is sent from a different TPS office.
    (D) The document is sent by mail, paid for by TPS.

Questions 167 and 168 refer to the following classified advertisement.

> Classic black leather motorcycle jacket—$85. Size 46. Bikers' envy. Like new. Must sell, need cash. (602) 789-6543, 10:00 A.M. – 6:00 P.M.

167. What is being sold?

    (A) A car
    (B) A jacket
    (C) A motorcycle
    (D) Black leather

168. Why is this item being sold?

    (A) The seller is moving.
    (B) The seller needs money.
    (C) The seller bought a new one.
    (D) The item needs some repair work.

GO ON TO THE NEXT PAGE

Questions 169–171 refer to the following facsimile message.

Fax to: Deborah Conrad   Reply to: Fax No. 45/09 681-2310

From: Andrew Collins
Date: 1/22

Message for Addressee

Deborah:

I have just broken my leg in a skiing accident and cannot return to Australia for 7–10 days. I would like you to assume all of my duties in my absence, including supervision of employees and conduct of daily meetings. I will communicate daily with you by fax, if at all possible. Please inform me immediately of any serious developments within the department. I will return as quickly as I can. Thank you for your help. I wish I were there instead of here.

Regards,

Andy

169. Why has Mr. Collins not returned to his office?

(A) He is injured.
(B) He is too busy.
(C) He is too tired.
(D) He has lost his ticket.

170. What does Mr. Collins want Ms. Conrad to do?

(A) Go skiing with him
(B) Take on his responsibilities
(C) Go quickly to Australia
(D) Find a new employee

171. Of what does Mr. Collins want to be kept informed?

(A) Ms. Conrad's opinions
(B) Any new company plans
(C) Any major office problem
(D) Australian currency fluctuations

Questions 172 and 173 refer to the following advertisement.

Shirgar horses are superb animals whose superiority as a breed is unchallenged. Their perfection did not come about by chance. Shirgar horses are the result of bloodlines so blue that they can be traced back for centuries.

So it is with the Neptune Motor Car, the champion of automobiles, the choice of automobile enthusiasts. There is no Neptune Motor Car "factory." Each car is still handcrafted at the Neptune facility by men who would better be termed artists than engineers. They create a car that dominates the road, but does so with speed, luxury, and finesse, rather than with gaudy ostentation.

The Neptune Motor Car—a creation of incomparable quality. A car that is not only to be driven, but savored.

172. What is stated as the reason for people to buy this car?

(A) Advanced technology
(B) Safety engineering
(C) Price
(D) Quality

173. What are Neptune Motor Car engineers compared to?

(A) Artists
(B) Soldiers
(C) Horse breeders
(D) Motor enthusiasts

GO ON TO THE NEXT PAGE

Questions 174–176 refer to the following guarantee.

National Computer Warehouse
Satisfaction Guaranteed!

If you are dissatisfied with your NCW computer purchase, return the product within 14 days in its original condition, with all packaging and manuals and the original sales receipt or invoice. We will exchange or give full credit. Software may be exchanged for the same product only. Software returns allowed only for defective merchandise or merchandise still in original wrapper. Labor and service charges are not refundable.

174. How long after a purchase does a person have to return an NCW computer product?

(A) One day
(B) One week
(C) Two weeks
(D) Thirty days

175. What is stated as grounds for returning an NCW computer product?

(A) Lack of satisfaction
(B) Better price elsewhere
(C) Malfunction of the product
(D) Upgrading to a better product

176. For what does National Computer Warehouse NOT give credit or exchange?

(A) Parts
(B) Labor
(C) Software
(D) Hardware

Questions 177 and 178 refer to the following advertisement.

> Route 66 Self-Storage: Over 30,000 sq. ft. of warehouse space, locked and virtually airtight vaults, various sizes available, low rents, packing supplies available at no extra charge. Telephone (021) 987-6543.

177. What type of business is being advertised?

(A) Packing
(B) Moving
(C) Storage
(D) Offices

178. Which of the following is NOT advertised as a reason to bring business to this firm?

(A) Security
(B) Reputation
(C) Low prices
(D) Free supplies

Questions 179 and 180 refer to the following promotion.

> The California avocado has more potassium than a banana, contains seventeen vitamins and minerals, and is cholesterol-free. That makes this fruit a healthy choice for a nutrition-packed snack. Buy California avocados today.

179. What is said to make the avocado a healthy food?

(A) It is fresh fruit.
(B) It contains no salt.
(C) It is organically grown.
(D) It has no cholesterol.

180. How is it suggested the avocado be eaten?

(A) In a salad
(B) As a light meal
(C) Instead of dessert
(D) Mixed with other fruits

Questions 181 and 182 refer to the following article.

> Currently, many companies are paying more attention to their software than to their employees. While modern technology is crucial to any business operation, neglect of human resources can damage a corporation quickly and sometimes irreparably. A number of studies show that worker satisfaction and motivation, for example, have a direct impact on productivity. Even small things, such as an extended coffee break or an occasional office party, can have noticeable effects on worker morale. Remember, even the most sophisticated machines still need human operators.

181. What does the writer say may prevent a corporation from becoming successful?

   (A) Neglect of employees
   (B) High overhead rates
   (C) Failure to adopt new technology quickly
   (D) Assigning too much importance to minor details

182. What does the writer say may affect productivity?

   (A) Employee morale
   (B) New kinds of software
   (C) Sophisticated machines
   (D) Coffee breaks that are too long

Questions 183–185 refer to the following classified advertisements.

VACANCIES/RENTALS

APT: 2-br. 201 Grand Ave. Smokeless building. Rent includes heat. Other utilities extra. Avail. immediately. Fourth floor. 10-minute walk to bus stop. $400, plus one-month-rent security deposit.

STUDIO: 378 Chestnut St. $250, no utilities incl. Non-smokers only. Second floor. Three blocks to bus stop and several stores. Avail. Dec. 10.

APT: 1-br. 745 Parkside Dr. Ground floor. No smokers. $475, all utilities incl. Newly renovated bldg. One block to bus. Avail. Jan. 1.

APT: 2-br. 28 Lenox Rd. $375, utils. incl. Near subway, bus. No pets or smokers. Third floor. Avail. Dec. 15.

183. In which apartment would a smoker be allowed?

(A) 201 Grand Ave.
(B) 745 Parkside Dr.
(C) 28 Lenox Rd.
(D) None

184. Which apartment is available for earliest occupancy?

(A) 201 Grand Ave.
(B) 378 Chestnut St.
(C) 745 Parkside Dr.
(D) 28 Lenox Rd.

185. Which apartment would be best for a physically handicapped person?

(A) 201 Grand Ave.
(B) 378 Chestnut St.
(C) 745 Parkside Dr.
(D) 28 Lenox Rd.

GO ON TO THE NEXT PAGE

Questions 186 and 187 refer to the following advertisement.

Beginning Tomorrow—Oriental Carpets

For seven days, handmade oriental carpets are on sale. All sizes, from Iran, Turkey, Afghanistan, and Pakistan. Bokharas, Balouchis, Isfahans, and Kilims. All authentic and exquisite examples of their kind. Some of these carpets are antique or used and reflect the conditions under which they were kept. At the Convention Center, beginning at 10:00 A.M.

186. What is being announced?

(A) A week-long oriental carpet sale
(B) A one-day sale of oriental carpets
(C) Arrival of a shipment of oriental carpets
(D) An exposition by oriental carpet manufacturers

187. What is said about the carpets?

(A) They are all new.
(B) They are not expensive.
(C) They are excellent reproductions.
(D) They may not be in good condition.

Questions 188–190 refer to the following communication.

Taipei Sports Equipment, Incorporated
497 Chang Hui Street
Suite 875
Taipei, Taiwan

Cable: TSI-891-4430 Tel: (03) 750-1966

Mr. Takashi Nagahara
Chief Executive Officer
Kobe Athletics Unlimited

Dear Mr. Nagahara:

I am glad to hear that you and Mr. Fujikawa will be visiting Taiwan in August. I received your letter, dated June 6, expressing interest in meeting with representatives of our company and touring our various facilities on your next visit to Taípei, August 16–19. We are pleased to be able to accommodate your schedule. My assistant, Francis Wu, is working now on a tentative itinerary for your visit. If you have any special requests, please have somebody contact Mr. Wu.

Within a week I will send you a draft for approval. My staff and I are looking forward to seeing you.

Sincerely yours,

Gao Chang An
Vice-President

188. Who is preparing Mr. Nagahara's visit?

(A) Mr. Nagahara
(B) Mr. Gao
(C) Mr. Fujikawa
(D) Mr. Wu

189. Where will the people meet?

(A) Kobe.
(B) Taipei.
(C) Tunghai.
(D) It is still uncertain.

190. When will Mr. Gao contact Mr. Nagahara?

(A) The same day
(B) The next day
(C) The following week
(D) By August

GO ON TO THE NEXT PAGE

Questions 191–193 refer to the following advertisement.

> Investment Opportunity: Diversified telemarketing/research firm needs capital for growth. Our services include computerized directory assistance, national change of address updating, telemarketing, and market research data collection. We are growing and profitable. Will consider equity or other form of participation. For information, contact Box 54, Circulation Management Magazine, 611 Broadway #321, New York, NY 10012. ALL REPLIES ARE KEPT CONFIDENTIAL.

191. Who has placed this advertisement?

    (A) A magazine
    (B) A telephone company
    (C) A marketing consultant
    (D) An unnamed telemarketing firm

192. What is the advertisement for?

    (A) Telephone service
    (B) Part-time employment
    (C) Records updating
    (D) Solicitation of investment capital

193. What will be done for people who respond to the advertisement?

    (A) Their names will be listed in the magazine.
    (B) Their replies will be kept secret.
    (C) Their resumes will be forwarded to other offices.
    (D) They will be invited for an interview.

Questions 194–196 refer to the following memorandum.

To: Albert Rawley
Chief Executive Officer
New Zealand Copper Corporation

From: Bill Patterson
Managing Director

Date: April 8, 19—

I have been disappointed with our progress here. As promised when we opened, we enjoy a low wage scale and productive workers. The red tape involved in conducting business here, however, is unacceptably burdensome and is apparently becoming worse.

More specifically, recently it has been very difficult to arrange export shipping. All forms of government-sponsored transportation, including trains, trucks, and ships, fail to keep to their schedules, and many do not travel, regardless of schedule.

As you well know, the key to maintaining good client relations is on-time delivery. By this letter I am requesting approval for funds to contract with a private transportation company, in an attempt to overcome this inertia. I will try this approach for six months. If matters do not improve, we should consider withdrawing from all manufacturing activity here.

I hope you understand the urgency of this situation and can give me a prompt reply. I have a company in mind. They are ready to move as soon as they have a contract.

194. What problem does Mr. Patterson have?

(A) Lack of raw materials
(B) Low worker productivity
(C) Difficulty in moving goods
(D) Managerial disorganization

195. Why does Mr. Patterson say he wants to take action?

(A) To increase profits
(B) To improve productivity
(C) To improve the company's image
(D) To ensure customer satisfaction

196. What does Mr. Patterson want to do?

(A) Increase wages
(B) Cease doing business
(C) Hire a private firm
(D) Move plants to other locations

GO ON TO THE NEXT PAGE

Questions 197 and 198 refer to the following memorandum.

To : All Staff
From : Management
Date : June 6, 19—
Subject: Company Policy on Smoking

We have received a number of complaints from employees concerning discarded tobacco waste on external walkways, around entrances, in the parking lots, and elsewhere on company grounds. Our inspection supports the validity of the complaints. To remedy the situation, we are placing additional receptacles for tobacco waste at strategic locations on the grounds, with the expectation that employees will respond positively to our effort to reduce this abuse of our environment. We will monitor the situation and hope that more severe measures to control tobacco waste will not be necessary. We appreciate employee cooperation in this matter.

197. What employee complaint has prompted this notice?

(A) People smoking in nonsmoking areas
(B) People smoking inside company buildings
(C) Smokers who want more smoking areas created
(D) Smokers not disposing of cigarette butts properly

198. What measure has the company taken to remedy the problem?

(A) Smoking is banned on all company property.
(B) Employees have been urged to be patient with one another.
(C) Containers for cigarette butts have been placed about on company grounds.
(D) Special ventilated smoking areas have been established.

Questions 199 and 200 refer to the following letter.

> Dear Mr. Park:
>
> Mr. John Pettybrook of our International Sales Division has passed along to me your proposal for the Richard Skelly personal development videos. I hope to be able to respond shortly, but first I must review other licensing agreements to ensure that there is no conflict in what you propose. In the meantime, please do not hesitate to contact me, should you have any questions.
>
> Sincerely,
>
> Karen Algood-Williams

199. What is the purpose of this letter?

    (A) To deny a request
    (B) To accept an offer
    (C) To acknowledge an offer
    (D) To make a request

200. What is the concern of the writer?

    (A) That her company may lose money
    (B) That other contracts would prevent her from doing something
    (C) That Mr. Pettybrook will not give his permission
    (D) That Mr. Park will refuse her proposal

Stop! This is the end of the test. If you finish before time is called, you can go back to Parts V, VI, and VII and check your work.

TEST 5—SCRIPT

Part I

1. (Man B)
   (A) I have to go to court today.
   (B) The courts are not occupied.
   (C) His tennis shoes are outside.
   (D) We are going to play catch.

2. (Woman)
   (A) The man is holding the rope.
   (B) The man has landed on his feet.
   (C) The man is handing over the ring.
   (D) The man is looking up the walk.

3. (Man B)
   (A) The man will not come close.
   (B) The man is left with a stack of shirts.
   (C) The shirts have been thrown in the wash.
   (D) The man is looking at the clothes.

4. (Man B)
   (A) The runners are on the track.
   (B) The road curves to the right.
   (C) The athletes have crossed the road.
   (D) The man ran past the store.

5. (Woman)
   (A) The cook is watching the kitchen crew.
   (B) Food is cooking in the pan.
   (C) The women are learning to cook.
   (D) The woman is washing the pan.

6. (Man B)
   (A) The bones are in a pile near the cliff.
   (B) The animal is climbing on the rocks.
   (C) The large bones are imbedded in stone.
   (D) The animal has been hit with a rock.

7. (Woman)
   (A) The man has his hands in his pockets.
   (B) The man is working on the locks.
   (C) The man is running up the stairs.
   (D) The man has backed into a ditch.

8. (Man B) (A) The baseball game is over.
(B) People are playing a game.
(C) They're unable to park.
(D) They're going to a game.

9. (Woman) (A) The books are about to be put on a shelf.
(B) The woman has walked away from the shelf.
(C) The woman is taking a book off the shelf.
(D) The shelves have come down on the books.

10. (Man B) (A) People pick flowers along the walk.
(B) The walks are lined with flowers.
(C) The man is selling flowers on the sidewalk.
(D) Flowers are growing on the sidewalk.

11. (Man B) (A) The taller the tree, the better.
(B) All three towers are very tall.
(C) The building is on a hill.
(D) The water tower is high above the trees.

12. (Man B) (A) The truck would like to leave.
(B) The trucks have gone into the woods.
(C) The truck is made of wood.
(D) The truck is carrying heavy logs.

13. (Woman) (A) The woman is heading downhill.
(B) The women are going through the office.
(C) The woman is looking in the cabinet.
(D) The women are looking for work.

14. (Woman) (A) He is traveling a long way.
(B) He is sweeping the room.
(C) The tires are very low.
(D) The man is sound asleep.

15. (Man B) (A) The street is being dug up.
(B) Men are working in the field.
(C) A man has fallen in the hole.
(D) The workers are sitting around.

16. (Woman)
(A) The room is for boxes only.
(B) The piles of boxes have been carried out.
(C) Some boxes are piled to the ceiling.
(D) The boxes were put in the trash.

17. (Man B)
(A) There is little traffic out.
(B) The houses are in a row.
(C) Pedestrians are crowding the walk.
(D) The woman has found her way.

18. (Woman)
(A) The woman is sitting on the walk.
(B) The woman is holding her arm.
(C) The woman is carrying flowers.
(D) The woman is bending over.

19. (Man B)
(A) The boats are going toward the shore.
(B) Boats are tied to the dock.
(C) The motorboats are pulling away.
(D) The boats are adrift in the river.

20. (Woman)
(A) The man is entering the barber shop.
(B) The man is getting a haircut.
(C) The men are standing on a chair.
(D) The man has found a place to sit down.

Part II

21. (Man B) Where is the nearest pharmacy?
(Woman)
(A) On Pelton Street, at the corner.
(B) At nine o'clock.
(C) You can go by taxi or bus.

22. (Man A) How many gas stations are there between here and Milltown?
(Woman)
(A) Yes, there are.
(B) There are only two.
(C) I think it's possible.

23. (Man B) Do you want to come to the opening on Monday?
(Woman)
(A) It's not open yet.
(B) There's an opening in our department.
(C) Gee, I'd love to go.

24. (Woman) Who is responsible for the Milan project?
(Man B) (A) Tom Travers, in the Design Division.
(B) Yes, I have many responsibilities.
(C) That project could be very profitable.

25. (Man B) Have you seen the new shopping arcade?
(Man A) (A) Yes, several people visited me yesterday.
(B) Did they get lost again?
(C) No. I'm so busy, I haven't been able to get out.

26. (Man A) Would you care for something to put on your toast?
(Man B) (A) I'll help you as soon as I finish here.
(B) Yes, I'd like some jam or marmalade, please.
(C) I think I'll need a size larger.

27. (Woman) How many times have you visited them in Prague?
(Man A) (A) At least five, maybe six.
(B) I'd rather not, if I can avoid it.
(C) My flight leaves at eleven thirty.

28. (Woman) Mr. Wilkes isn't in. May I take a message?
(Man B) (A) Please have one of the chocolates.
(B) Please have him call John at the office.
(C) Yes. That will be four dollars and ten cents.

29. (Man A) How do you manage to make your products so popular?
(Woman) (A) I don't care for any, thank you.
(B) We target our advertising very carefully.
(C) No, I'm really not very popular.

30. (Man A) Where will the meeting be held?
(Man B) (A) We'll meet on Monday.
(B) In Frankfurt.
(C) Only once a week.

31. (Woman) Does this bus go downtown?
(Man B) (A) No, it's up to you.
(B) I was there yesterday, thanks.
(C) No. You'll have to catch the Number 73 across the street.

32. (Man A) Would you care for something to drink?
(Woman)
(A) Yes, I really care.
(B) I like it done carefully.
(C) Yes, please. What do you have?

33. (Woman) When do you plan to leave for your Asia trip?
(Man A)
(A) No, in fact, it's really quite narrow.
(B) Yes, we already have a plan.
(C) As soon as I get my visas.

34. (Woman) Do you have any idea what time it is?
(Man B)
(A) Yes, it's half past one.
(B) No, I'm sorry, they've already left.
(C) I've had several good ideas.

35. (Woman) How will the crisis affect their position?
(Man A)
(A) Not at all, or so they say.
(B) Yes, it's quite serious.
(C) We have serious misgivings about it.

36. (Man B) Were you able to meet your deadline?
(Woman)
(A) Yes, but just barely.
(B) No, it wasn't listed.
(C) Yes, isn't that a shame?

37. (Man A) Did profits go up this quarter?
(Man B)
(A) No, they weren't listed.
(B) No, in fact they dropped 1 percent.
(C) Yes, but he's already returned.

38. (Woman) Do you have change for a twenty?
(Man B)
(A) Yes, I think I want to move to a new apartment.
(B) I'm sorry. I have no small bills at all.
(C) That sounds very inexpensive to me.

39. (Man B) I didn't know your father works for Time-Plus.
(Woman)
(A) Yes. He's been with them since 1975.
(B) I think he's still looking for it.
(C) No, I heard it's very near.

40. (Man A) Will we be getting any new office equipment this year?
(Man B)
(A) Yes, he certainly learns fast.
(B) No. He says he's going to quit.
(C) We budgeted for two PCs and some file cabinets.

41. (Man B) When did they turn down our offer?
(Woman)
(A) I think they turned right.
(B) They responded yesterday.
(C) It's been going down since Monday.

42. (Man A) What's the deadline for sending in payment?
(Man B)
(A) We have until the end of the month.
(B) Yes, I think the line's dead.
(C) We haven't sent it yet.

43. (Man B) How can I help you?
(Woman)
(A) Thank you, you've been very kind.
(B) I'm looking for the registration desk.
(C) I'll be there in a minute.

44. (Man B) How was the dispute finally settled?
(Man A)
(A) They do, but not often enough.
(B) They moved in last week.
(C) Everyone compromised, but no one was happy with it.

45. (Woman) I'd like to go visit my parents this weekend.
(Man B)
(A) Yes, I enjoyed their visit too.
(B) That's a good idea. We haven't been there for a while.
(C) I hope they can stay longer than last time.

46. (Man A) Have you seen my umbrella?
(Woman)
(A) They're in a vase on the table.
(B) It's a very good show.
(C) Yes. I put it in the closet a couple of days ago.

47. (Woman) Bill, what's the square root of 225?
(Man B)
(A) I don't know, but there's a table in the back of my engineering book.
(B) I thought it was round and a lot bigger than that.
(C) It's right in the middle of town.

48. (Man A) They should have reduced their operating costs long ago, don't you think?
(Woman)
(A) Yes, but I'm feeling much better, thank you.
(B) It may be expensive, but it's worth the money.
(C) Yes, and now it's going to cost them much more.

49. (Woman) There's somebody at the door. Can you get it?
(Man B)
(A) The windows need cleaning, too.
(B) I've been waiting a long time.
(C) In a minute, as soon as I get off the phone.

50. (Man B) Will their closing have any effect on us?
(Man A)
(A) We don't expect it to.
(B) No, we can dress any way we want.
(C) Yes, they've been good to us.

Part III

51. (Woman) May I help you, sir?
(Man A) Yes. Can I get a cup of coffee?
(Woman) Coffee is served only in the lobby, on the first floor.

52. (Man B) What are rents like here?
(Man A) A little expensive. It's safe and comfortable on the west side, less so on the east.
(Man B) I'd like to take a look at something on the west side. I need only two bedrooms.

53. (Man A) It's not like Bill to be late for an appointment.
(Man B) You're right. He's always punctual.
(Man A) Well, we can't start the meeting until he gets here.

54. (Woman) I'm looking for the housewares section. What floor is it on?
(Man A) The fourth floor. You can take the stairs, in the rear of the store, or use the elevator, over there.
(Woman) I'll take the elevator. It's closer.

55. (Woman) Where did our doctor move his office to?
(Man B) That new glass building downtown.
(Woman) How convenient! That's only a block from my office. I can walk it.

56. (Man A) I'm sorry I'm late. Traffic was backed up for an hour because of the storm.
(Man B) That's o.k. I was caught in it myself and just got in.
(Man A) Well, maybe we should start. We don't have a lot of time.

57. (Man B) Oh, what a beautiful day!
(Woman) I know. But even this weather can't change the way I feel. I just lost my job.
(Man B) I'm sorry to hear that, and they say it's really hard to get a job right now. I hope things work out for you.

58. (Woman) I have to buy something for a man, forty-five, who I don't know very well. Do you have any suggestions?
(Man B) If you know how he dresses, a man can always use a new necktie.
(Woman) That's a good idea. He's very conservative.

59. (Man B) Will you have time to go over this sales report later?
(Man A) Yes. I should be free at ten.
(Man B) Good. I'll ask Paul to sit in on the meeting, too. I know he wants to see what we're doing.

60. (Woman) I sent a package to my friend in Taiwan a month ago, and she hasn't received it yet.
(Man B) It should have arrived by now. Did you insure it?
(Woman) No, but I guess I should have. I just assumed it would arrive all right.

61. (Woman) Did you design this room yourself?
(Man B) Yes, I couldn't afford a contractor, so I drew up some plans, talked to a lot of people, and then did the work.
(Woman) It looks as if an architect did it.

62. (Man B) Is the Post Office open on Independence Day?
(Man A) For half a day only. We close at noon.
(Man B) Good. I can still send mail out that morning.

63. (Man B) The neighbors are always talking about moving. What's wrong with where they are?
(Woman) They'd like to be closer to their family.
(Man B) I can understand that, but I'm surprised they'd be willing to give up their jobs and say good-bye to where they've lived for twenty years.

64. (Man A) How can I help you?
(Man B) I'd like to cash this check and open an account.
(Man A) Very well. You'll have to see an officer first. Come this way, please.

65. (Woman) DiVito's Pizza. Can I take your order?
(Man A) Yes. This is Bill Gates over at Consolidated. We'd like a large pepperoni pizza and three large sodas. Can you deliver them here to the office?
(Woman) Sure. That'll be twelve dollars and thirty cents. We'll be there in about 45 minutes. Be sure to call Security so we can get in.

66. (Woman) I'm concerned with how we'll be able to fix anything that might go wrong with it and where we get spare parts.
(Man A) You needn't worry. We have everything necessary right here for all repairs and maintenance servicing.
(Woman) That's comforting to hear.

67. (Man B) You need a boarding pass to go beyond this point.
(Woman) I realize that, but I want to say good-bye to my son. He's only ten.
(Man B) I'm sorry, Ma'am, but you'll have to say good-bye here. I can't let you past.

68. (Man A) Nurse, who'll get the results of the tests?
(Man B) Probably Dr. Morgan, head of surgery. He'll discuss them with you after he consults with other physicians.
(Man A) Well, at least I'm in good hands.

69. (Woman) Yes, this is the Catalog Department. How may I help you?
(Man B) I'd like to place an order for an overcoat from your fall catalog.
(Woman) Fine. I'll need the item number, the catalog page it appears on, your size, and the color.

70. (Man B) When do you leave for Manila?
(Woman) I still don't know. I have to get several of these files together before I can go, and they're very complicated.
(Man B) I hope you can get away soon. There's a lot that has to be taken care of in our office there, and only you can do it.

71. (Woman) Look at that! Our stock is already down almost 10 points. Shouldn't we sell?
(Man B) No, don't sell. It'll go back up again before close.
(Woman) I sure hope you're right. I'd hate for it to go down more.

72. (Man A) My company's doing fine, but I'm concerned about my personal finances and my retirement.
(Woman) Well, this bank doesn't deal only with large clients. We're here to serve individuals as well.
(Man A) Well, perhaps you can help.

73. (Man B) This is an interesting trade show, don't you think?
(Man A) Yes. I'm particularly interested in those new automatic packaging machines they're showing.
(Man B) So am I. We've been thinking of buying one, and I was asked to get price estimates.

74. (Man B) Are all of these policy statements up-to-date?
(Woman) Yes, I added recent changes just yesterday.
(Man B) Good. There's no hurry, but at some point I'd like you to make me a copy for reference.

75. (Man B) Ever since we had that bad publicity, things haven't gone well. We're losing old clients, and we're getting no new ones.
(Woman) We made some bad decisions and we're paying the price. We have to work on regaining public trust.
(Man B) That'll take time, and we may not be able to do it.

76. (Woman) Who's your most reliable partner in Germany right now?
(Man A) Lately we've been working closely with the Rhinehart Banking Group. We've had no problems with them.
(Woman) I've heard some good things about Rhinehart myself. We're looking for someone to work with, and they may be able to do what we want. It's not very complicated.

77. (Woman) Can you stop at mother's house on your way home from work and take her television to be repaired? It stopped working again.
(Man B) Of course. Does she know I'll be stopping by?
(Woman) Not yet, but I'll call her later. If there's any problem, I'll reach you at work.

78. (Woman) I'd like to prequalify for a mortgage loan. Is that possible?
(Man B) I think so. Please sit down. I'll need to get your financial history and information on the property you want to buy.
(Woman) Here's a completed application. It should give you all of the information you need.

79. (Man B) I understand we're going to begin program trading on the futures market.
(Woman) Yes. It's worked well for Japanese traders. I want to see what it does for us.
(Man B) It may be just what we need. Then again, if you're wrong, it could wind up costing us a lot of money.

80. (Woman) The fax machine isn't working, and I need to get a copy of this letter over to Bill this afternoon.
(Man B) There's another machine in General Affairs. Why don't you ask if they'll let you send it from there?
(Woman) Of course. Why didn't I think of that?

Part IV

(Man A) Questions 81 through 83 refer to the following talk.

(Man B) Ladies and gentlemen, welcome to the Harlan Company's newest shipbuilding yard, the largest in the nation and the fourth-largest in the world. Here, the most up-to-date technology is used to produce the highest-quality, lowest-cost ships in the world. We are about to embark on a tour that will take you to just a few of our interesting facilities. The tour takes only an hour and a half, but many of our visitors say the memory will last a lifetime. We hope you enjoy it. Please board the trams and follow me.

(Man A) Now read question 81 in your test book and answer it.

(Man A) Now read question 82 in your test book and answer it.

(Man A) Now read question 83 in your test book and answer it.

(Man A) Questions 84 and 85 refer to the following announcement.

(Woman) Attention, customers! A man's brown leather wallet has been found in the Electronics Department and is in the manager's office. If you have lost a man's wallet, come to the manager's office at the front of the store to identify the lost item.

(Man A) Now read question 84 in your test book and answer it.

(Man A) Now read question 85 in your test book and answer it.

(Man A) Questions 86 and 87 refer to the following request.

(Man B) Hi, everyone. My name's Mike Allison. I'm addressing you today on behalf of the local fire department. As many of you know, each year at this time we go door-to-door asking for donations for the Fireman's Fund. Our fund was established in 1946 and since then has helped many local needy families with medical bills, necessary home repairs, food, and clothing. Someone from the fire department will be visiting your home soon. Be generous. Dig deep. Your donation will be appreciated.

(Man A) Now read question 86 in your test book and answer it.

(Man A) Now read question 87 in your test book and answer it.

(Man A) Questions 88 and 89 refer to the following advertisement.

(Woman) Europe Air is pleased to announce the expansion of its routes to South America. New non-stop flights depart daily from Paris and Brussels, going to Mexico, Lima, Rio de Janeiro, and Buenos Aires. Experience the romance and glamour of South America any day of the week—through the efficiency, comfort, and convenience of Europe Air. Phone your travel agent or representative today.

(Man A) Now read question 88 in your test book and answer it.

(Man A) Now read question 89 in your test book and answer it.

(Man A) Questions 90 through 92 refer to the following talk.

(Woman) Ladies and gentlemen, I am privileged to introduce to you Dr. Elizabeth R. Tuttle, the executive director of Hi-Tech Medicine, Inc., one of our nation's foremost biological research centers. Having spent her entire professional career on the frontier of medical research, Dr. Tuttle will speak to us today about recent progress in the development of genetic models. Please welcome her with a warm round of applause!

(Man A) Now read question 90 in your test book and answer it.

(Man A) Now read question 91 in your test book and answer it.

(Man A) Now read question 92 in your test book and answer it.

(Man A) Questions 93 and 94 refer to the following announcement.

(Woman) Attention, all building occupants! In a few minutes we will conduct a fire drill to test evacuation procedures. When you hear the alarm, please close any open windows and leave the building by designated routes as quickly as possible. Close all doors behind you. Use only the stairs. Do not attempt to use the elevator. All employees will meet in the parking lot. This is only a drill.

(Man A) Now read question 93 in your test book and answer it.

(Man A) Now read question 94 in your test book and answer it.

(Man A) Questions 95 through 97 refer to the following report.

(Man B) This morning at dawn, *Trekkie*, the newest of space shuttles, was launched from Cape Canaveral. While *Trekkie* is no smaller than previous shuttlecraft, not counting its fuel, it weighs 30 percent less than previous craft and has 6 percent more interior space. All equipment has been downsized, thanks to developments in electronics. The shuttle's heavy ceramic underside, previously necessary because of extreme heat generated on reentry, has been replaced with new, highly heat-resistant coated fabrics. These fabrics have been years in development and are a tremendous breakthrough in weight reduction for the craft. *Trekkie* is the prototype for shuttles that will be used to establish stations in space, far into the future.

(Man A) Now read question 95 in your test book and answer it.

(Man A) Now read question 96 in your test book and answer it.

(Man A) Now read question 97 in your test book and answer it.

(Man A) Questions 98 through 100 refer to the following announcement.

(Man B) I am H. Harry Kaplan, and this is the afternoon "Brief Update" of the news. In the bitter race for 11th district supervisor, after the final count Lester Burl has squeaked by incumbent Mark Prowse by only two percentage points.

In other local news, the Tenth Street overpass will be closed for two days, starting at noon tomorrow, for utility crews to repair a water main.

Finally, the weather: Today's high was seventy-three degrees. Expect slightly cooler temperatures with showers tonight. There will be more rain tomorrow, with a high of only sixty-two.

This is H. Harry Kaplan for "Brief Update." Listen for the complete day's news at ten tonight.

(Man A) Now read question 98 in your test book and answer it.

(Man A) Now read question 99 in your test book and answer it.

(Man A) Now read question 100 in your test book and answer it.

This is the end of the Listening Comprehension portion of the test. Turn to Part V in your test book.

TEST 5 COMPARISON SCORES

The score range for the TOEIC is 10 to 990, 5 to 495 for listening and 5 to 495 for reading. This is a converted score, otherwise known as a scaled score, arrived at by converting an examinee's raw score by a formula that changes with every test. The raw score is merely the number of questions answered correctly. On the TOEIC, there is no penalty for answering a question incorrectly.

Converted scores are reported, rather than raw scores, because the developers of the TOEIC make a statistical adjustment for the relative ease or difficulty of each test. This procedure ensures that scores are equivalent over time and do not fluctuate because one or another test may be easier or more difficult than others.

The raw scores that appear below, for this test and for this test only, correspond to a total mean converted TOEIC score of 500, 250 for listening and 250 for reading. Other tests in this book have mean scores calculated on different formulas.

These scores are provided so, if they like, students can compare their performance on this test with a performance that would produce a total converted score of 500. Raw part scores of above the scores provided here would convert to a score of above 500, while raw part scores of below the scores provided here would convert to a score of below 500.

Part	Mean Raw Score
I	16
II	19
III	18
IV	11
Mean Listening	64
V	25
VI	10
VII	28
Mean Reading	63
Mean Total	127

Converted Scores for Above Mean Scores

Mean Listening	250
Mean Reading	250
Mean Total	500

ANSWER KEY FOR TEST 5—LISTENING

Key: Part I

1. (B) The courts are not occupied.
2. (A) The man is holding the rope.
3. (D) The man is looking at the clothes.
4. (A) The runners are on the track.
5. (B) Food is cooking in the pan.
6. (C) The large bones are imbedded in stone.
7. (A) The man has his hands in his pockets.
8. (B) People are playing a game.
9. (C) The woman is taking a book off the shelf.
10. (C) The man is selling flowers on the sidewalk.
11. (D) The water tower is high above the trees.
12. (D) The truck is carrying heavy logs.
13. (C) The woman is looking in the cabinet.
14. (D) The man is sound asleep.
15. (A) The street is being dug up.
16. (C) Some boxes are piled to the ceiling.
17. (A) There is little traffic out.
18. (D) The woman is bending over.
19. (B) Boats are tied to the dock.
20. (B) The man is getting a haircut.

Key: Part II

21. (A) On Pelton Street, at the corner.
22. (B) There are only two.
23. (C) Gee, I'd love to go.
24. (A) Tom Travers, in the Design Division.
25. (C) No. I'm so busy, I haven't been able to get out.
26. (B) Yes, I'd like some jam or marmalade, please.
27. (A) At least five, maybe six.
28. (B) Please have him call John at the office.
29. (B) We target our advertising very carefully.
30. (B) In Frankfurt.
31. (C) No. You'll have to catch the Number 73 across the street.
32. (C) Yes, please. What do you have?
33. (C) As soon as I get my visas.
34. (A) Yes, it's half past one.
35. (A) Not at all, or so they say.
36. (A) Yes, but just barely.
37. (B) No, in fact they dropped 1 percent.
38. (B) I'm sorry. I have no small bills at all.
39. (A) Yes. He's been with them since 1975.
40. (C) We budgeted for two PCs and some file cabinets.
41. (B) They responded yesterday.
42. (A) We have until the end of the month.
43. (B) I'm looking for the registration desk.
44. (C) Everyone compromised, but no one was happy with it.
45. (B) That's a good idea. We haven't been there for a while.
46. (C) Yes. I put it in the closet a couple of days ago.
47. (A) I don't know, but there's a table in the back of my engineering book.
48. (C) Yes, and now it's going to cost them much more.
49. (C) In a minute, as soon as I get off the phone.
50. (A) We don't expect it to.

Key: Part III

51. (B) To get a cup of coffee
52. (B) Housing
53. (C) He is usually on time.
54. (B) By taking the elevator
55. (A) One block
56. (D) They were stopped in traffic.
57. (D) She is out of work.
58. (A) Buy a gift
59. (D) The men will discuss a sales report.
60. (A) It did not arrive.
61. (D) The speaker
62. (A) Post Office hours
63. (D) They want to be near their family.
64. (D) In a bank
65. (B) At work
66. (A) Repairs
67. (C) She did not have a boarding pass.
68. (C) The head of surgery
69. (A) Place an order
70. (B) She does not know.
71. (A) Sell
72. (D) His financial future
73. (C) Buy new equipment
74. (B) Make photocopies
75. (C) It no longer enjoys a good reputation.
76. (A) A corporate relationship
77. (C) Help his mother-in-law
78. (B) Borrow some money
79. (D) Investment trading techniques
80. (D) Speak with someone in General Affairs

Key: Part IV

81. (C) At a shipyard
82. (A) Very large
83. (B) One and a half hours
84. (B) A wallet
85. (B) At the manager's office
86. (D) The fire department
87. (C) Money
88. (D) To Latin America
89. (D) Daily departures
90. (B) Executive director
91. (A) Medical research
92. (D) Welcome Dr. Tuttle
93. (A) To test evacuation procedures
94. (D) Shut doors as they leave
95. (A) It is lighter.
96. (B) Fabric
97. (C) It will be used to establish space stations.
98. (C) Lester Burl
99. (B) It will be temporarily closed.
100. (A) Rain

ANSWER KEY FOR TEST 5—READING

Key: Part V

101. (C) venture
102. (D) delivered
103. (C) popular
104. (D) apologized for
105. (D) compared with
106. (B) accepted
107. (D) was considered
108. (D) several
109. (C) every
110. (B) looking
111. (B) approved
112. (C) attempt
113. (A) keep out
114. (D) found
115. (C) lasted
116. (B) enforced
117. (B) endure
118. (A) applied
119. (D) overwhelmed
120. (A) were once
121. (B) about
122. (C) absenteeism
123. (D) confidential
124. (A) recall
125. (A) On
126. (D) cleared
127. (C) place
128. (C) found resources
129. (A) Few of
130. (A) collapsed
131. (B) meal
132. (D) deliberately
133. (B) combined
134. (C) departure
135. (B) debate
136. (D) showed up for
137. (D) speculative
138. (C) residence
139. (A) ties
140. (C) across

Key: Part VI

141. (D) development
142. (D) had been contacted
143. (C) become
144. (C) dropped
145. (A) not uncommon that
146. (B) trouble
147. (C) do not
148. (D) needed to
149. (A) be
150. (B) an
151. (B) were
152. (C) had become used to
153. (B) commuters entering
154. (C) potential
155. (C) most companies, new companies
156. (C) taking
157. (A) were
158. (A) living
159. (C) lack of credit
160. (A) service

Key: Part VII

161. (C) 7
162. (A) For six hours
163. (D) More than forty
164. (A) Admission is free.
165. (A) Anywhere in the world
166. (B) No fee is charged.
167. (B) A jacket
168. (B) The seller needs money.
169. (A) He is injured.
170. (B) Take on his responsibilities
171. (C) Any major office problem
172. (D) Quality
173. (A) Artists
174. (C) Two weeks
175. (A) Lack of satisfaction
176. (B) Labor
177. (C) Storage
178. (B) Reputation
179. (D) It has no cholesterol.
180. (B) As a light meal
181. (A) Neglect of employees
182. (A) Employee morale
183. (D) None
184. (A) 201 Grand Ave.
185. (C) 745 Parkside Dr.
186. (A) A week-long oriental carpet sale
187. (D) They may not be in good condition.
188. (D) Mr. Wu
189. (B) Taipei
190. (C) The following week
191. (D) An unnamed telemarketing firm
192. (D) Solicitation of investment capital
193. (B) Their replies will be kept secret.
194. (C) Difficulty in moving goods
195. (D) To ensure customer satisfaction
196. (C) Hire a private firm
197. (D) Smokers not disposing of cigarette butts properly
198. (C) Containers for cigarette butts have been placed about on company grounds.
199. (C) To acknowledge an offer
200. (B) That other contracts would prevent her from doing something

TOEIC®
TEST 6

LISTENING COMPREHENSION

In this section of the test, you will have the chance to show how well you understand spoken English. There are four parts to this section, with special directions for each part.

Part I

Directions: For each question, you will see a picture in your test book and you will hear four short statements. The statements will be spoken just one time. They will not be printed in your test book, so you must listen carefully to understand what the speaker says.

When you hear the four statements, look at the picture in your test book and choose the statement that best describes what you see in the picture. Then, on your answer sheet, find the number of the question and mark your answer.

Look at the sample below.

Now listen to the four statements.

Sample Answer

Ⓐ ● Ⓒ Ⓓ

Statement (B), "They're having a meeting," best describes what you see in the picture. Therefore, you should choose answer (B).

1. 

2. 

3.

4.

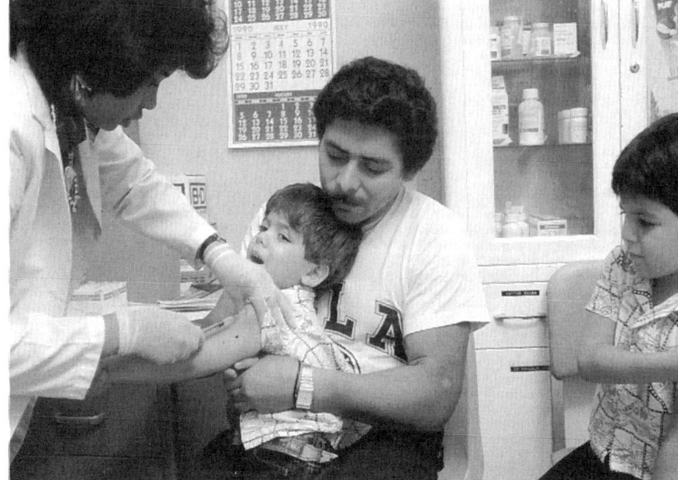

5. 

6. 

GO ON TO THE NEXT PAGE

7.

8.

9.

10.

GO ON TO THE NEXT PAGE

11.

12.

13.

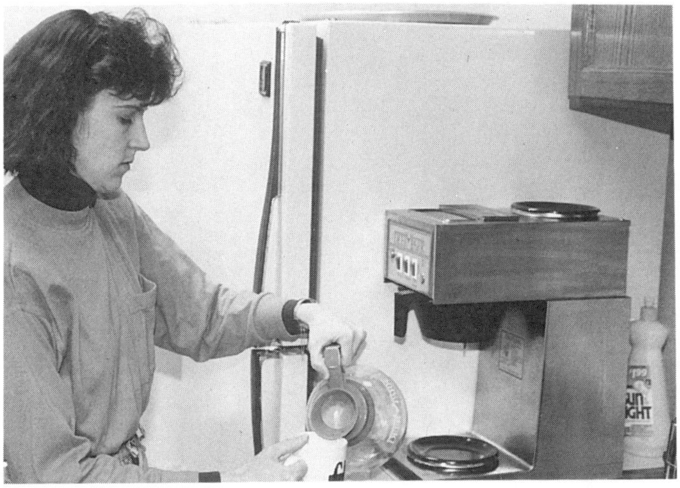

14.

15.

16.

17.

18.

GO ON TO THE NEXT PAGE

19.

20.

Part II

Directions: In this part of the test you will hear a question spoken in English, followed by three responses, also spoken in English. The question and the responses will be spoken just one time. They will not be printed in your test book, so you must listen carefully to understand what the speakers say. You are to choose the best response to each question.

Now listen to a sample question:

You will hear:

You will also hear:

Sample Answer

● Ⓑ Ⓒ

The best response to the question "How are you?" is choice (A) "I am fine, thank you." Therefore, you should choose answer (A).

21. Mark your answer on your answer sheet.
22. Mark your answer on your answer sheet.
23. Mark your answer on your answer sheet.
24. Mark your answer on your answer sheet.
25. Mark your answer on your answer sheet.
26. Mark your answer on your answer sheet.
27. Mark your answer on your answer sheet.
28. Mark your answer on your answer sheet.
29. Mark your answer on your answer sheet.
30. Mark your answer on your answer sheet.
31. Mark your answer on your answer sheet.
32. Mark your answer on your answer sheet.
33. Mark your answer on your answer sheet.
34. Mark your answer on your answer sheet.
35. Mark your answer on your answer sheet.
36. Mark your answer on your answer sheet.
37. Mark your answer on your answer sheet.
38. Mark your answer on your answer sheet.
39. Mark your answer on your answer sheet.
40. Mark your answer on your answer sheet.
41. Mark your answer on your answer sheet.
42. Mark your answer on your answer sheet.
43. Mark your answer on your answer sheet.
44. Mark your answer on your answer sheet.
45. Mark your answer on your answer sheet.
46. Mark your answer on your answer sheet.
47. Mark your answer on your answer sheet.
48. Mark your answer on your answer sheet.
49. Mark your answer on your answer sheet.
50. Mark your answer on your answer sheet.

GO ON TO THE NEXT PAGE

Part III

Directions: In this part of the test, you will hear 30 short conversations between two people. The conversations will not be printed in your test book. You will hear the conversations only once, so you must listen carefully to understand what the speakers say.

In your test book you will read a question about each conversation. The question will be followed by four answers. You are to choose the best answer to each question and mark it on your answer sheet.

51. What is said about the new employee?

    (A) He is very young.
    (B) He is good looking.
    (C) He is a fast worker.
    (D) He will contribute a lot.

52. What had the man requested?

    (A) A report
    (B) A letter
    (C) A magazine
    (D) A newspaper

53. What is the man going to do?

    (A) Retire
    (B) Buy a company
    (C) Begin a new job
    (D) Take a vacation

54. Why does the man need a chair?

    (A) He is old.
    (B) He is tired.
    (C) He hurt his knee.
    (D) His ankle is broken.

55. What are the speakers discussing?

    (A) A park
    (B) A school
    (C) A church
    (D) A factory

56. What is the man trying to do?

    (A) Rent a car
    (B) Pay a fine
    (C) Get a new driver's license
    (D) Make a collect telephone call

57. What happened to John?

    (A) He did not go to class.
    (B) He came late to class.
    (C) He had to leave class early.
    (D) He forgot which day he was to go to class.

58. What will Lily do?

    (A) Be in a play
    (B) Go on a trip
    (C) Make a speech
    (D) Open a business

59. Where does this situation take place?

    (A) In a bank
    (B) In a hotel
    (C) In a store
    (D) In an office

60. What is the man going to do on the weekend?

    (A) Visit relatives
    (B) Go to Los Angeles
    (C) Conduct some business
    (D) Take the children to the zoo

61. What did the man ask for?

(A) A room
(B) The time
(C) Lighting
(D) Directions

62. What are the speakers discussing?

(A) Legal expenses
(B) Zoning restrictions
(C) Property development
(D) Water and electricity

63. How is the trade fair different from others?

(A) It is much larger.
(B) It is not as specialized.
(C) It will feature special seminars.
(D) There will be cash prizes for visitors.

64. What did Bob do?

(A) He died.
(B) He became ill.
(C) He lost his hearing.
(D) He refused to leave.

65. What does Maganya do?

(A) She acts.
(B) She sings.
(C) She dances.
(D) She tells stories.

66. How did Jim perform as a councilman?

(A) He did a good job.
(B) He was not very effective.
(C) He always did as he was told.
(D) He was often away on business.

67. What is the woman trying to do?

(A) Cash a check
(B) Deposit a check
(C) Send money by wire
(D) Take money out of an account

68. What is the man worried about?

(A) He does not play golf.
(B) He has to work on Saturday.
(C) He will be unable to have lunch.
(D) He has an appointment in the afternoon.

69. What are the speakers discussing?

(A) Art
(B) Health
(C) Employment
(D) Construction

70. What did people think about Henry?

(A) He was always on time.
(B) He was a good worker.
(C) He was not a very nice person.
(D) He was not qualified for his job.

71. Why did the man arrive late for work?

(A) He was late leaving his house.
(B) Road construction held up traffic.
(C) A friend asked him for a ride to work.
(D) There was an accident on the expressway.

72. What are the speakers discussing?

(A) A piece of art
(B) Carpet for the home
(C) The design of a house
(D) A color to paint a living room

GO ON TO THE NEXT PAGE

73. What has become of Jordan?

(A) He left on vacation.
(B) He has been promoted.
(C) He has had an operation.
(D) He has not been heard from.

74. Where was the file found?

(A) On a desk
(B) In Mike's office
(C) In the storage room
(D) In the operations room

75. Why is Dame Charlotte excited?

(A) She was given two tickets to a play.
(B) She was selected for a role in a play.
(C) She went to the opening of a new theater.
(D) She was invited by Alpert to attend a play.

76. Where are the speakers?

(A) On a bus
(B) On an airplane
(C) In a restaurant
(D) In an automobile

77. What happened to the man at work?

(A) He worked until after 6 o'clock.
(B) His meeting was canceled.
(C) His meeting ended earlier than expected.
(D) He left a meeting early so he could go out to dinner.

78. What have the speakers decided to do?

(A) Reduce production of E-3 printers
(B) Lay off printer production line workers
(C) Sell the printer inventory at discounted prices
(D) Review printer production schedules with sales people

79. What is the man's problem?

(A) He loses things.
(B) He is always in a hurry.
(C) He is late for a meeting.
(D) He does not know what to do.

80. What is creating problems for the speakers?

(A) A loan
(B) An accident
(C) A new product
(D) Currency exchange rates

Part IV

Directions: In this part of the test, you will hear several short talks. Each will be spoken just one time. They will not be printed in your test book, so you must listen carefully to understand and remember what is said.

In your test book you will read two or more questions about each short talk. The questions will be followed by four answers. You are to choose the best answer to each question and mark it on your answer sheet.

81. How many different flavors does Old World soup come in?

(A) One
(B) Three
(C) Four
(D) Five

82. What is said to encourage listeners to buy Old World soups?

(A) The price is low.
(B) The soup is healthy.
(C) The flavors are new.
(D) It is easy to prepare.

83. Where can Old World soups be bought?

(A) At the Old World Soup Restaurant
(B) In a variety of restaurants
(C) In certain gourmet food stores
(D) At a lot of grocery stores

84. In which of the following is Deltrans involved?

(A) Aerospace
(B) Telephone systems
(C) Vehicle manufacture
(D) Shipping

85. What does the speaker say she will do?

(A) Sell a product
(B) Tell about her products
(C) Negotiate a deal
(D) Endorse a political candidate

86. How does the speaker say the company is perceived?

(A) As an automobile manufacturer
(B) As a communications specialist
(C) As a multinational corporation
(D) As an unfair employer

87. Why are schools and government offices closing early?

(A) Heavy snow is expected.
(B) There is a power failure.
(C) There has been a major accident.
(D) Floods have destroyed bridges and highways.

88. Who should call the Red Cross?

(A) All boat owners
(B) Owners of some four-wheel-drive vehicles
(C) Public transportation operators
(D) People not able to get to safety

89. What is the drug Rindamal supposed to do?

(A) Cure colds
(B) Slow aging
(C) Grow hair
(D) Stop smoking

GO ON TO THE NEXT PAGE

90. Who discovered the drug?

(A) A scientist working in his home laboratory
(B) A major drug company
(C) The National Health Agency
(D) University researchers

91. What is the base substance of the drug?

(A) Animal fats
(B) Natural acids
(C) Vegetable matter
(D) Petroleum

92. What does this comment concern?

(A) A request for a loan
(B) A plan to reduce costs
(C) The acceptance of an offer
(D) The establishment of credit

93. What reason does the speaker give for the decision?

(A) A lot of money is involved.
(B) Her friend is an honest person.
(C) The program is not of interest to her.
(D) She owes it to her friend.

94. What is the subject to be discussed?

(A) An offensive topic
(B) A newspaper article
(C) Psychological counseling
(D) Obscenity on the radio

95. What are listeners urged to do?

(A) Listen to the speakers
(B) Telephone the radio station
(C) Write a letter
(D) Purchase a product

96. How does the speaker assess the survey results?

(A) As very good
(B) As better than average
(C) As satisfactory
(D) As disappointing

97. What aspect of the product does the speaker address?

(A) Price
(B) Quality
(C) Packaging
(D) Distribution

98. What will happen soon?

(A) A party will be held.
(B) A survey will be taken.
(C) A meeting will be held.
(D) A new product will be introduced.

99. What does the speaker suggest?

(A) Increasing production
(B) Using profits more wisely
(C) Selling off some companies
(D) Creating a new product line

100. What does the speaker say about his company?

(A) It has a good marketing strategy.
(B) It has an innovative product line.
(C) It is losing money.
(D) It is growing too quickly.

This is the end of the Listening Comprehension portion of the test. Turn to Part V in your test book.

YOU WILL HAVE ONE HOUR AND FIFTEEN MINUTES TO COMPLETE PARTS V, VI, AND VII OF THE TEST.

READING

In this section of the test, you will have a chance to show how well you understand written English. There are three parts to this section, with special directions for each part.

Part V

Directions: Questions 101–140 are incomplete sentences. Four words or phrases, marked (A), (B), (C), (D), are given beneath each sentence. You are to choose the one word or phrase that best completes the sentence. Then, on your answer sheet, find the number of the question and mark your answer.

Example

Because the equipment is very delicate, it must be handled with ———.

(A) caring
(B) careful
(C) care
(D) carefully

Sample Answer

The sentence should read, "Because the equipment is very delicate, it must be handled with care." Therefore, you should choose answer (C).

As soon as you understand the directions, begin work on the questions.

101. The earnings report showed that it had not been ——— a great year after all.

(A) so
(B) such
(C) some
(D) somewhat

102. The man ——— a pair of diamond earrings as a present for his wife's birthday.

(A) selected
(B) picketed
(C) reviewed
(D) identified

103. As a ———, everyone who had invested with him lost 90 percent of of their investment.

(A) more
(B) result
(C) change
(D) resulting

104. A recent ——— in corporate organization is to reduce the number of levels of management.

(A) tread
(B) bend
(C) brand
(D) trend

105. It rained ———, creating difficult travel conditions.

(A) in day
(B) all day
(C) some day
(D) tomorrow

106. Residents were ——— to learn that property taxes would remain unchanged for another year.

(A) enjoyed
(B) relieved
(C) deserted
(D) enlightened

107. The company gave us ——— license to publish their books.

(A) a rightful
(B) a principal
(C) an inclusive
(D) an exclusive

108. Business kept them ——— the road much of the time.

(A) at
(B) in
(C) on
(D) by

109. The evening news comes on at nine o'clock and ——— only thirty minutes.

(A) lasts
(B) stops
(C) starts
(D) begins

110. The most dangerous chemicals were ——— in a special room in the back of the laboratory.

(A) stored
(B) stayed
(C) keeping
(D) containers

111. At least the weather was nice, which was ——— to be thankful for.

(A) any
(B) some
(C) anything
(D) something

112. She suggested ——— read the ballot carefully.

(A) him
(B) he to
(C) that to
(D) that he

113. They can wait ——— the first for delivery of the shipment.

(A) in
(B) and
(C) until
(D) before

114. The driver ——— the intersection cautiously.

(A) reach
(B) create
(C) appeared
(D) approached

115. The project ——— smoothly until the final phase, when major problems developed.

(A) went
(B) goes
(C) were
(D) going

116. No one ——— whether the new design would improve the equipment's performance.

(A) could say
(B) would call
(C) will know
(D) made known

117. The number of sales personnel who leave the company ——— very small.

(A) is
(B) are
(C) were
(D) have been

118. Patent ——— for the new product will be difficult to obtain.

(A) time
(B) care
(C) rights
(D) negotiation

119. Journalism is a career often ——— by people who want to influence others with their writing.

(A) choice
(B) decide
(C) chosen
(D) prepared

120. The ABC Company bought out ——— of the competition, creating a monopoly.

(A) all
(B) some
(C) entire
(D) almost

121. The filling station on Main Street is open twenty-four hours ——— day.

(A) a
(B) in
(C) all
(D) for

122. The inauguration of the soft drink bottling ——— was scheduled for Monday, October 10.

(A) faculty
(B) plankton
(C) facility
(D) plantation

123. Neither Henry nor his brother Jules ——— English when they were young.

(A) spoke
(B) speaks
(C) have spoken
(D) were speaking

124. ——— has to supervise the final phase of the construction.

(A) Anyone
(B) Someone
(C) Anybody
(D) Sometime

GO ON TO THE NEXT PAGE

125. Three flights ——— canceled due to poor weather conditions over the Pacific.

(A) has
(B) has been
(C) have been
(D) having been

126. They needed an ——— replacement for the employee who went into the hospital.

(A) another
(B) operable
(C) immediate
(D) indifferent

127. Accountants must remind clients not to ——— old tax records.

(A) throw off
(B) throw away
(C) discarded
(D) disposed of

128. The students took a tour of a ——— factory and saw how automobile window glass is made.

(A) close
(B) nearby
(C) next to
(D) together

129. The unreliability of links for direct communication required that all messages be ——— from station to station.

(A) past
(B) posted
(C) relayed
(D) indicated

130. The administration ——— to answer the charges, claiming that they were politically motivated.

(A) denied
(B) refused
(C) rejected
(D) accounted

131. The team ——— to take first place.

(A) diverse
(B) reversed
(C) observed
(D) deserved

132. The pilot had never ——— that particular aircraft.

(A) fled
(B) flown
(C) flied
(D) flowed

133. He did not recall ——— them at the reception.

(A) the met
(B) having met
(C) him to meet
(D) that he meet

134. Australia has ——— population per square mile of any populated continent.

(A) fewer
(B) little
(C) the least
(D) much less

135. When the team was in Paris, the president called them ——.

(A) in Seoul
(B) the stadium
(C) at California
(D) from New Brunswick

136. The hurricane —— the resort so badly that it had to be completely rebuilt.

(A) killed
(B) buried
(C) damaged
(D) deserted

137. This year, like last, staff —— to fill all of the year-end orders before the December 31 deadline.

(A) fast
(B) runs
(C) hurry
(D) rushed

138. Innovative marketing —— sell the new baby food product.

(A) helped
(B) guided
(C) tutored
(D) increased

139. The company's retrenchment plan failed to —— investors, and its stock continued to decline.

(A) impress
(B) dismiss
(C) determine
(D) encourage

140. A recent court ruling —— the issue of competitors sharing pricing in preparing proposals.

(A) said
(B) ruled
(C) spoke to
(D) explained to

GO ON TO THE NEXT PAGE

Part VI

Directions: In Questions 141–160 each sentence has four words or phrases underlined. The four underlined parts of the sentence are marked (A), (B), (C), (D). You are to identify the one underlined word or phrase that should be corrected or rewritten. Then, on your answer sheet, find the number of the question and mark your answer.

Example

All employee are required to wear their
A B
identification badges while at work.
C D

Sample Answer

● Ⓑ Ⓒ Ⓓ

Choice (A), the underlined word "employee," is not correct in this sentence. This sentence should read, "All employees are required to wear their identification badges while at work." Therefore, you should choose answer (A).

As soon as you understand the directions, begin work on the questions.

141. Of all of the problem areas in the city,
A
traffics move slowest around the
B C
west-side circle and across the bridge.
D

142. A new model car is introduced during
A B
the past month, but did not receive
C
good reviews.
D

143. The men sat late into the night,
A B
drinking coffee and talk.
C D

144. They hid their intentions until it was
A
too late for an effective counter-
campaign to be mounted, thus ensuring
B C
their victorious.
D

145. The last winter I went skiing with
A
some of my friends, but one of them
B
broke his leg and had to be taken to
C D
the hospital.

146. It has been five years since Mr. Tate
A
first began manage the office property
B C
at 5th and Cedar.
D

147. The air by the cellar under the fort was
A B C
very damp.
D

148. Because of the grow number of
A
customers, store management decided
B
to add an information desk, located
C D
near the main entrance.

149. The publication was subject to the
A
usual limitations on size, paper, and
pricing, but where it excellent was in
B C
the quality of its illustrations.
D

150. Drinking coffee is popular among
A
Westerners in general, but many people
have turned it into an art form
B C
involved elaborate equipment.
D

151. A written proposal are needed to sell
A
any product or service to the
government, even if the government has
B C
formally solicited an offer.
D

152. I would have gladly given him the
A
money I owe him if he has come to
B
my office as he said he would.
C D

153. She should have gone to visit her
A B
mother before many months ago.
C D

154. Paychecks are issued on the first and
A
the fifteenth of every month, except
B
when either of those days goes on a
C D
Saturday, a Sunday, or a holiday.

155. Frequent reading can help increasing
A B C
a person's vocabulary.
D

GO ON TO THE NEXT PAGE

156. Theater reviewers often find themselves
A
are being carried away by their own wit
B C
and the power of their position, a
combination of flaws that is fatal for an
D
impartial review.

157. The old man was still strong but agile
A B
at the advanced age of 96, dancing at a
C
birthday party given in his honor.
D

158. The applicant qualifications did not
A
meet the requirements for the position,
B C
which he found very disappointing.
D

159. While he is only a five-years-old, he
A B
shows a lot of athletic ability and
C
enjoys all kinds of sports.
D

160. One of the members of the audience
were invited to join the performers
A B
on stage to help with the act.
C D

Part VII

Directions: Questions 161–200 are based on a variety of reading material (for example, announcements, paragraphs, advertisements, and the like). You are to choose the one best answer, (A), (B), (C), or (D), to each question. Then, on your answer sheet, find the number of the question and mark your answer. Answer all questions following a passage on the basis of what is stated or implied in that passage.

Read the following example.

> The Museum of Technology is a "hands-on" museum, designed for people to experience science at work. Visitors are encouraged to use, test, and handle the objects on display. Special demonstrations are scheduled for the first and second Wednesdays of each month at 1:30 P.M. Open Tuesday–Friday, 2:30–4:30 P.M., Saturday 11:00 A.M.–4:30 P.M., and Sunday 1:00–4:30 P.M.
>
> When during the month can visitors see special demonstrations?
>
> (A) Every weekend
> (B) The first two Wednesdays
> (C) One afternoon a week
> (D) Every other Wednesday

Sample Answer

Ⓐ ● Ⓒ Ⓓ

The passage says that the demonstrations are scheduled for the first and second Wednesdays of the month. Therefore, you should choose answer (B).

As soon as you understand the directions, begin work on the questions.

GO ON TO THE NEXT PAGE

Questions 161–163 refer to the following advertisement.

CREST's Pro Carpet Cleaning
$14 a room (But hurry—2 weeks only!)

2 Rooms Only $28!
6 Rooms Only $84!

For thoroughly clean carpets, we move and replace most furniture. We pretreat problem and traffic areas at no extra cost.

Call Dept. 89, Mon. to Sat. 8:30 A.M. to 5:00 P.M.
(234) 765-1234

161. With this offer, how much would it cost to have the carpet in three rooms cleaned?

(A) $35.00
(B) $42.00
(C) $49.00
(D) $56.00

162. For how long is this offer available?

(A) One week
(B) Two weeks
(C) One month
(D) Two months

163. What does Crest do to carpet areas that become particularly dirty?

(A) They pretreat the area.
(B) They shampoo the area twice.
(C) They repair or replace damaged carpet.
(D) They provide a special chemical treatment, at additional cost.

Questions 164–167 refer to the following letter.

Intelfex, Inc.
1655 Sea Harbor Rd.
Orlando, FL

February 8, 19—

Eastern Bank
P.O. Box 345
Bahrain

Gentlemen:

Intelfex is looking for agents to market and sell its products in Bahrain. Your branch in Orlando has told us that you may be able to help us.

We are a large manufacturer of cellular telephones. At present, we export only to Europe and Latin America, but we would like to start exporting to the Gulf countries.

We would appreciate it if you could forward this letter and copies of the enclosed product literature to any companies you know of in Bahrain that might be interested in representing us.

Sincerely yours,

Robert J. Winston
Export Division

Encs.

164. What is Intelfex's business?

(A) Banking
(B) Shipping
(C) Intelligence
(D) Manufacturing

165. What is Intelfex looking for?

(A) Employees
(B) An auditor
(C) New representatives
(D) Financing for their company

166. In what areas of the world does Intelfex do business?

(A) Asia
(B) South Africa & Europe
(C) North and Central America
(D) Latin America and Europe

167. What is enclosed with the letter?

(A) A resume
(B) Sample product
(C) An annual report
(D) Product literature

Questions 168–170 refer to the following notice.

ATTENTION, CUSTOMERS

In honor of Founders' Day, Saturday, July 23, and to thank our loyal patrons, we will be giving all customers one free ice-cream cone with every cone purchased. Also, a $10 gift certificate will be awarded to the tenth, fiftieth, and one-hundredth customers entering our store on Founders' Day.

Hours will be extended from our usual 10:00 A.M. to 6:00 P.M. to 9:00 A.M. to 9:00 P.M. to commemorate this special day in our store's history.

Harold T. Roberts, Owner

168. What is the purpose of this notice?

(A) To inform customers about a free drawing
(B) To announce the shop's grand opening
(C) To advertise an Independence Day special
(D) To explain plans for Founders' Day

169. What will the fiftieth person through the door receive?

(A) A ten-dollar gift certificate
(B) Two free ice-cream cones
(C) A free drink with an order
(D) A coupon for an ice-cream cone

170. For how many additional hours will the store remain open on July 23?

(A) One
(B) Three
(C) Four
(D) Five

Questions 171–173 refer to the following notice.

NOTICE OF VIOLATION

Parking fines are payable in person in the Office of the Clerk, City Hall, on weekdays from 9:00 A.M. to 5:00 P.M. Notice of intent to contest any violation must be delivered to the court, either in person or by mail, within ten days of the summons. All fines are doubled if not paid within 30 days of the issuance of the summons and no notice of intent to contest is filed. Fines must be paid in cash. No personal checks or credit cards will be accepted.

171. When must a person file a notice to contest a violation?

(A) After paying the fine
(B) Within 10 days of the violation
(C) Within 30 days of the violation
(D) Weekdays between 9:00 A.M. and 5:00 P.M.

172. What happens if a $10.00 fine is not paid within the time allowed?

(A) The person must contest.
(B) The fine is raised to $20.00.
(C) The person must file a notice.
(D) The person responsible is arrested.

173. How are fines paid?

(A) By mail
(B) By check
(C) In cash
(D) In ten days

GO ON TO THE NEXT PAGE

Questions 174–176 refer to the following letter.

Center for Educational Progress
367 Market Street
San Francisco, CA 94170

Professor Robert A. Handy
Department of Education
University of North Carolina
Chapel Hill, NC 27510

Dear Professor Handy:

We are very pleased that you have offered to make a presentation at the 4th California Conference on Bilingual Education. Your talk, "Parents and Bilingualism," is certain to be of great interest to many of the conference attendees, as your work in this field is quite well known.

The enclosed materials will tell you more about the conference schedule. Included, also, is a Presenter's Information Package.

The Center will reimburse you against receipts for all travel and accommodation expenses associated with the conference. Please feel free to make a collect call to my assistant, Ms. Aletha Jones, at (415) 855-2457 if you have any questions in this regard.

Thank you again for your participation. Your presentation is sure to help make our program a success.

Yours,

Steven P. Ryan, Ed.D.
Director

Enclosures:

174. What does Dr. Handy's field appear to be?

(A) Worker education
(B) Adult education
(C) Second-language education
(D) College education

175. What did Dr. Handy receive from Dr. Ryan?

(A) A research report
(B) An invitation to speak at a conference
(C) An information packet
(D) A presenter's fee

176. Who will pay Dr. Handy's expenses?

(A) Dr. Handy, himself
(B) The State of California
(C) The University of North Carolina
(D) The Center for Educational Progress

Questions 177–179 refer to the following report.

> Miami. Oct 10. Residents of St. Croix in the U.S. Virgin Islands have begun to stockpile water, food, batteries, and candles as newly formed tropical storm Floyd gains momentum.
>
> Business is "pretty heavy," said Lynn Holster, manager of Gandhi's Hardware, the island's only hardware store.
>
> Tiny St. Croix is expected to be hit by the storm by midnight Tuesday, local time, but no one can yet predict how severe the storm will be. On Oct. 10 at 3:00 A.M. EST, Floyd's wind speed was 85 mph, well above hurricane level. Local residents remember that St. Croix was hit by hurricanes Denise and Gilbert in 1988 and by Hugo in 1989.

177. What are residents of St. Croix doing to prepare for the hurricane?

(A) Evacuating the island
(B) Buying emergency supplies
(C) Taking refuge in a hardware store
(D) Putting boards over windows and doors

178. How many other hurricanes are reported to have hit St. Croix in recent years?

(A) One
(B) Two
(C) Three
(D) Four

179. What is the name of the hurricane that is expected to hit the island?

(A) Floyd
(B) Denise
(C) Gilbert
(D) Hugo

GO ON TO THE NEXT PAGE

Questions 180–182 refer to the following job posting.

REGIONAL PRODUCTION MANAGER

The Blacksquire Clothing Group is looking for a regional production manager for our Eastern European operations. Blacksquire Eastern Europe is involved in a number of apparel production sites throughout the region that support, exclusively, export to North America and Japan.

The successful candidate will necessarily have more than ten years experience in production and be fluent in English. One other major European language, particularly Polish or German, would be helpful.

Competitive salary and benefits.

Contact: Frederick Radice, Blacksquire Clothing,
944 Solidarinosc Street, Gdansk 003-478, Poland.
Phone: (39) 721-7740 Fax: (39) 721-1219

180. Which of the following describes Blacksquire Group operations in Eastern Europe?

(A) Manufacture for export
(B) Design and manufacture for local markets
(C) Manufacture of up-scale imported designs
(D) Manufacture to market under other labels

181. Which of the following is a requirement for this position?

(A) Technical training
(B) Production background
(C) International experience
(D) Fluency in two languages

182. Where is the open position located?

(A) Japan
(B) Poland
(C) North America
(D) The Czech Republic

Questions 183–185 refer to the following report.

> The TFX and Hess companies will merge their computer networking services subsidiaries to form a new company, to be called Advantis. Advantis will be controlled by its computer-maker parent, TFX. The company will offer telephone and data transmission services to major companies. Such services appeal to companies that do not want to invest capital to build their own data networks. The merger will take place in November. Service to customers will be available by the first of the year.

183. Which companies are planning to merge two of their subsidiary companies?

(A) TFX and Hess
(B) TFX and Advantis
(C) Hess and Advantis
(D) Hess and Computer Data

184. Who will be the clientele of the new company?

(A) Small companies
(B) Major businesses
(C) Government agencies
(D) Computer networking companies

185. When will the new company be able to begin providing services?

(A) In January
(B) In November
(C) In December
(D) Immediately

GO ON TO THE NEXT PAGE

Questions 186–188 refer to the following article.

Lemon grass—an indispensable part of Thai cuisine. Stalks are bought in bundles of about 6–8 and are usually 7–8 inches/ 18–20cm long. Ends are trimmed and the stalk finely sliced. One average stalk will give approximately 3tbs/45ml finely sliced lemon grass. Stalks will last quite well for 2–3 weeks in a refrigerator, and chopped lemon grass can be put in a plastic bag and frozen. Chopped lemon grass is also available dried in small packets.

186. How should a cook prepare lemon grass for use in cooking?

(A) Slice and cook immediately, to preserve flavor.
(B) Soak the grass in salt water and then chop.
(C) Trim the ends and slice the grass finely.
(D) Scrub the stalks clean and boil them.

187. How much lemon grass will three average stalks yield?

(A) 1 tbs or 15 ml
(B) 3 tbs or 45 ml
(C) 6 tbs or 90 ml
(D) 9 tbs or 135 ml

188. How can lemon grass be stored to preserve its flavor?

(A) In a dark place
(B) In a plastic bag
(C) In a cold place
(D) In an airtight container

Questions 189–191 refer to the following memorandum.

To: All Benvoek Diamond Employees and Dependents

From: Dieter Vanderwaal
Director
Personnel

It has come to my attention that many Benvoek employees are concerned about the growing number of public disruptions going on across the country. I have been personally informed by President Mobele, however, that the state is fundamentally sound, stable, and safe. President Mobele has also informed me that he expects the situation to improve as the summer weather passes.

In the meantime, all Benvoek employees and their dependents are encouraged to keep a low profile to avoid being identified as foreigners. Also, it would not be wise to venture unaccompanied into the rural areas at this time.

189. As what is this memorandum intended to serve?

(A) A threat
(B) A warning
(C) An invitation
(D) A correction

190. With whom does Mr. Vanderwaal claim to have spoken?

(A) A writer
(B) A professor
(C) A public official
(D) A business associate

191. When does Mr. Vanderwaal say the situation may change?

(A) After the summer.
(B) The following year.
(C) Almost immediately.
(D) It is unclear.

GO ON TO THE NEXT PAGE

Questions 192 and 193 refer to the following announcement.

European Capital Markets Conference

The *European Economic Journal* is pleased to announce the Fifth European Capital Markets Conference. This annual conference has come to serve as the most important public forum for leading policy makers and international accounting, consulting, and legal institutions, to discuss new directions in the European region. This year's conference will highlight developments and opportunities resulting from the opening up of the pan-European bond, stock, currency, and futures markets.

192. Which of the following is mentioned as a party interested in this conference?

(A) Lawyers
(B) Writers
(C) Scholars
(D) Advertisers

193. What is a key topic of discussion at the conference?

(A) Trade negotiation
(B) Vocational education
(C) Market liberalization
(D) Privatization of industries

Questions 194–197 refer to the following letter.

May 7, 19—

Mr. Jan Michaels
Michaels Valve and Pump Co.
200 Valley Blvd.
Sunspot, AZ

Dear Mr. Michaels:

This letter is to inform you of an embarrassing situation that has arisen, due to the inexperience of one of our warehousemen. It seems that your April 15 order for 55 units of our PQ-108 pump with a 3/4 hp motor was mistakenly put in a bin with back orders.

You requested immediate shipment. We discovered the error only today and have already packed the pumps for shipping. They will be picked up later today by Consolidated Freight and should arrive in a few days.

We very much regret this error. As you know from past experience, we value our association with you and would do nothing knowingly to jeopardize it.

Please accept our apologies. We hope this delay has not caused you great inconvenience.

Yours,
Alfred Nolan, President
Nolan Pumps

194. What became of the original order?

(A) It was lost in the mail.
(B) It was misplaced at Nolan Pumps.
(C) It was sent to the wrong address.
(D) It was not clearly written.

195. When was the order filled?

(A) On March 4
(B) On April 15
(C) On May 7
(D) The day before

196. Why is Mr. Nolan worried?

(A) Because Michaels is a new customer
(B) Because Michaels seems to always receive poor service
(C) Because Michaels complained to him personally
(D) Because he is afraid of losing Michaels' business

197. Who was responsible for the problem?

(A) Mr. Nolan
(B) The post office
(C) A new employee
(D) Consolidated Freight

Questions 198–200 refer to the following notice.

> The Export Processing Zone (EPZ) is an attractive investment opportunity for both domestic and international enterprises. Wages are determined only by the market, and strikes are prohibited. Products produced in the zone may be exported locally up to a value equivalent to 5 percent of wages to local hires. There are no restrictions on importation of either labor or capital into the zone, but foreign managers must train local counterparts. Income derived from activities in the EPZ is granted a five-year tax holiday and may be repatriated or reinvested. For reinvested capital, during the initial five-year period, additional special concessions are available.

198. Which of the following statements concerning labor in the zone is true?

    (A) Wages are controlled.
    (B) Strikes are not allowed.
    (C) Only local labor may be hired.
    (D) Local hires may import products.

199. Which of the following is stated as a benefit of investment in the EPZ?

    (A) Trained local managers
    (B) Major market concessions
    (C) Unlimited remittances of profits
    (D) Availability of a skilled work force

200. Why would somebody want to reinvest capital earned in the EPZ?

    (A) To get an additional 5-year tax holiday
    (B) To be allowed to export locally
    (C) To avoid having to train local managers
    (D) For incentives that are not stated

Stop! This is the end of the test. If you finish before time is called, you can go back to Parts V, VI, and VII and check your work.

TEST 6—SCRIPT

Part I

1. (Man B)
(A) She is looking to the west.
(B) The games are not far away.
(C) People went home after the game.
(D) The men are playing a game of chess.

2. (Woman)
(A) The young men are sitting on the wall.
(B) The people are starting to dance.
(C) From here you can see a long way.
(D) It's hard to work in the dark.

3. (Woman)
(A) The woman is waiting for the car to back out.
(B) The woman is parking her car in the lot.
(C) The woman is turning right, into the lot.
(D) The woman is pushing a shopping cart in the parking lot.

4. (Man B)
(A) The machine has been damaged.
(B) The doctor is holding the child.
(C) They have been misplaced.
(D) The children are being vaccinated.

5. (Man B)
(A) The man is working at his computer.
(B) The men are carrying the plants.
(C) The men are repairing the computers.
(D) The plans are sitting on the computer.

6. (Man B)
(A) The man is meeting with his followers.
(B) Men are working in the field of flowers.
(C) The man is trying to grow some flowers.
(D) Men are going to plant the flowers.

7. (Woman)
(A) They look for the rags.
(B) They carried a couple of bags.
(C) The couple are carrying many bags.
(D) The group has found its bags.

8. (Man B)
(A) They have traveled very far.
(B) The trail is not well marked.
(C) The train is stopping at the station.
(D) Rain is falling on the tracks.

9. (Woman)
(A) The weather is very hot.
(B) People have all gone inside.
(C) The woman is reading the paper.
(D) The man is walking away from the woman.

10. (Man B)
(A) Water is running down the road.
(B) Traffic is close to the river.
(C) The road is closed to traffic.
(D) The flood is nearly up to road level.

11. (Woman)
(A) People are buying fruit.
(B) The woman is working in marketing.
(C) This drink tastes like fruit.
(D) The dress is bright orange.

12. (Man B)
(A) The couple are walking toward their car.
(B) The man is waiting for a train.
(C) The man is standing in the subway car.
(D) The couple are looking for a place to sit.

13. (Woman)
(A) The women are drinking coffee.
(B) The woman is pouring a cup of coffee.
(C) The woman is about to make some coffee.
(D) The woman has served the coffee.

14. (Man B)
(A) The child is watching the fight.
(B) The women are talking to one another.
(C) The garage was there before the fence went up.
(D) Their hats have blown away.

15. (Woman)
(A) The man is holding up the flag shop.
(B) The man is looking up at the banner.
(C) The man is standing under the flag pole.
(D) The man is putting up a flag in front of his house.

16. (Man B)
(A) The walkway is being mopped.
(B) People are standing in line.
(C) The windows are being cleaned.
(D) Men are entering the building.

17. (Man B)
(A) The man is carrying some rolls.
(B) The man is talking on the phone.
(C) The man is leaning against the post.
(D) The man is running up the street.

18. (Man B)
(A) The man is pulling into the gas station.
(B) The man has his hand on the tank of gas.
(C) The man is putting gas in his car.
(D) The man's car is running out of gas.

19. (Man B)
(A) The man is watching the flies.
(B) Important documents are locked in the file box.
(C) A file is missing from the drawer.
(D) The drawer is full of files.

20. (Woman)
(A) The parents are reading to their children.
(B) The man is feeding the girl.
(C) The children are buying books.
(D) The family is eating together.

Part II

21. (Man A) Can I see you again sometime soon?
(Woman)
(A) He's not here.
(B) You'll be late for your meeting.
(C) I'd like that. Maybe this Saturday?

22. (Man B) Excuse me. Can you tell me what time it is?
(Woman)
(A) It's best if you go early.
(B) It's about to begin.
(C) It's five thirty-five.

23. (Man B) Who's the new man in the office?
(Man A)
(A) His name is Jim Miller.
(B) I think we need to hire someone.
(C) Yes. They told me to come here.

24. (Man B) How long was the meeting?
(Woman)
(A) It lasted more than an hour.
(B) Almost fifty meters.
(C) They met in the Board Room.

25. (Man B) Did you hear about John's promotion?
(Man A)
(A) Yes, I've always liked visiting there.
(B) No, I won't be able to attend.
(C) Yes, I heard about it this morning.

26. (Man A) Do you know where we put the report on Upton?
(Man B)
(A) You should notify the police.
(B) Yes. I sent the whole file over to the main office.
(C) I'd say somewhere between ten and fifteen.

27. (Man B) That decision isn't necessarily final, is it?
(Man A)
(A) No, I suppose not.
(B) Yes, you were.
(C) I certainly will.

28. (Man B) Are these strawberries fresh?
(Man A)
(A) I love strawberries.
(B) Yes, we picked them this morning.
(C) No, they're Spanish.

29. (Man A) What time does the bus come by?
(Man B)
(A) This is only the second time.
(B) The next one's at two-thirty.
(C) I have a quarter to three.

30. (Man B) Do you have any idea how much these desks will cost?
(Man A)
(A) I prefer to sit near the window.
(B) List price on them is three hundred ten dollars.
(C) I left my ID at home, but everyone knows me.

31. (Man B) Our computer files are in total disarray. Can you organize them for us?
(Woman)
(A) If you give me enough time, I'm sure I can straighten them out.
(B) Sir, I don't think we should listen to them.
(C) That was very nice of them. I'll send a thank-you note.

32. (Man B) Would you be able to repair this clock?
(Man A)
(A) I don't know where they put it.
(B) You don't think it's that late, do you?
(C) Maybe, but it's old, and parts for it will be hard to find.

33. (Man B) Are we supposed to meet them in the lobby, or out front?
(Woman)
(A) The design is not a pretty one.
(B) I'm sure they said to wait in the lobby.
(C) I'd prefer something light, perhaps just a salad.

34. (Man A) Are there any tickets left for the eight o'clock show on Friday?
(Woman)
(A) No, it's at nine o'clock.
(B) Yes, they just left.
(C) I'm sorry. The entire weekend is sold out.

35. (Woman) May I use your phone for a local call?
(Man B)
(A) We applied for a telephone yesterday.
(B) Yes. It's next to the cash register.
(C) They say it's long distance.

36. (Man A) Can I give you a ride somewhere?
(Man B)
(A) Yes, I've just come from the Post Office.
(B) No, thanks. I'm just out for a walk.
(C) I believe there's a taxi stand across the street.

37. (Woman) Do you have time to go to the store for me?
(Man B)
(A) I do if I hurry. What do you need?
(B) Yes. It's three-fifteen.
(C) It starts at one o'clock.

38. (Woman) Do you sell staples for this kind of stapler?
(Man B)
(A) I like all fruit, but especially apples.
(B) I'll need to see some identification.
(C) Yes. Look in aisle four, with the fixatives.

39. (Man A) What day of the week is New Year's on this year?
(Woman)
(A) All day Tuesday.
(B) In four weeks.
(C) It's on a Friday.

40. (Man B) Where is the Hanson file?
(Woman)
(A) It's about five centimeters thick.
(B) It's the building just past the Post Office.
(C) It's in the cabinet in the back office.

41. (Man A) How many cartons do we have in our inventory?
(Woman)
(A) Enough to last six weeks at our current sales level.
(B) They're all pretty funny, I'd say.
(C) No, they haven't invented anything.

42. (Man A) When can I pick up my ticket?
(Woman)
(A) At the Overseas Travel desk.
(B) Wednesday morning, if that's convenient.
(C) I'm afraid I haven't seen it.

43. (Woman) Do you know what consultants will be coming in?
(Man B)
(A) I didn't think they were here yet.
(B) If so, we'll be able to leave early.
(C) They're the same people who came in last year.

44. (Woman) Have you tried the restaurant down the street?
(Man B)
(A) Yes, we went there yesterday.
(B) I think it's down that street, over there.
(C) We've been trying, but if you insist.

45. (Man B) I really like your hair like that.
(Woman)
(A) Why, thank you. But I'm not so sure I care for it.
(B) I wouldn't care to, thank you.
(C) I'm sorry. I'm busy and have to stay here.

46. (Woman) I have a friend in the hospital, and I'd like to get her a gift. Could you suggest something?
(Man B)
(A) You could give her a gown, or maybe a book.
(B) Yes, he's been there for over a week.
(C) Please, don't worry. Everything will be just fine.

47. (Woman) Will you call our top twenty customers and ask if they'll serve on the product council we're setting up?
(Man A)
(A) I was able to reach only about half of them.
(B) The council met last night and decided against it.
(C) I'd be glad to, and I know they'll appreciate it.

48. (Man B) Have sales increased this week?
(Woman)
(A) I haven't seen the latest figures.
(B) Yes, we sometimes have sales.
(C) We would like to sell it.

49. (Woman) Does your department have anyone to recommend to replace Billings after he retires?
(Man B)
(A) Yes, your resume came in yesterday.
(B) We have two people, either of whom would be very good.
(C) Of course I'm looking forward to retiring.

50. (Man B) Can your company promote our new product?
(Woman)
(A) Yes, I was promoted to supervisor.
(B) Well, it depends on what your market is.
(C) Yes, your company can do it.

Part III

51. (Man A) What do you think of the new man in our department?
(Woman) You mean Charlie? He'll be a real asset to the company.
(Man A) I agree. We could use some fresh ideas.

52. (Woman) Here's the paper you asked for.
(Man A) Is that yesterday's or today's?
(Woman) It's today's, just delivered.

53. (Man B) Did I tell you? I got a new job.
(Woman) No! What's the name of the company?
(Man B) Simmons Finance. I start on the first.

54. (Man A) Here, let me get you a chair. What happened to you?
(Man B) I broke my ankle skiing.
(Man A) That must hurt. I'm sorry to hear it.

55. (Woman) Did you hear? They're tearing down the old grammar school.
(Man B) No! That great old building? It seemed that we spent a lifetime there.
(Woman) That's it. I really enjoyed those years.

56. (Man A) My name is Jones. I've reserved a car.
(Woman) I'll need to see your driver's license and a major credit card, Mr. Jones. Would you like full-size, compact, or mini?
(Man A) I'd like a compact, but it has to have air conditioning.

57. (Man A) John, class begins at 10 o'clock, and you should be here.
(Man B) I know, but I missed my bus. I'm sorry.
(Man A) That's no excuse. It's disruptive for others, and you have to come on time.

58. (Woman) Did Lily tell you she was asked to speak at the school Parents' Night?
(Man B) No, but I'm not surprised they chose her. She's a good speaker.
(Woman) She sure is. In that, she takes after you. You've always been a good speaker.

59. (Man A) I'd like to transfer one hundred dollars from my savings to my checking account.
(Woman) Of course. Please fill out this transfer slip.
(Man A) Is there a pen here that I can use?

60. (Man A) We're going to Los Angeles for the weekend.
(Woman) Do you have relatives there?
(Man A) No, Mary and I just want to get away from everything and do some sightseeing.

61. (Man A) I'm looking for the Crown Hotel.
(Man B) You need to turn right at this light. It's two blocks down, on your right.
(Man A) Thanks. I've been driving around for twenty minutes trying to find it. I was about to give up.

62. (Man A) Wilson is thinking about developing that unused land. As it is, it's just sitting there costing him money.
(Man B) That may be, but for now it'll cost him even more to develop it.
(Man A) He knows that, but he thinks in the long run he'll come out ahead.

63. (Man B) What does this trade fair have that's so special?
(Woman) It's not just another display of high-tech hardware. In a series of seminars, we're going to address problems common to our client industries, such as engineering marketing and patent protection.
(Man B) In that case, it may be worth attending.

64. (Woman) Bob has a terrible cold today.
(Man A) Well, he shouldn't go around in this weather without a coat. I must have told him a hundred times.
(Woman) Yes, I always tell him, too, but he refuses to listen.

65. (Man B) Has Maganya been asked to perform for the president?
(Woman) Yes. She was invited to give a special performance for him and some of his guests this weekend.
(Man B) She must be very excited, but then she does have a beautiful voice. It's no wonder they always ask her to sing.

66. (Man A) Did you hear that Jim failed to get re-elected to the council?
(Man B) Yes, it's too bad. I thought he was doing a pretty good job.
(Man A) I did, too, but his replacement has a lot of business experience. He should do just fine.

67. (Woman) I've been asked to deposit this check in my brother's savings account.
(Man B) You may, but you'll have to complete a deposit slip. Here, I'll show you. For savings, you need this blue slip.
(Woman) Yes, he said I'd have to fill out something.

68. (Man B) On Saturdays we usually play a round of golf. Would you like to join us this week?
(Man A) I'd like to, but I have to be back by two o'clock. Would that be a problem?
(Man B) No, you'll have time. We always finish by lunch, have a bite at the club, and leave by one.

69. (Man A) I'm afraid the position for which you applied has been filled.
(Man B) I see. Would it be possible to apply for another?
(Man A) I'm sorry, but that was the only position we had open. We'll keep your name on file, in case something comes up.

70. (Woman) Did you hear that Henry is leaving the company?
(Man B) Yes. That's too bad. I was under the impression he was on a fast track to the top.
(Woman) It sure looked that way. Everyone was always saying what a good job he was doing. He must have done something wrong.

71. (Man B) I came into town on the South Expressway. The traffic was backed up as far as the ballpark.
(Woman) There was a bad accident on a curve, and only one lane was open. Some people sat in traffic for two hours.
(Man B) I guess it's a good thing I came in early. I lost only twenty minutes.

72. (Woman) This painting goes with nothing we have in the house. The colors are all wrong.
(Man B) Darling, you don't buy a painting because the colors match your drapes. You buy it for other, more aesthetic, qualities.
(Woman) That's fine, if you want to put it in a closet or hang it in a gallery. But in our living room, it has to match the drapes.

73. (Man B) How did Jordan's surgery go?
(Man A) There were some complications, but he's doing fine. He'll be in the hospital another week.
(Man B) Well, I'm glad to hear everything's o.k.

74. (Woman) That data file we were looking for is in Mike's office.
(Man A) I thought it was supposed to be in the operations room.
(Woman) I did, too. Mike must have needed it for something he's working on.

75. (Man B) Has Dame Charlotte been given the lead in the new Alpert play?
(Man A) Yes, and I understand she's quite excited about it.
(Man B) I'm really looking forward to seeing her perform. Although I don't care for her in person, on stage she's great.

76. (Woman) What time will we be eating lunch?
(Man B) While you were sleeping, the driver announced we'll stop at about 12:30.
(Woman) I can hardly wait. I'm starved.

77. (Woman) I thought you were working until six.
(Man B) I was supposed to, but we finished our meeting at five and were let go.
(Woman) Good. We can leave early for dinner.

78. (Man B) Did you know that our inventory of E-3 printers isn't moving very fast and it's growing?

(Man A) No, I didn't know that. Let's cut back production until we ship some out.

(Man B) All right. There are other jobs I can put people on for the short term. We'll start tomorrow.

79. (Man B) Why can I never find my keys when I'm in a hurry?

(Woman) It's because you can never find anything, regardless of whether you're in a hurry.

(Man B) Well, in that case, there's probably nothing I can do about it, and I shouldn't worry.

80. (Man A) What are the chances for further appreciation of the yen? This is killing our business!

(Woman) We don't expect it to go any higher for the time being.

(Man A) That's good news, but a lot of damage has already been done.

Part IV

(Man A) Questions 81 through 83 refer to the following advertisement.

(Man B) For a taste of times gone by, try Old World homemade soup, now on your grocery store shelves. Available in five varieties, Old World soups are made with only the finest natural ingredients. They contain no preservatives. That makes Old World soups your best choice for a healthy and nutritious meal. Old World soups: try all five of them. This is the taste your grandfather came home to. Now available at grocery stores everywhere.

(Man A) Now read question 81 in your test book and answer it.

(Man A) Now read question 82 in your test book and answer it.

(Man A) Now read question 83 in your test book and answer it.

(Man A) Questions 84 through 86 refer to the following briefing.

(Woman) Thank you, gentlemen, for your time. I've joined you today to say a few words about my company, Deltrans. We know that most people think of Deltrans as only a car company. Those people are less than 20 percent right. At Deltrans, we also design and manufacture a variety of transport systems: rail cars, buses, and aircraft, to name a few. Today I will introduce you to some of our less well-known product lines.

(Man A) Now read Question 84 in your test book and answer it.

(Man A) Now read Question 85 in your test book and answer it.

(Man A) Now read Question 86 in your test book and answer it.

(Man A) Questions 87 and 88 refer to the following bulletin.

(Man B) Due to the heavy snowfall, which is expected to get worse as the day goes on, all schools and government offices will close at 1:00 P.M. All motorists are advised to get off the roads as soon as possible and avoid driving until further notice. All public transportation will be operating on a reduced schedule, as weather permits. Any owner of a four-wheel-drive vehicle with a CB radio who would like to volunteer in case of an emergency should contact the Red Cross at 768-2391.

(Man A) Now read question 87 in your test book and answer it.

(Man A) Now read question 88 in your test book and answer it.

(Man A) Questions 89 through 91 refer to the following announcement.

(Woman) The National Health Agency announced yesterday that a new drug, found in an everyday household plant, a cactus, has been claimed to cure the common cold in laboratory experiments. Discovered by researchers at Commonwealth University, the drug, Rindamal, is extracted by a fairly simple process. Three major drug companies have expressed interest in marketing the anti-cold drug, should the early findings of its powers be substantiated with further testing.

(Man A) Now read question 89 in your test book and answer it.

(Man A) Now read question 90 in your test book and answer it.

(Man A) Now read question 91 in your test book and answer it.

(Man A) Questions 92 and 93 refer to the following explanation.

(Woman) I'm sorry, but I'm afraid that we have to decline your loan request. Although your company is sound, the amount you're asking for is too large for the collateral you can put up. We could consider lending such a large amount to only a few of our major corporate customers. If, however, you would like to apply for a smaller amount, we would probably be able to accommodate you.

(Man A) Now read question 92 in your test book and answer it.

(Man A) Now read question 93 in your test book and answer it.

(Man A) Questions 94 and 95 refer to the following announcement.

(Man B) Today we are going to discuss indelicate subject matter. No, not indelicate subjects, but the developing trend of discussing, on-the-air, matters that many people find offensive. Our guests today include a psychologist, a radio announcer who has been labeled obscene by the *Post*, and you, our audience, who we hope will phone in and air your views. We'll begin by asking Dr. Edward Blitz to define the problem for us.

(Man A) Now read question 94 in your test book and answer it.

(Man A) Now read question 95 in your test book and answer it.

(Man A) Questions 96 through 98 refer to the following report.

(Man B) The results of our customer product-satisfaction survey are in, but they are not encouraging. They reveal a serious lack of satisfaction among our customers with our new cleaning solvent. For instance, out of 78 companies responding to the survey, only 37, or fewer than half, expressed satisfaction with our product. We are going to have to work harder on quality control and also upon salvaging our name with customers. In the next two days we will call a meeting of the product management team to discuss this matter.

(Man A) Now read question 96 in your test book and answer it.

(Man A) Now read question 97 in your test book and answer it.

(Man A) Now read question 98 in your test book and answer it.

(Man A) Questions 99 and 100 refer to the following report.

(Woman) As a result of an overall drop in profits last year, a loss of an unprecedented 27 percent over the previous year, our Audit Division has reviewed all of our businesses from the point of view of profitability. Their findings tell us that we should sell off some of our less-profitable holdings, with the Fresh Day Food Corporation heading the list. The complete list and financial data are provided in Appendix A of the report in your file. All of our indicators tell us that by doing this, we can consolidate our remaining holdings and prevent further major losses.

(Man A) Now read question 99 in your test book and answer it.

(Man A) Now read question 100 in your test book and answer it.

This is the end of the Listening Comprehension portion of the test. Turn to Part V in your test book.

TEST 6 COMPARISON SCORES

The score range for the TOEIC is 10 to 990, 5 to 495 for listening and 5 to 495 for reading. This is a converted score, otherwise known as a scaled score, arrived at by converting an examinee's raw score by a formula that changes with every test. The raw score is merely the number of questions answered correctly. On the TOEIC, there is no penalty for answering a question incorrectly.

Converted scores are reported, rather than raw scores, because the developers of the TOEIC make a statistical adjustment for the relative ease or difficulty of each test. This procedure ensures that scores are equivalent over time and do not fluctuate because one or another test may be easier or more difficult than others.

The raw scores that appear below, for this test and for this test only, correspond to a total mean converted TOEIC score of 500, 250 for listening and 250 for reading. Other tests in this book have mean scores calculated on different formulas.

These scores are provided so, if they like, students can compare their performance on this test with a performance that would produce a total converted score of 500. Raw part scores of above the scores provided here would convert to a score of above 500, while raw part scores of below the scores provided here would convert to a score of below 500.

Part	Mean Raw Score
I	15
II	19
III	19
IV	11
Mean Listening	64
V	25
VI	11
VII	27
Mean Reading	63
Mean Total	127

Converted Scores for Above Mean Scores

Mean Listening	250
Mean Reading	250
Mean Total	500

ANSWER KEY FOR TEST 6—LISTENING

Key: Part I

1. (D) The men are playing a game of chess.
2. (A) The young men are sitting on the wall.
3. (D) The woman is pushing a shopping cart in the parking lot.
4. (D) The children are getting vaccinated.
5. (A) The man is working at his computer.
6. (B) Men are working in the field of flowers.
7. (C) The couple are carrying many bags.
8. (C) The train is stopping at the station.
9. (D) The man is walking away from the woman.
10. (C) The road is closed to traffic.
11. (A) People are buying fruit.
12. (C) The man is standing in the subway car.
13. (B) The woman is pouring a cup of coffee.
14. (B) The women are talking to one another.
15. (B) The man is looking up at the banner.
16. (A) The walkway is being mopped.
17. (B) The man is talking on the phone.
18. (C) The man is putting gas in his car.
19. (D) The drawer is full of files.
20. (A) The parents are reading to their children.

Key: Part II

21. (C) I'd like that. Maybe this Saturday?
22. (C) It's five thirty-five.
23. (A) His name is Jim Miller.
24. (A) It lasted more than an hour.
25. (C) Yes, I heard about it this morning.
26. (B) Yes. I sent the whole file over to the main office.
27. (A) No, I suppose not.
28. (B) Yes, we picked them this morning.
29. (B) The next one's at two-thirty.
30. (B) List price on them is three hundred ten dollars.
31. (A) If you give me enough time, I'm sure I can straighten them out.
32. (C) Maybe, but it's old, and parts for it will be hard to find.
33. (B) I'm sure they said to wait in the lobby.
34. (C) I'm sorry. The entire weekend is sold out.
35. (B) Yes. It's next to the cash register.
36. (B) No, thanks. I'm just out for a walk.
37. (A) I do if I hurry. What do you need?
38. (C) Yes. Look in aisle four, with the fixatives.
39. (C) It's on a Friday.
40. (C) It's in the cabinet in the back office.
41. (A) Enough to last six weeks at our current sales level.
42. (B) Wednesday morning, if that's convenient.
43. (C) They're the same people who came in last year.
44. (A) Yes, we went there yesterday.
45. (A) Why, thank you. But I'm not so sure I care for it.
46. (A) You could give her a gown, or maybe a book.
47. (C) I'd be glad to, and I know they'll appreciate it.
48. (A) I haven't seen the latest figures.
49. (B) We have two people, either of whom would be very good.
50. (B) Well, it depends on what your market is.

Key: Part III

51. (D) He will contribute a lot.
52. (D) A newspaper
53. (C) Begin a new job
54. (D) His ankle is broken.
55. (B) A school
56. (A) Rent a car
57. (B) He came late to class.
58. (C) Make a speech
59. (A) In a bank
60. (B) Go to Los Angeles
61. (D) Directions
62. (C) Property development
63. (C) It will feature special seminars.
64. (B) He became ill.
65. (B) She sings.
66. (A) He did a good job.
67. (B) Deposit a check
68. (D) He has an appointment in the afternoon.
69. (C) Employment
70. (B) He was a good worker.
71. (D) There was an accident on the expressway.
72. (A) A piece of art
73. (C) He has had an operation.
74. (B) In Mike's office
75. (B) She was selected for a role in a play.
76. (A) On a bus
77. (C) His meeting ended earlier than expected.
78. (A) Reduce production of E-3 printers
79. (A) He loses things.
80. (D) Currency exchange rates

Key: Part IV

81. (D) Five
82. (B) The soup is healthy.
83. (D) At a lot of grocery stores
84. (C) Vehicle manufacture
85. (B) Tell about her products
86. (A) As an automobile manufacturer
87. (A) Heavy snow is expected.
88. (B) Owners of some four-wheel-drive vehicles
89. (A) Cure colds
90. (D) University researchers
91. (C) Vegetable matter
92. (A) A request for a loan
93. (A) A lot of money is involved.
94. (D) Obscenity on the radio
95. (B) Telephone the radio station
96. (D) As disappointing
97. (B) Quality
98. (C) A meeting will be held.
99. (C) Selling off some companies
100. (C) It is losing money.

ANSWER KEY FOR TEST 6—READING

Key: Part V

101. (B) such
102. (A) selected
103. (B) result
104. (D) trend
105. (B) all day
106. (B) relieved
107. (D) an exclusive
108. (C) on
109. (A) lasts
110. (A) stored
111. (D) something
112. (D) that he
113. (C) until
114. (D) approached
115. (A) went
116. (A) could say
117. (A) is
118. (C) rights
119. (C) chosen
120. (A) all
121. (A) a
122. (C) facility
123. (A) spoke
124. (B) Someone
125. (C) have been
126. (C) immediate
127. (B) throw away
128. (B) nearby
129. (C) relayed
130. (B) refused
131. (D) deserved
132. (B) flown
133. (B) having met
134. (C) the least
135. (D) from New Brunswick
136. (C) damaged
137. (D) rushed
138. (A) helped
139. (A) impress
140. (C) spoke to

Key: Part VI

141. (B) traffic moves
142. (A) was
143. (D) talking
144. (D) victory
145. (A) Last winter
146. (C) began managing
147. (B) in
148. (A) growing
149. (B) it was excellent, it showed excellence, it excelled
150. (D) involving
151. (A) is needed, is required
152. (B) he had come
153. (C) many
154. (D) falls, comes, is
155. (C) increase
156. (B) carried, being carried
157. (B) and
158. (A) applicant's qualifications
159. (B) five-year-old
160. (A) was

Key: Part VII

161. (B) $42.00
162. (B) Two weeks
163. (A) They pretreat the area.
164. (D) Manufacturing
165. (C) New representatives
166. (D) Latin America and Europe
167. (D) Product literature
168. (D) To explain plans for Founders' Day
169. (A) A ten-dollar gift certificate
170. (C) Four
171. (B) Within 10 days of the violation
172. (B) The fine is raised to $20.00.
173. (C) In cash
174. (C) Second-language education
175. (C) An information packet
176. (D) The Center for Educational Progress
177. (B) Buying emergency supplies
178. (C) Three
179. (A) Floyd
180. (A) Manufacture for export
181. (B) Production background
182. (B) Poland
183. (A) TFX and Hess
184. (B) Major businesses
185. (A) In January
186. (C) Trim the ends and slice the grass finely.
187. (D) 9 tbs or 135 ml
188. (C) In a cold place
189. (B) A warning
190. (C) A public official
191. (A) After the summer
192. (A) Lawyers
193. (C) Market liberalization
194. (B) It was misplaced at Nolan Pumps.
195. (C) On May 7
196. (D) Because he is afraid of losing Michaels' business
197. (C) A new employee
198. (B) Strikes are not allowed.
199. (C) Unlimited remittances of profits
200. (D) For incentives that are not stated

Answer Sheet—TOEIC® Test 1

Listening (Parts I–IV)

1. Ⓐ Ⓑ Ⓒ Ⓓ
2. Ⓐ Ⓑ Ⓒ Ⓓ
3. Ⓐ Ⓑ Ⓒ Ⓓ
4. Ⓐ Ⓑ Ⓒ Ⓓ
5. Ⓐ Ⓑ Ⓒ Ⓓ
6. Ⓐ Ⓑ Ⓒ Ⓓ
7. Ⓐ Ⓑ Ⓒ Ⓓ
8. Ⓐ Ⓑ Ⓒ Ⓓ
9. Ⓐ Ⓑ Ⓒ Ⓓ
10. Ⓐ Ⓑ Ⓒ Ⓓ
11. Ⓐ Ⓑ Ⓒ Ⓓ
12. Ⓐ Ⓑ Ⓒ Ⓓ
13. Ⓐ Ⓑ Ⓒ Ⓓ
14. Ⓐ Ⓑ Ⓒ Ⓓ
15. Ⓐ Ⓑ Ⓒ Ⓓ
16. Ⓐ Ⓑ Ⓒ Ⓓ
17. Ⓐ Ⓑ Ⓒ Ⓓ
18. Ⓐ Ⓑ Ⓒ Ⓓ
19. Ⓐ Ⓑ Ⓒ Ⓓ
20. Ⓐ Ⓑ Ⓒ Ⓓ
21. Ⓐ Ⓑ Ⓒ
22. Ⓐ Ⓑ Ⓒ
23. Ⓐ Ⓑ Ⓒ
24. Ⓐ Ⓑ Ⓒ
25. Ⓐ Ⓑ Ⓒ
26. Ⓐ Ⓑ Ⓒ
27. Ⓐ Ⓑ Ⓒ
28. Ⓐ Ⓑ Ⓒ
29. Ⓐ Ⓑ Ⓒ
30. Ⓐ Ⓑ Ⓒ
31. Ⓐ Ⓑ Ⓒ
32. Ⓐ Ⓑ Ⓒ
33. Ⓐ Ⓑ Ⓒ
34. Ⓐ Ⓑ Ⓒ
35. Ⓐ Ⓑ Ⓒ
36. Ⓐ Ⓑ Ⓒ
37. Ⓐ Ⓑ Ⓒ
38. Ⓐ Ⓑ Ⓒ
39. Ⓐ Ⓑ Ⓒ
40. Ⓐ Ⓑ Ⓒ
41. Ⓐ Ⓑ Ⓒ
42. Ⓐ Ⓑ Ⓒ
43. Ⓐ Ⓑ Ⓒ
44. Ⓐ Ⓑ Ⓒ
45. Ⓐ Ⓑ Ⓒ
46. Ⓐ Ⓑ Ⓒ
47. Ⓐ Ⓑ Ⓒ
48. Ⓐ Ⓑ Ⓒ
49. Ⓐ Ⓑ Ⓒ
50. Ⓐ Ⓑ Ⓒ
51. Ⓐ Ⓑ Ⓒ Ⓓ
52. Ⓐ Ⓑ Ⓒ Ⓓ
53. Ⓐ Ⓑ Ⓒ Ⓓ
54. Ⓐ Ⓑ Ⓒ Ⓓ
55. Ⓐ Ⓑ Ⓒ Ⓓ
56. Ⓐ Ⓑ Ⓒ Ⓓ
57. Ⓐ Ⓑ Ⓒ Ⓓ
58. Ⓐ Ⓑ Ⓒ Ⓓ
59. Ⓐ Ⓑ Ⓒ Ⓓ
60. Ⓐ Ⓑ Ⓒ Ⓓ
61. Ⓐ Ⓑ Ⓒ Ⓓ
62. Ⓐ Ⓑ Ⓒ Ⓓ
63. Ⓐ Ⓑ Ⓒ Ⓓ
64. Ⓐ Ⓑ Ⓒ Ⓓ
65. Ⓐ Ⓑ Ⓒ Ⓓ
66. Ⓐ Ⓑ Ⓒ Ⓓ
67. Ⓐ Ⓑ Ⓒ Ⓓ
68. Ⓐ Ⓑ Ⓒ Ⓓ
69. Ⓐ Ⓑ Ⓒ Ⓓ
70. Ⓐ Ⓑ Ⓒ Ⓓ
71. Ⓐ Ⓑ Ⓒ Ⓓ
72. Ⓐ Ⓑ Ⓒ Ⓓ
73. Ⓐ Ⓑ Ⓒ Ⓓ
74. Ⓐ Ⓑ Ⓒ Ⓓ
75. Ⓐ Ⓑ Ⓒ Ⓓ
76. Ⓐ Ⓑ Ⓒ Ⓓ
77. Ⓐ Ⓑ Ⓒ Ⓓ
78. Ⓐ Ⓑ Ⓒ Ⓓ
79. Ⓐ Ⓑ Ⓒ Ⓓ
80. Ⓐ Ⓑ Ⓒ Ⓓ
81. Ⓐ Ⓑ Ⓒ Ⓓ
82. Ⓐ Ⓑ Ⓒ Ⓓ
83. Ⓐ Ⓑ Ⓒ Ⓓ
84. Ⓐ Ⓑ Ⓒ Ⓓ
85. Ⓐ Ⓑ Ⓒ Ⓓ
86. Ⓐ Ⓑ Ⓒ Ⓓ
87. Ⓐ Ⓑ Ⓒ Ⓓ
88. Ⓐ Ⓑ Ⓒ Ⓓ
89. Ⓐ Ⓑ Ⓒ Ⓓ
90. Ⓐ Ⓑ Ⓒ Ⓓ
91. Ⓐ Ⓑ Ⓒ Ⓓ
92. Ⓐ Ⓑ Ⓒ Ⓓ
93. Ⓐ Ⓑ Ⓒ Ⓓ
94. Ⓐ Ⓑ Ⓒ Ⓓ
95. Ⓐ Ⓑ Ⓒ Ⓓ
96. Ⓐ Ⓑ Ⓒ Ⓓ
97. Ⓐ Ⓑ Ⓒ Ⓓ
98. Ⓐ Ⓑ Ⓒ Ⓓ
99. Ⓐ Ⓑ Ⓒ Ⓓ
100. Ⓐ Ⓑ Ⓒ Ⓓ

Reading (Parts V–VII)

101. Ⓐ Ⓑ Ⓒ Ⓓ
102. Ⓐ Ⓑ Ⓒ Ⓓ
103. Ⓐ Ⓑ Ⓒ Ⓓ
104. Ⓐ Ⓑ Ⓒ Ⓓ
105. Ⓐ Ⓑ Ⓒ Ⓓ
106. Ⓐ Ⓑ Ⓒ Ⓓ
107. Ⓐ Ⓑ Ⓒ Ⓓ
108. Ⓐ Ⓑ Ⓒ Ⓓ
109. Ⓐ Ⓑ Ⓒ Ⓓ
110. Ⓐ Ⓑ Ⓒ Ⓓ
111. Ⓐ Ⓑ Ⓒ Ⓓ
112. Ⓐ Ⓑ Ⓒ Ⓓ
113. Ⓐ Ⓑ Ⓒ Ⓓ
114. Ⓐ Ⓑ Ⓒ Ⓓ
115. Ⓐ Ⓑ Ⓒ Ⓓ
116. Ⓐ Ⓑ Ⓒ Ⓓ
117. Ⓐ Ⓑ Ⓒ Ⓓ
118. Ⓐ Ⓑ Ⓒ Ⓓ
119. Ⓐ Ⓑ Ⓒ Ⓓ
120. Ⓐ Ⓑ Ⓒ Ⓓ
121. Ⓐ Ⓑ Ⓒ Ⓓ
122. Ⓐ Ⓑ Ⓒ Ⓓ
123. Ⓐ Ⓑ Ⓒ Ⓓ
124. Ⓐ Ⓑ Ⓒ Ⓓ
125. Ⓐ Ⓑ Ⓒ Ⓓ
126. Ⓐ Ⓑ Ⓒ Ⓓ
127. Ⓐ Ⓑ Ⓒ Ⓓ
128. Ⓐ Ⓑ Ⓒ Ⓓ
129. Ⓐ Ⓑ Ⓒ Ⓓ
130. Ⓐ Ⓑ Ⓒ Ⓓ
131. Ⓐ Ⓑ Ⓒ Ⓓ
132. Ⓐ Ⓑ Ⓒ Ⓓ
133. Ⓐ Ⓑ Ⓒ Ⓓ
134. Ⓐ Ⓑ Ⓒ Ⓓ
135. Ⓐ Ⓑ Ⓒ Ⓓ
136. Ⓐ Ⓑ Ⓒ Ⓓ
137. Ⓐ Ⓑ Ⓒ Ⓓ
138. Ⓐ Ⓑ Ⓒ Ⓓ
139. Ⓐ Ⓑ Ⓒ Ⓓ
140. Ⓐ Ⓑ Ⓒ Ⓓ
141. Ⓐ Ⓑ Ⓒ Ⓓ
142. Ⓐ Ⓑ Ⓒ Ⓓ
143. Ⓐ Ⓑ Ⓒ Ⓓ
144. Ⓐ Ⓑ Ⓒ Ⓓ
145. Ⓐ Ⓑ Ⓒ Ⓓ
146. Ⓐ Ⓑ Ⓒ Ⓓ
147. Ⓐ Ⓑ Ⓒ Ⓓ
148. Ⓐ Ⓑ Ⓒ Ⓓ
149. Ⓐ Ⓑ Ⓒ Ⓓ
150. Ⓐ Ⓑ Ⓒ Ⓓ
151. Ⓐ Ⓑ Ⓒ Ⓓ
152. Ⓐ Ⓑ Ⓒ Ⓓ
153. Ⓐ Ⓑ Ⓒ Ⓓ
154. Ⓐ Ⓑ Ⓒ Ⓓ
155. Ⓐ Ⓑ Ⓒ Ⓓ
156. Ⓐ Ⓑ Ⓒ Ⓓ
157. Ⓐ Ⓑ Ⓒ Ⓓ
158. Ⓐ Ⓑ Ⓒ Ⓓ
159. Ⓐ Ⓑ Ⓒ Ⓓ
160. Ⓐ Ⓑ Ⓒ Ⓓ
161. Ⓐ Ⓑ Ⓒ Ⓓ
162. Ⓐ Ⓑ Ⓒ Ⓓ
163. Ⓐ Ⓑ Ⓒ Ⓓ
164. Ⓐ Ⓑ Ⓒ Ⓓ
165. Ⓐ Ⓑ Ⓒ Ⓓ
166. Ⓐ Ⓑ Ⓒ Ⓓ
167. Ⓐ Ⓑ Ⓒ Ⓓ
168. Ⓐ Ⓑ Ⓒ Ⓓ
169. Ⓐ Ⓑ Ⓒ Ⓓ
170. Ⓐ Ⓑ Ⓒ Ⓓ
171. Ⓐ Ⓑ Ⓒ Ⓓ
172. Ⓐ Ⓑ Ⓒ Ⓓ
173. Ⓐ Ⓑ Ⓒ Ⓓ
174. Ⓐ Ⓑ Ⓒ Ⓓ
175. Ⓐ Ⓑ Ⓒ Ⓓ
176. Ⓐ Ⓑ Ⓒ Ⓓ
177. Ⓐ Ⓑ Ⓒ Ⓓ
178. Ⓐ Ⓑ Ⓒ Ⓓ
179. Ⓐ Ⓑ Ⓒ Ⓓ
180. Ⓐ Ⓑ Ⓒ Ⓓ
181. Ⓐ Ⓑ Ⓒ Ⓓ
182. Ⓐ Ⓑ Ⓒ Ⓓ
183. Ⓐ Ⓑ Ⓒ Ⓓ
184. Ⓐ Ⓑ Ⓒ Ⓓ
185. Ⓐ Ⓑ Ⓒ Ⓓ
186. Ⓐ Ⓑ Ⓒ Ⓓ
187. Ⓐ Ⓑ Ⓒ Ⓓ
188. Ⓐ Ⓑ Ⓒ Ⓓ
189. Ⓐ Ⓑ Ⓒ Ⓓ
190. Ⓐ Ⓑ Ⓒ Ⓓ
191. Ⓐ Ⓑ Ⓒ Ⓓ
192. Ⓐ Ⓑ Ⓒ Ⓓ
193. Ⓐ Ⓑ Ⓒ Ⓓ
194. Ⓐ Ⓑ Ⓒ Ⓓ
195. Ⓐ Ⓑ Ⓒ Ⓓ
196. Ⓐ Ⓑ Ⓒ Ⓓ
197. Ⓐ Ⓑ Ⓒ Ⓓ
198. Ⓐ Ⓑ Ⓒ Ⓓ
199. Ⓐ Ⓑ Ⓒ Ⓓ
200. Ⓐ Ⓑ Ⓒ Ⓓ

Answer Sheet—TOEIC® Test 2

Listening (Parts I–IV)

No.	Answer	No.	Answer	No.	Answer	No.	Answer
1.	Ⓐ Ⓑ Ⓒ Ⓓ	26.	Ⓐ Ⓑ Ⓒ	51.	Ⓐ Ⓑ Ⓒ Ⓓ	76.	Ⓐ Ⓑ Ⓒ Ⓓ
2.	Ⓐ Ⓑ Ⓒ Ⓓ	27.	Ⓐ Ⓑ Ⓒ	52.	Ⓐ Ⓑ Ⓒ Ⓓ	77.	Ⓐ Ⓑ Ⓒ Ⓓ
3.	Ⓐ Ⓑ Ⓒ Ⓓ	28.	Ⓐ Ⓑ Ⓒ	53.	Ⓐ Ⓑ Ⓒ Ⓓ	78.	Ⓐ Ⓑ Ⓒ Ⓓ
4.	Ⓐ Ⓑ Ⓒ Ⓓ	29.	Ⓐ Ⓑ Ⓒ	54.	Ⓐ Ⓑ Ⓒ Ⓓ	79.	Ⓐ Ⓑ Ⓒ Ⓓ
5.	Ⓐ Ⓑ Ⓒ Ⓓ	30.	Ⓐ Ⓑ Ⓒ	55.	Ⓐ Ⓑ Ⓒ Ⓓ	80.	Ⓐ Ⓑ Ⓒ Ⓓ
6.	Ⓐ Ⓑ Ⓒ Ⓓ	31.	Ⓐ Ⓑ Ⓒ	56.	Ⓐ Ⓑ Ⓒ Ⓓ	81.	Ⓐ Ⓑ Ⓒ Ⓓ
7.	Ⓐ Ⓑ Ⓒ Ⓓ	32.	Ⓐ Ⓑ Ⓒ	57.	Ⓐ Ⓑ Ⓒ Ⓓ	82.	Ⓐ Ⓑ Ⓒ Ⓓ
8.	Ⓐ Ⓑ Ⓒ Ⓓ	33.	Ⓐ Ⓑ Ⓒ	58.	Ⓐ Ⓑ Ⓒ Ⓓ	83.	Ⓐ Ⓑ Ⓒ Ⓓ
9.	Ⓐ Ⓑ Ⓒ Ⓓ	34.	Ⓐ Ⓑ Ⓒ	59.	Ⓐ Ⓑ Ⓒ Ⓓ	84.	Ⓐ Ⓑ Ⓒ Ⓓ
10.	Ⓐ Ⓑ Ⓒ Ⓓ	35.	Ⓐ Ⓑ Ⓒ	60.	Ⓐ Ⓑ Ⓒ Ⓓ	85.	Ⓐ Ⓑ Ⓒ Ⓓ
11.	Ⓐ Ⓑ Ⓒ Ⓓ	36.	Ⓐ Ⓑ Ⓒ	61.	Ⓐ Ⓑ Ⓒ Ⓓ	86.	Ⓐ Ⓑ Ⓒ Ⓓ
12.	Ⓐ Ⓑ Ⓒ Ⓓ	37.	Ⓐ Ⓑ Ⓒ	62.	Ⓐ Ⓑ Ⓒ Ⓓ	87.	Ⓐ Ⓑ Ⓒ Ⓓ
13.	Ⓐ Ⓑ Ⓒ Ⓓ	38.	Ⓐ Ⓑ Ⓒ	63.	Ⓐ Ⓑ Ⓒ Ⓓ	88.	Ⓐ Ⓑ Ⓒ Ⓓ
14.	Ⓐ Ⓑ Ⓒ Ⓓ	39.	Ⓐ Ⓑ Ⓒ	64.	Ⓐ Ⓑ Ⓒ Ⓓ	89.	Ⓐ Ⓑ Ⓒ Ⓓ
15.	Ⓐ Ⓑ Ⓒ Ⓓ	40.	Ⓐ Ⓑ Ⓒ	65.	Ⓐ Ⓑ Ⓒ Ⓓ	90.	Ⓐ Ⓑ Ⓒ Ⓓ
16.	Ⓐ Ⓑ Ⓒ Ⓓ	41.	Ⓐ Ⓑ Ⓒ	66.	Ⓐ Ⓑ Ⓒ Ⓓ	91.	Ⓐ Ⓑ Ⓒ Ⓓ
17.	Ⓐ Ⓑ Ⓒ Ⓓ	42.	Ⓐ Ⓑ Ⓒ	67.	Ⓐ Ⓑ Ⓒ Ⓓ	92.	Ⓐ Ⓑ Ⓒ Ⓓ
18.	Ⓐ Ⓑ Ⓒ Ⓓ	43.	Ⓐ Ⓑ Ⓒ	68.	Ⓐ Ⓑ Ⓒ Ⓓ	93.	Ⓐ Ⓑ Ⓒ Ⓓ
19.	Ⓐ Ⓑ Ⓒ Ⓓ	44.	Ⓐ Ⓑ Ⓒ	69.	Ⓐ Ⓑ Ⓒ Ⓓ	94.	Ⓐ Ⓑ Ⓒ Ⓓ
20.	Ⓐ Ⓑ Ⓒ Ⓓ	45.	Ⓐ Ⓑ Ⓒ	70.	Ⓐ Ⓑ Ⓒ Ⓓ	95.	Ⓐ Ⓑ Ⓒ Ⓓ
21.	Ⓐ Ⓑ Ⓒ	46.	Ⓐ Ⓑ Ⓒ	71.	Ⓐ Ⓑ Ⓒ Ⓓ	96.	Ⓐ Ⓑ Ⓒ Ⓓ
22.	Ⓐ Ⓑ Ⓒ	47.	Ⓐ Ⓑ Ⓒ	72.	Ⓐ Ⓑ Ⓒ Ⓓ	97.	Ⓐ Ⓑ Ⓒ Ⓓ
23.	Ⓐ Ⓑ Ⓒ	48.	Ⓐ Ⓑ Ⓒ	73.	Ⓐ Ⓑ Ⓒ Ⓓ	98.	Ⓐ Ⓑ Ⓒ Ⓓ
24.	Ⓐ Ⓑ Ⓒ	49.	Ⓐ Ⓑ Ⓒ	74.	Ⓐ Ⓑ Ⓒ Ⓓ	99.	Ⓐ Ⓑ Ⓒ Ⓓ
25.	Ⓐ Ⓑ Ⓒ	50.	Ⓐ Ⓑ Ⓒ	75.	Ⓐ Ⓑ Ⓒ Ⓓ	100.	Ⓐ Ⓑ Ⓒ Ⓓ

Reading (Parts V–VII)

No.	Answer	No.	Answer	No.	Answer	No.	Answer
101.	Ⓐ Ⓑ Ⓒ Ⓓ	126.	Ⓐ Ⓑ Ⓒ Ⓓ	151.	Ⓐ Ⓑ Ⓒ Ⓓ	176.	Ⓐ Ⓑ Ⓒ Ⓓ
102.	Ⓐ Ⓑ Ⓒ Ⓓ	127.	Ⓐ Ⓑ Ⓒ Ⓓ	152.	Ⓐ Ⓑ Ⓒ Ⓓ	177.	Ⓐ Ⓑ Ⓒ Ⓓ
103.	Ⓐ Ⓑ Ⓒ Ⓓ	128.	Ⓐ Ⓑ Ⓒ Ⓓ	153.	Ⓐ Ⓑ Ⓒ Ⓓ	178.	Ⓐ Ⓑ Ⓒ Ⓓ
104.	Ⓐ Ⓑ Ⓒ Ⓓ	129.	Ⓐ Ⓑ Ⓒ Ⓓ	154.	Ⓐ Ⓑ Ⓒ Ⓓ	179.	Ⓐ Ⓑ Ⓒ Ⓓ
105.	Ⓐ Ⓑ Ⓒ Ⓓ	130.	Ⓐ Ⓑ Ⓒ Ⓓ	155.	Ⓐ Ⓑ Ⓒ Ⓓ	180.	Ⓐ Ⓑ Ⓒ Ⓓ
106.	Ⓐ Ⓑ Ⓒ Ⓓ	131.	Ⓐ Ⓑ Ⓒ Ⓓ	156.	Ⓐ Ⓑ Ⓒ Ⓓ	181.	Ⓐ Ⓑ Ⓒ Ⓓ
107.	Ⓐ Ⓑ Ⓒ Ⓓ	132.	Ⓐ Ⓑ Ⓒ Ⓓ	157.	Ⓐ Ⓑ Ⓒ Ⓓ	182.	Ⓐ Ⓑ Ⓒ Ⓓ
108.	Ⓐ Ⓑ Ⓒ Ⓓ	133.	Ⓐ Ⓑ Ⓒ Ⓓ	158.	Ⓐ Ⓑ Ⓒ Ⓓ	183.	Ⓐ Ⓑ Ⓒ Ⓓ
109.	Ⓐ Ⓑ Ⓒ Ⓓ	134.	Ⓐ Ⓑ Ⓒ Ⓓ	159.	Ⓐ Ⓑ Ⓒ Ⓓ	184.	Ⓐ Ⓑ Ⓒ Ⓓ
110.	Ⓐ Ⓑ Ⓒ Ⓓ	135.	Ⓐ Ⓑ Ⓒ Ⓓ	160.	Ⓐ Ⓑ Ⓒ Ⓓ	185.	Ⓐ Ⓑ Ⓒ Ⓓ
111.	Ⓐ Ⓑ Ⓒ Ⓓ	136.	Ⓐ Ⓑ Ⓒ Ⓓ	161.	Ⓐ Ⓑ Ⓒ Ⓓ	186.	Ⓐ Ⓑ Ⓒ Ⓓ
112.	Ⓐ Ⓑ Ⓒ Ⓓ	137.	Ⓐ Ⓑ Ⓒ Ⓓ	162.	Ⓐ Ⓑ Ⓒ Ⓓ	187.	Ⓐ Ⓑ Ⓒ Ⓓ
113.	Ⓐ Ⓑ Ⓒ Ⓓ	138.	Ⓐ Ⓑ Ⓒ Ⓓ	163.	Ⓐ Ⓑ Ⓒ Ⓓ	188.	Ⓐ Ⓑ Ⓒ Ⓓ
114.	Ⓐ Ⓑ Ⓒ Ⓓ	139.	Ⓐ Ⓑ Ⓒ Ⓓ	164.	Ⓐ Ⓑ Ⓒ Ⓓ	189.	Ⓐ Ⓑ Ⓒ Ⓓ
115.	Ⓐ Ⓑ Ⓒ Ⓓ	140.	Ⓐ Ⓑ Ⓒ Ⓓ	165.	Ⓐ Ⓑ Ⓒ Ⓓ	190.	Ⓐ Ⓑ Ⓒ Ⓓ
116.	Ⓐ Ⓑ Ⓒ Ⓓ	141.	Ⓐ Ⓑ Ⓒ Ⓓ	166.	Ⓐ Ⓑ Ⓒ Ⓓ	191.	Ⓐ Ⓑ Ⓒ Ⓓ
117.	Ⓐ Ⓑ Ⓒ Ⓓ	142.	Ⓐ Ⓑ Ⓒ Ⓓ	167.	Ⓐ Ⓑ Ⓒ Ⓓ	192.	Ⓐ Ⓑ Ⓒ Ⓓ
118.	Ⓐ Ⓑ Ⓒ Ⓓ	143.	Ⓐ Ⓑ Ⓒ Ⓓ	168.	Ⓐ Ⓑ Ⓒ Ⓓ	193.	Ⓐ Ⓑ Ⓒ Ⓓ
119.	Ⓐ Ⓑ Ⓒ Ⓓ	144.	Ⓐ Ⓑ Ⓒ Ⓓ	169.	Ⓐ Ⓑ Ⓒ Ⓓ	194.	Ⓐ Ⓑ Ⓒ Ⓓ
120.	Ⓐ Ⓑ Ⓒ Ⓓ	145.	Ⓐ Ⓑ Ⓒ Ⓓ	170.	Ⓐ Ⓑ Ⓒ Ⓓ	195.	Ⓐ Ⓑ Ⓒ Ⓓ
121.	Ⓐ Ⓑ Ⓒ Ⓓ	146.	Ⓐ Ⓑ Ⓒ Ⓓ	171.	Ⓐ Ⓑ Ⓒ Ⓓ	196.	Ⓐ Ⓑ Ⓒ Ⓓ
122.	Ⓐ Ⓑ Ⓒ Ⓓ	147.	Ⓐ Ⓑ Ⓒ Ⓓ	172.	Ⓐ Ⓑ Ⓒ Ⓓ	197.	Ⓐ Ⓑ Ⓒ Ⓓ
123.	Ⓐ Ⓑ Ⓒ Ⓓ	148.	Ⓐ Ⓑ Ⓒ Ⓓ	173.	Ⓐ Ⓑ Ⓒ Ⓓ	198.	Ⓐ Ⓑ Ⓒ Ⓓ
124.	Ⓐ Ⓑ Ⓒ Ⓓ	149.	Ⓐ Ⓑ Ⓒ Ⓓ	174.	Ⓐ Ⓑ Ⓒ Ⓓ	199.	Ⓐ Ⓑ Ⓒ Ⓓ
125.	Ⓐ Ⓑ Ⓒ Ⓓ	150.	Ⓐ Ⓑ Ⓒ Ⓓ	175.	Ⓐ Ⓑ Ⓒ Ⓓ	200.	Ⓐ Ⓑ Ⓒ Ⓓ

Answer Sheet—TOEIC® Test 3

Listening (Parts I–IV)

1. Ⓐ Ⓑ Ⓒ Ⓓ
2. Ⓐ Ⓑ Ⓒ Ⓓ
3. Ⓐ Ⓑ Ⓒ Ⓓ
4. Ⓐ Ⓑ Ⓒ Ⓓ
5. Ⓐ Ⓑ Ⓒ Ⓓ
6. Ⓐ Ⓑ Ⓒ Ⓓ
7. Ⓐ Ⓑ Ⓒ Ⓓ
8. Ⓐ Ⓑ Ⓒ Ⓓ
9. Ⓐ Ⓑ Ⓒ Ⓓ
10. Ⓐ Ⓑ Ⓒ Ⓓ
11. Ⓐ Ⓑ Ⓒ Ⓓ
12. Ⓐ Ⓑ Ⓒ Ⓓ
13. Ⓐ Ⓑ Ⓒ Ⓓ
14. Ⓐ Ⓑ Ⓒ Ⓓ
15. Ⓐ Ⓑ Ⓒ Ⓓ
16. Ⓐ Ⓑ Ⓒ Ⓓ
17. Ⓐ Ⓑ Ⓒ Ⓓ
18. Ⓐ Ⓑ Ⓒ Ⓓ
19. Ⓐ Ⓑ Ⓒ Ⓓ
20. Ⓐ Ⓑ Ⓒ Ⓓ
21. Ⓐ Ⓑ Ⓒ
22. Ⓐ Ⓑ Ⓒ
23. Ⓐ Ⓑ Ⓒ
24. Ⓐ Ⓑ Ⓒ
25. Ⓐ Ⓑ Ⓒ
26. Ⓐ Ⓑ Ⓒ
27. Ⓐ Ⓑ Ⓒ
28. Ⓐ Ⓑ Ⓒ
29. Ⓐ Ⓑ Ⓒ
30. Ⓐ Ⓑ Ⓒ
31. Ⓐ Ⓑ Ⓒ
32. Ⓐ Ⓑ Ⓒ
33. Ⓐ Ⓑ Ⓒ
34. Ⓐ Ⓑ Ⓒ
35. Ⓐ Ⓑ Ⓒ
36. Ⓐ Ⓑ Ⓒ
37. Ⓐ Ⓑ Ⓒ
38. Ⓐ Ⓑ Ⓒ
39. Ⓐ Ⓑ Ⓒ
40. Ⓐ Ⓑ Ⓒ
41. Ⓐ Ⓑ Ⓒ
42. Ⓐ Ⓑ Ⓒ
43. Ⓐ Ⓑ Ⓒ
44. Ⓐ Ⓑ Ⓒ
45. Ⓐ Ⓑ Ⓒ
46. Ⓐ Ⓑ Ⓒ
47. Ⓐ Ⓑ Ⓒ
48. Ⓐ Ⓑ Ⓒ
49. Ⓐ Ⓑ Ⓒ
50. Ⓐ Ⓑ Ⓒ
51. Ⓐ Ⓑ Ⓒ Ⓓ
52. Ⓐ Ⓑ Ⓒ Ⓓ
53. Ⓐ Ⓑ Ⓒ Ⓓ
54. Ⓐ Ⓑ Ⓒ Ⓓ
55. Ⓐ Ⓑ Ⓒ Ⓓ
56. Ⓐ Ⓑ Ⓒ Ⓓ
57. Ⓐ Ⓑ Ⓒ Ⓓ
58. Ⓐ Ⓑ Ⓒ Ⓓ
59. Ⓐ Ⓑ Ⓒ Ⓓ
60. Ⓐ Ⓑ Ⓒ Ⓓ
61. Ⓐ Ⓑ Ⓒ Ⓓ
62. Ⓐ Ⓑ Ⓒ Ⓓ
63. Ⓐ Ⓑ Ⓒ Ⓓ
64. Ⓐ Ⓑ Ⓒ Ⓓ
65. Ⓐ Ⓑ Ⓒ Ⓓ
66. Ⓐ Ⓑ Ⓒ Ⓓ
67. Ⓐ Ⓑ Ⓒ Ⓓ
68. Ⓐ Ⓑ Ⓒ Ⓓ
69. Ⓐ Ⓑ Ⓒ Ⓓ
70. Ⓐ Ⓑ Ⓒ Ⓓ
71. Ⓐ Ⓑ Ⓒ Ⓓ
72. Ⓐ Ⓑ Ⓒ Ⓓ
73. Ⓐ Ⓑ Ⓒ Ⓓ
74. Ⓐ Ⓑ Ⓒ Ⓓ
75. Ⓐ Ⓑ Ⓒ Ⓓ
76. Ⓐ Ⓑ Ⓒ Ⓓ
77. Ⓐ Ⓑ Ⓒ Ⓓ
78. Ⓐ Ⓑ Ⓒ Ⓓ
79. Ⓐ Ⓑ Ⓒ Ⓓ
80. Ⓐ Ⓑ Ⓒ Ⓓ
81. Ⓐ Ⓑ Ⓒ Ⓓ
82. Ⓐ Ⓑ Ⓒ Ⓓ
83. Ⓐ Ⓑ Ⓒ Ⓓ
84. Ⓐ Ⓑ Ⓒ Ⓓ
85. Ⓐ Ⓑ Ⓒ Ⓓ
86. Ⓐ Ⓑ Ⓒ Ⓓ
87. Ⓐ Ⓑ Ⓒ Ⓓ
88. Ⓐ Ⓑ Ⓒ Ⓓ
89. Ⓐ Ⓑ Ⓒ Ⓓ
90. Ⓐ Ⓑ Ⓒ Ⓓ
91. Ⓐ Ⓑ Ⓒ Ⓓ
92. Ⓐ Ⓑ Ⓒ Ⓓ
93. Ⓐ Ⓑ Ⓒ Ⓓ
94. Ⓐ Ⓑ Ⓒ Ⓓ
95. Ⓐ Ⓑ Ⓒ Ⓓ
96. Ⓐ Ⓑ Ⓒ Ⓓ
97. Ⓐ Ⓑ Ⓒ Ⓓ
98. Ⓐ Ⓑ Ⓒ Ⓓ
99. Ⓐ Ⓑ Ⓒ Ⓓ
100. Ⓐ Ⓑ Ⓒ Ⓓ

Reading (Parts V–VII)

101. Ⓐ Ⓑ Ⓒ Ⓓ
102. Ⓐ Ⓑ Ⓒ Ⓓ
103. Ⓐ Ⓑ Ⓒ Ⓓ
104. Ⓐ Ⓑ Ⓒ Ⓓ
105. Ⓐ Ⓑ Ⓒ Ⓓ
106. Ⓐ Ⓑ Ⓒ Ⓓ
107. Ⓐ Ⓑ Ⓒ Ⓓ
108. Ⓐ Ⓑ Ⓒ Ⓓ
109. Ⓐ Ⓑ Ⓒ Ⓓ
110. Ⓐ Ⓑ Ⓒ Ⓓ
111. Ⓐ Ⓑ Ⓒ Ⓓ
112. Ⓐ Ⓑ Ⓒ Ⓓ
113. Ⓐ Ⓑ Ⓒ Ⓓ
114. Ⓐ Ⓑ Ⓒ Ⓓ
115. Ⓐ Ⓑ Ⓒ Ⓓ
116. Ⓐ Ⓑ Ⓒ Ⓓ
117. Ⓐ Ⓑ Ⓒ Ⓓ
118. Ⓐ Ⓑ Ⓒ Ⓓ
119. Ⓐ Ⓑ Ⓒ Ⓓ
120. Ⓐ Ⓑ Ⓒ Ⓓ
121. Ⓐ Ⓑ Ⓒ Ⓓ
122. Ⓐ Ⓑ Ⓒ Ⓓ
123. Ⓐ Ⓑ Ⓒ Ⓓ
124. Ⓐ Ⓑ Ⓒ Ⓓ
125. Ⓐ Ⓑ Ⓒ Ⓓ
126. Ⓐ Ⓑ Ⓒ Ⓓ
127. Ⓐ Ⓑ Ⓒ Ⓓ
128. Ⓐ Ⓑ Ⓒ Ⓓ
129. Ⓐ Ⓑ Ⓒ Ⓓ
130. Ⓐ Ⓑ Ⓒ Ⓓ
131. Ⓐ Ⓑ Ⓒ Ⓓ
132. Ⓐ Ⓑ Ⓒ Ⓓ
133. Ⓐ Ⓑ Ⓒ Ⓓ
134. Ⓐ Ⓑ Ⓒ Ⓓ
135. Ⓐ Ⓑ Ⓒ Ⓓ
136. Ⓐ Ⓑ Ⓒ Ⓓ
137. Ⓐ Ⓑ Ⓒ Ⓓ
138. Ⓐ Ⓑ Ⓒ Ⓓ
139. Ⓐ Ⓑ Ⓒ Ⓓ
140. Ⓐ Ⓑ Ⓒ Ⓓ
141. Ⓐ Ⓑ Ⓒ Ⓓ
142. Ⓐ Ⓑ Ⓒ Ⓓ
143. Ⓐ Ⓑ Ⓒ Ⓓ
144. Ⓐ Ⓑ Ⓒ Ⓓ
145. Ⓐ Ⓑ Ⓒ Ⓓ
146. Ⓐ Ⓑ Ⓒ Ⓓ
147. Ⓐ Ⓑ Ⓒ Ⓓ
148. Ⓐ Ⓑ Ⓒ Ⓓ
149. Ⓐ Ⓑ Ⓒ Ⓓ
150. Ⓐ Ⓑ Ⓒ Ⓓ
151. Ⓐ Ⓑ Ⓒ Ⓓ
152. Ⓐ Ⓑ Ⓒ Ⓓ
153. Ⓐ Ⓑ Ⓒ Ⓓ
154. Ⓐ Ⓑ Ⓒ Ⓓ
155. Ⓐ Ⓑ Ⓒ Ⓓ
156. Ⓐ Ⓑ Ⓒ Ⓓ
157. Ⓐ Ⓑ Ⓒ Ⓓ
158. Ⓐ Ⓑ Ⓒ Ⓓ
159. Ⓐ Ⓑ Ⓒ Ⓓ
160. Ⓐ Ⓑ Ⓒ Ⓓ
161. Ⓐ Ⓑ Ⓒ Ⓓ
162. Ⓐ Ⓑ Ⓒ Ⓓ
163. Ⓐ Ⓑ Ⓒ Ⓓ
164. Ⓐ Ⓑ Ⓒ Ⓓ
165. Ⓐ Ⓑ Ⓒ Ⓓ
166. Ⓐ Ⓑ Ⓒ Ⓓ
167. Ⓐ Ⓑ Ⓒ Ⓓ
168. Ⓐ Ⓑ Ⓒ Ⓓ
169. Ⓐ Ⓑ Ⓒ Ⓓ
170. Ⓐ Ⓑ Ⓒ Ⓓ
171. Ⓐ Ⓑ Ⓒ Ⓓ
172. Ⓐ Ⓑ Ⓒ Ⓓ
173. Ⓐ Ⓑ Ⓒ Ⓓ
174. Ⓐ Ⓑ Ⓒ Ⓓ
175. Ⓐ Ⓑ Ⓒ Ⓓ
176. Ⓐ Ⓑ Ⓒ Ⓓ
177. Ⓐ Ⓑ Ⓒ Ⓓ
178. Ⓐ Ⓑ Ⓒ Ⓓ
179. Ⓐ Ⓑ Ⓒ Ⓓ
180. Ⓐ Ⓑ Ⓒ Ⓓ
181. Ⓐ Ⓑ Ⓒ Ⓓ
182. Ⓐ Ⓑ Ⓒ Ⓓ
183. Ⓐ Ⓑ Ⓒ Ⓓ
184. Ⓐ Ⓑ Ⓒ Ⓓ
185. Ⓐ Ⓑ Ⓒ Ⓓ
186. Ⓐ Ⓑ Ⓒ Ⓓ
187. Ⓐ Ⓑ Ⓒ Ⓓ
188. Ⓐ Ⓑ Ⓒ Ⓓ
189. Ⓐ Ⓑ Ⓒ Ⓓ
190. Ⓐ Ⓑ Ⓒ Ⓓ
191. Ⓐ Ⓑ Ⓒ Ⓓ
192. Ⓐ Ⓑ Ⓒ Ⓓ
193. Ⓐ Ⓑ Ⓒ Ⓓ
194. Ⓐ Ⓑ Ⓒ Ⓓ
195. Ⓐ Ⓑ Ⓒ Ⓓ
196. Ⓐ Ⓑ Ⓒ Ⓓ
197. Ⓐ Ⓑ Ⓒ Ⓓ
198. Ⓐ Ⓑ Ⓒ Ⓓ
199. Ⓐ Ⓑ Ⓒ Ⓓ
200. Ⓐ Ⓑ Ⓒ Ⓓ

Answer Sheet—TOEIC® Test 4

Listening (Parts I–IV)

1. Ⓐ Ⓑ Ⓒ Ⓓ
2. Ⓐ Ⓑ Ⓒ Ⓓ
3. Ⓐ Ⓑ Ⓒ Ⓓ
4. Ⓐ Ⓑ Ⓒ Ⓓ
5. Ⓐ Ⓑ Ⓒ Ⓓ
6. Ⓐ Ⓑ Ⓒ Ⓓ
7. Ⓐ Ⓑ Ⓒ Ⓓ
8. Ⓐ Ⓑ Ⓒ Ⓓ
9. Ⓐ Ⓑ Ⓒ Ⓓ
10. Ⓐ Ⓑ Ⓒ Ⓓ
11. Ⓐ Ⓑ Ⓒ Ⓓ
12. Ⓐ Ⓑ Ⓒ Ⓓ
13. Ⓐ Ⓑ Ⓒ Ⓓ
14. Ⓐ Ⓑ Ⓒ Ⓓ
15. Ⓐ Ⓑ Ⓒ Ⓓ
16. Ⓐ Ⓑ Ⓒ Ⓓ
17. Ⓐ Ⓑ Ⓒ Ⓓ
18. Ⓐ Ⓑ Ⓒ Ⓓ
19. Ⓐ Ⓑ Ⓒ Ⓓ
20. Ⓐ Ⓑ Ⓒ Ⓓ
21. Ⓐ Ⓑ Ⓒ
22. Ⓐ Ⓑ Ⓒ
23. Ⓐ Ⓑ Ⓒ
24. Ⓐ Ⓑ Ⓒ
25. Ⓐ Ⓑ Ⓒ
26. Ⓐ Ⓑ Ⓒ
27. Ⓐ Ⓑ Ⓒ
28. Ⓐ Ⓑ Ⓒ
29. Ⓐ Ⓑ Ⓒ
30. Ⓐ Ⓑ Ⓒ
31. Ⓐ Ⓑ Ⓒ
32. Ⓐ Ⓑ Ⓒ
33. Ⓐ Ⓑ Ⓒ
34. Ⓐ Ⓑ Ⓒ
35. Ⓐ Ⓑ Ⓒ
36. Ⓐ Ⓑ Ⓒ
37. Ⓐ Ⓑ Ⓒ
38. Ⓐ Ⓑ Ⓒ
39. Ⓐ Ⓑ Ⓒ
40. Ⓐ Ⓑ Ⓒ
41. Ⓐ Ⓑ Ⓒ
42. Ⓐ Ⓑ Ⓒ
43. Ⓐ Ⓑ Ⓒ
44. Ⓐ Ⓑ Ⓒ
45. Ⓐ Ⓑ Ⓒ
46. Ⓐ Ⓑ Ⓒ
47. Ⓐ Ⓑ Ⓒ
48. Ⓐ Ⓑ Ⓒ
49. Ⓐ Ⓑ Ⓒ
50. Ⓐ Ⓑ Ⓒ
51. Ⓐ Ⓑ Ⓒ Ⓓ
52. Ⓐ Ⓑ Ⓒ Ⓓ
53. Ⓐ Ⓑ Ⓒ Ⓓ
54. Ⓐ Ⓑ Ⓒ Ⓓ
55. Ⓐ Ⓑ Ⓒ Ⓓ
56. Ⓐ Ⓑ Ⓒ Ⓓ
57. Ⓐ Ⓑ Ⓒ Ⓓ
58. Ⓐ Ⓑ Ⓒ Ⓓ
59. Ⓐ Ⓑ Ⓒ Ⓓ
60. Ⓐ Ⓑ Ⓒ Ⓓ
61. Ⓐ Ⓑ Ⓒ Ⓓ
62. Ⓐ Ⓑ Ⓒ Ⓓ
63. Ⓐ Ⓑ Ⓒ Ⓓ
64. Ⓐ Ⓑ Ⓒ Ⓓ
65. Ⓐ Ⓑ Ⓒ Ⓓ
66. Ⓐ Ⓑ Ⓒ Ⓓ
67. Ⓐ Ⓑ Ⓒ Ⓓ
68. Ⓐ Ⓑ Ⓒ Ⓓ
69. Ⓐ Ⓑ Ⓒ Ⓓ
70. Ⓐ Ⓑ Ⓒ Ⓓ
71. Ⓐ Ⓑ Ⓒ Ⓓ
72. Ⓐ Ⓑ Ⓒ Ⓓ
73. Ⓐ Ⓑ Ⓒ Ⓓ
74. Ⓐ Ⓑ Ⓒ Ⓓ
75. Ⓐ Ⓑ Ⓒ Ⓓ
76. Ⓐ Ⓑ Ⓒ Ⓓ
77. Ⓐ Ⓑ Ⓒ Ⓓ
78. Ⓐ Ⓑ Ⓒ Ⓓ
79. Ⓐ Ⓑ Ⓒ Ⓓ
80. Ⓐ Ⓑ Ⓒ Ⓓ
81. Ⓐ Ⓑ Ⓒ Ⓓ
82. Ⓐ Ⓑ Ⓒ Ⓓ
83. Ⓐ Ⓑ Ⓒ Ⓓ
84. Ⓐ Ⓑ Ⓒ Ⓓ
85. Ⓐ Ⓑ Ⓒ Ⓓ
86. Ⓐ Ⓑ Ⓒ Ⓓ
87. Ⓐ Ⓑ Ⓒ Ⓓ
88. Ⓐ Ⓑ Ⓒ Ⓓ
89. Ⓐ Ⓑ Ⓒ Ⓓ
90. Ⓐ Ⓑ Ⓒ Ⓓ
91. Ⓐ Ⓑ Ⓒ Ⓓ
92. Ⓐ Ⓑ Ⓒ Ⓓ
93. Ⓐ Ⓑ Ⓒ Ⓓ
94. Ⓐ Ⓑ Ⓒ Ⓓ
95. Ⓐ Ⓑ Ⓒ Ⓓ
96. Ⓐ Ⓑ Ⓒ Ⓓ
97. Ⓐ Ⓑ Ⓒ Ⓓ
98. Ⓐ Ⓑ Ⓒ Ⓓ
99. Ⓐ Ⓑ Ⓒ Ⓓ
100. Ⓐ Ⓑ Ⓒ Ⓓ

Reading (Parts V–VII)

101. Ⓐ Ⓑ Ⓒ Ⓓ
102. Ⓐ Ⓑ Ⓒ Ⓓ
103. Ⓐ Ⓑ Ⓒ Ⓓ
104. Ⓐ Ⓑ Ⓒ Ⓓ
105. Ⓐ Ⓑ Ⓒ Ⓓ
106. Ⓐ Ⓑ Ⓒ Ⓓ
107. Ⓐ Ⓑ Ⓒ Ⓓ
108. Ⓐ Ⓑ Ⓒ Ⓓ
109. Ⓐ Ⓑ Ⓒ Ⓓ
110. Ⓐ Ⓑ Ⓒ Ⓓ
111. Ⓐ Ⓑ Ⓒ Ⓓ
112. Ⓐ Ⓑ Ⓒ Ⓓ
113. Ⓐ Ⓑ Ⓒ Ⓓ
114. Ⓐ Ⓑ Ⓒ Ⓓ
115. Ⓐ Ⓑ Ⓒ Ⓓ
116. Ⓐ Ⓑ Ⓒ Ⓓ
117. Ⓐ Ⓑ Ⓒ Ⓓ
118. Ⓐ Ⓑ Ⓒ Ⓓ
119. Ⓐ Ⓑ Ⓒ Ⓓ
120. Ⓐ Ⓑ Ⓒ Ⓓ
121. Ⓐ Ⓑ Ⓒ Ⓓ
122. Ⓐ Ⓑ Ⓒ Ⓓ
123. Ⓐ Ⓑ Ⓒ Ⓓ
124. Ⓐ Ⓑ Ⓒ Ⓓ
125. Ⓐ Ⓑ Ⓒ Ⓓ
126. Ⓐ Ⓑ Ⓒ Ⓓ
127. Ⓐ Ⓑ Ⓒ Ⓓ
128. Ⓐ Ⓑ Ⓒ Ⓓ
129. Ⓐ Ⓑ Ⓒ Ⓓ
130. Ⓐ Ⓑ Ⓒ Ⓓ
131. Ⓐ Ⓑ Ⓒ Ⓓ
132. Ⓐ Ⓑ Ⓒ Ⓓ
133. Ⓐ Ⓑ Ⓒ Ⓓ
134. Ⓐ Ⓑ Ⓒ Ⓓ
135. Ⓐ Ⓑ Ⓒ Ⓓ
136. Ⓐ Ⓑ Ⓒ Ⓓ
137. Ⓐ Ⓑ Ⓒ Ⓓ
138. Ⓐ Ⓑ Ⓒ Ⓓ
139. Ⓐ Ⓑ Ⓒ Ⓓ
140. Ⓐ Ⓑ Ⓒ Ⓓ
141. Ⓐ Ⓑ Ⓒ Ⓓ
142. Ⓐ Ⓑ Ⓒ Ⓓ
143. Ⓐ Ⓑ Ⓒ Ⓓ
144. Ⓐ Ⓑ Ⓒ Ⓓ
145. Ⓐ Ⓑ Ⓒ Ⓓ
146. Ⓐ Ⓑ Ⓒ Ⓓ
147. Ⓐ Ⓑ Ⓒ Ⓓ
148. Ⓐ Ⓑ Ⓒ Ⓓ
149. Ⓐ Ⓑ Ⓒ Ⓓ
150. Ⓐ Ⓑ Ⓒ Ⓓ
151. Ⓐ Ⓑ Ⓒ Ⓓ
152. Ⓐ Ⓑ Ⓒ Ⓓ
153. Ⓐ Ⓑ Ⓒ Ⓓ
154. Ⓐ Ⓑ Ⓒ Ⓓ
155. Ⓐ Ⓑ Ⓒ Ⓓ
156. Ⓐ Ⓑ Ⓒ Ⓓ
157. Ⓐ Ⓑ Ⓒ Ⓓ
158. Ⓐ Ⓑ Ⓒ Ⓓ
159. Ⓐ Ⓑ Ⓒ Ⓓ
160. Ⓐ Ⓑ Ⓒ Ⓓ
161. Ⓐ Ⓑ Ⓒ Ⓓ
162. Ⓐ Ⓑ Ⓒ Ⓓ
163. Ⓐ Ⓑ Ⓒ Ⓓ
164. Ⓐ Ⓑ Ⓒ Ⓓ
165. Ⓐ Ⓑ Ⓒ Ⓓ
166. Ⓐ Ⓑ Ⓒ Ⓓ
167. Ⓐ Ⓑ Ⓒ Ⓓ
168. Ⓐ Ⓑ Ⓒ Ⓓ
169. Ⓐ Ⓑ Ⓒ Ⓓ
170. Ⓐ Ⓑ Ⓒ Ⓓ
171. Ⓐ Ⓑ Ⓒ Ⓓ
172. Ⓐ Ⓑ Ⓒ Ⓓ
173. Ⓐ Ⓑ Ⓒ Ⓓ
174. Ⓐ Ⓑ Ⓒ Ⓓ
175. Ⓐ Ⓑ Ⓒ Ⓓ
176. Ⓐ Ⓑ Ⓒ Ⓓ
177. Ⓐ Ⓑ Ⓒ Ⓓ
178. Ⓐ Ⓑ Ⓒ Ⓓ
179. Ⓐ Ⓑ Ⓒ Ⓓ
180. Ⓐ Ⓑ Ⓒ Ⓓ
181. Ⓐ Ⓑ Ⓒ Ⓓ
182. Ⓐ Ⓑ Ⓒ Ⓓ
183. Ⓐ Ⓑ Ⓒ Ⓓ
184. Ⓐ Ⓑ Ⓒ Ⓓ
185. Ⓐ Ⓑ Ⓒ Ⓓ
186. Ⓐ Ⓑ Ⓒ Ⓓ
187. Ⓐ Ⓑ Ⓒ Ⓓ
188. Ⓐ Ⓑ Ⓒ Ⓓ
189. Ⓐ Ⓑ Ⓒ Ⓓ
190. Ⓐ Ⓑ Ⓒ Ⓓ
191. Ⓐ Ⓑ Ⓒ Ⓓ
192. Ⓐ Ⓑ Ⓒ Ⓓ
193. Ⓐ Ⓑ Ⓒ Ⓓ
194. Ⓐ Ⓑ Ⓒ Ⓓ
195. Ⓐ Ⓑ Ⓒ Ⓓ
196. Ⓐ Ⓑ Ⓒ Ⓓ
197. Ⓐ Ⓑ Ⓒ Ⓓ
198. Ⓐ Ⓑ Ⓒ Ⓓ
199. Ⓐ Ⓑ Ⓒ Ⓓ
200. Ⓐ Ⓑ Ⓒ Ⓓ

Answer Sheet—TOEIC® Test 5

Listening (Parts I–IV)

1. (A) (B) (C) (D)
2. (A) (B) (C) (D)
3. (A) (B) (C) (D)
4. (A) (B) (C) (D)
5. (A) (B) (C) (D)
6. (A) (B) (C) (D)
7. (A) (B) (C) (D)
8. (A) (B) (C) (D)
9. (A) (B) (C) (D)
10. (A) (B) (C) (D)
11. (A) (B) (C) (D)
12. (A) (B) (C) (D)
13. (A) (B) (C) (D)
14. (A) (B) (C) (D)
15. (A) (B) (C) (D)
16. (A) (B) (C) (D)
17. (A) (B) (C) (D)
18. (A) (B) (C) (D)
19. (A) (B) (C) (D)
20. (A) (B) (C) (D)
21. (A) (B) (C)
22. (A) (B) (C)
23. (A) (B) (C)
24. (A) (B) (C)
25. (A) (B) (C)
26. (A) (B) (C)
27. (A) (B) (C)
28. (A) (B) (C)
29. (A) (B) (C)
30. (A) (B) (C)
31. (A) (B) (C)
32. (A) (B) (C)
33. (A) (B) (C)
34. (A) (B) (C)
35. (A) (B) (C)
36. (A) (B) (C)
37. (A) (B) (C)
38. (A) (B) (C)
39. (A) (B) (C)
40. (A) (B) (C)
41. (A) (B) (C)
42. (A) (B) (C)
43. (A) (B) (C)
44. (A) (B) (C)
45. (A) (B) (C)
46. (A) (B) (C)
47. (A) (B) (C)
48. (A) (B) (C)
49. (A) (B) (C)
50. (A) (B) (C)
51. (A) (B) (C) (D)
52. (A) (B) (C) (D)
53. (A) (B) (C) (D)
54. (A) (B) (C) (D)
55. (A) (B) (C) (D)
56. (A) (B) (C) (D)
57. (A) (B) (C) (D)
58. (A) (B) (C) (D)
59. (A) (B) (C) (D)
60. (A) (B) (C) (D)
61. (A) (B) (C) (D)
62. (A) (B) (C) (D)
63. (A) (B) (C) (D)
64. (A) (B) (C) (D)
65. (A) (B) (C) (D)
66. (A) (B) (C) (D)
67. (A) (B) (C) (D)
68. (A) (B) (C) (D)
69. (A) (B) (C) (D)
70. (A) (B) (C) (D)
71. (A) (B) (C) (D)
72. (A) (B) (C) (D)
73. (A) (B) (C) (D)
74. (A) (B) (C) (D)
75. (A) (B) (C) (D)
76. (A) (B) (C) (D)
77. (A) (B) (C) (D)
78. (A) (B) (C) (D)
79. (A) (B) (C) (D)
80. (A) (B) (C) (D)
81. (A) (B) (C) (D)
82. (A) (B) (C) (D)
83. (A) (B) (C) (D)
84. (A) (B) (C) (D)
85. (A) (B) (C) (D)
86. (A) (B) (C) (D)
87. (A) (B) (C) (D)
88. (A) (B) (C) (D)
89. (A) (B) (C) (D)
90. (A) (B) (C) (D)
91. (A) (B) (C) (D)
92. (A) (B) (C) (D)
93. (A) (B) (C) (D)
94. (A) (B) (C) (D)
95. (A) (B) (C) (D)
96. (A) (B) (C) (D)
97. (A) (B) (C) (D)
98. (A) (B) (C) (D)
99. (A) (B) (C) (D)
100. (A) (B) (C) (D)

Reading (Parts V–VII)

101. (A) (B) (C) (D)
102. (A) (B) (C) (D)
103. (A) (B) (C) (D)
104. (A) (B) (C) (D)
105. (A) (B) (C) (D)
106. (A) (B) (C) (D)
107. (A) (B) (C) (D)
108. (A) (B) (C) (D)
109. (A) (B) (C) (D)
110. (A) (B) (C) (D)
111. (A) (B) (C) (D)
112. (A) (B) (C) (D)
113. (A) (B) (C) (D)
114. (A) (B) (C) (D)
115. (A) (B) (C) (D)
116. (A) (B) (C) (D)
117. (A) (B) (C) (D)
118. (A) (B) (C) (D)
119. (A) (B) (C) (D)
120. (A) (B) (C) (D)
121. (A) (B) (C) (D)
122. (A) (B) (C) (D)
123. (A) (B) (C) (D)
124. (A) (B) (C) (D)
125. (A) (B) (C) (D)
126. (A) (B) (C) (D)
127. (A) (B) (C) (D)
128. (A) (B) (C) (D)
129. (A) (B) (C) (D)
130. (A) (B) (C) (D)
131. (A) (B) (C) (D)
132. (A) (B) (C) (D)
133. (A) (B) (C) (D)
134. (A) (B) (C) (D)
135. (A) (B) (C) (D)
136. (A) (B) (C) (D)
137. (A) (B) (C) (D)
138. (A) (B) (C) (D)
139. (A) (B) (C) (D)
140. (A) (B) (C) (D)
141. (A) (B) (C) (D)
142. (A) (B) (C) (D)
143. (A) (B) (C) (D)
144. (A) (B) (C) (D)
145. (A) (B) (C) (D)
146. (A) (B) (C) (D)
147. (A) (B) (C) (D)
148. (A) (B) (C) (D)
149. (A) (B) (C) (D)
150. (A) (B) (C) (D)
151. (A) (B) (C) (D)
152. (A) (B) (C) (D)
153. (A) (B) (C) (D)
154. (A) (B) (C) (D)
155. (A) (B) (C) (D)
156. (A) (B) (C) (D)
157. (A) (B) (C) (D)
158. (A) (B) (C) (D)
159. (A) (B) (C) (D)
160. (A) (B) (C) (D)
161. (A) (B) (C) (D)
162. (A) (B) (C) (D)
163. (A) (B) (C) (D)
164. (A) (B) (C) (D)
165. (A) (B) (C) (D)
166. (A) (B) (C) (D)
167. (A) (B) (C) (D)
168. (A) (B) (C) (D)
169. (A) (B) (C) (D)
170. (A) (B) (C) (D)
171. (A) (B) (C) (D)
172. (A) (B) (C) (D)
173. (A) (B) (C) (D)
174. (A) (B) (C) (D)
175. (A) (B) (C) (D)
176. (A) (B) (C) (D)
177. (A) (B) (C) (D)
178. (A) (B) (C) (D)
179. (A) (B) (C) (D)
180. (A) (B) (C) (D)
181. (A) (B) (C) (D)
182. (A) (B) (C) (D)
183. (A) (B) (C) (D)
184. (A) (B) (C) (D)
185. (A) (B) (C) (D)
186. (A) (B) (C) (D)
187. (A) (B) (C) (D)
188. (A) (B) (C) (D)
189. (A) (B) (C) (D)
190. (A) (B) (C) (D)
191. (A) (B) (C) (D)
192. (A) (B) (C) (D)
193. (A) (B) (C) (D)
194. (A) (B) (C) (D)
195. (A) (B) (C) (D)
196. (A) (B) (C) (D)
197. (A) (B) (C) (D)
198. (A) (B) (C) (D)
199. (A) (B) (C) (D)
200. (A) (B) (C) (D)

Answer Sheet—TOEIC® Test 6

Listening (Parts I–IV)

1. Ⓐ Ⓑ Ⓒ Ⓓ
2. Ⓐ Ⓑ Ⓒ Ⓓ
3. Ⓐ Ⓑ Ⓒ Ⓓ
4. Ⓐ Ⓑ Ⓒ Ⓓ
5. Ⓐ Ⓑ Ⓒ Ⓓ
6. Ⓐ Ⓑ Ⓒ Ⓓ
7. Ⓐ Ⓑ Ⓒ Ⓓ
8. Ⓐ Ⓑ Ⓒ Ⓓ
9. Ⓐ Ⓑ Ⓒ Ⓓ
10. Ⓐ Ⓑ Ⓒ Ⓓ
11. Ⓐ Ⓑ Ⓒ Ⓓ
12. Ⓐ Ⓑ Ⓒ Ⓓ
13. Ⓐ Ⓑ Ⓒ Ⓓ
14. Ⓐ Ⓑ Ⓒ Ⓓ
15. Ⓐ Ⓑ Ⓒ Ⓓ
16. Ⓐ Ⓑ Ⓒ Ⓓ
17. Ⓐ Ⓑ Ⓒ Ⓓ
18. Ⓐ Ⓑ Ⓒ Ⓓ
19. Ⓐ Ⓑ Ⓒ Ⓓ
20. Ⓐ Ⓑ Ⓒ Ⓓ
21. Ⓐ Ⓑ Ⓒ
22. Ⓐ Ⓑ Ⓒ
23. Ⓐ Ⓑ Ⓒ
24. Ⓐ Ⓑ Ⓒ
25. Ⓐ Ⓑ Ⓒ
26. Ⓐ Ⓑ Ⓒ
27. Ⓐ Ⓑ Ⓒ
28. Ⓐ Ⓑ Ⓒ
29. Ⓐ Ⓑ Ⓒ
30. Ⓐ Ⓑ Ⓒ
31. Ⓐ Ⓑ Ⓒ
32. Ⓐ Ⓑ Ⓒ
33. Ⓐ Ⓑ Ⓒ
34. Ⓐ Ⓑ Ⓒ
35. Ⓐ Ⓑ Ⓒ
36. Ⓐ Ⓑ Ⓒ
37. Ⓐ Ⓑ Ⓒ
38. Ⓐ Ⓑ Ⓒ
39. Ⓐ Ⓑ Ⓒ
40. Ⓐ Ⓑ Ⓒ
41. Ⓐ Ⓑ Ⓒ
42. Ⓐ Ⓑ Ⓒ
43. Ⓐ Ⓑ Ⓒ
44. Ⓐ Ⓑ Ⓒ
45. Ⓐ Ⓑ Ⓒ
46. Ⓐ Ⓑ Ⓒ
47. Ⓐ Ⓑ Ⓒ
48. Ⓐ Ⓑ Ⓒ
49. Ⓐ Ⓑ Ⓒ
50. Ⓐ Ⓑ Ⓒ
51. Ⓐ Ⓑ Ⓒ Ⓓ
52. Ⓐ Ⓑ Ⓒ Ⓓ
53. Ⓐ Ⓑ Ⓒ Ⓓ
54. Ⓐ Ⓑ Ⓒ Ⓓ
55. Ⓐ Ⓑ Ⓒ Ⓓ
56. Ⓐ Ⓑ Ⓒ Ⓓ
57. Ⓐ Ⓑ Ⓒ Ⓓ
58. Ⓐ Ⓑ Ⓒ Ⓓ
59. Ⓐ Ⓑ Ⓒ Ⓓ
60. Ⓐ Ⓑ Ⓒ Ⓓ
61. Ⓐ Ⓑ Ⓒ Ⓓ
62. Ⓐ Ⓑ Ⓒ Ⓓ
63. Ⓐ Ⓑ Ⓒ Ⓓ
64. Ⓐ Ⓑ Ⓒ Ⓓ
65. Ⓐ Ⓑ Ⓒ Ⓓ
66. Ⓐ Ⓑ Ⓒ Ⓓ
67. Ⓐ Ⓑ Ⓒ Ⓓ
68. Ⓐ Ⓑ Ⓒ Ⓓ
69. Ⓐ Ⓑ Ⓒ Ⓓ
70. Ⓐ Ⓑ Ⓒ Ⓓ
71. Ⓐ Ⓑ Ⓒ Ⓓ
72. Ⓐ Ⓑ Ⓒ Ⓓ
73. Ⓐ Ⓑ Ⓒ Ⓓ
74. Ⓐ Ⓑ Ⓒ Ⓓ
75. Ⓐ Ⓑ Ⓒ Ⓓ
76. Ⓐ Ⓑ Ⓒ Ⓓ
77. Ⓐ Ⓑ Ⓒ Ⓓ
78. Ⓐ Ⓑ Ⓒ Ⓓ
79. Ⓐ Ⓑ Ⓒ Ⓓ
80. Ⓐ Ⓑ Ⓒ Ⓓ
81. Ⓐ Ⓑ Ⓒ Ⓓ
82. Ⓐ Ⓑ Ⓒ Ⓓ
83. Ⓐ Ⓑ Ⓒ Ⓓ
84. Ⓐ Ⓑ Ⓒ Ⓓ
85. Ⓐ Ⓑ Ⓒ Ⓓ
86. Ⓐ Ⓑ Ⓒ Ⓓ
87. Ⓐ Ⓑ Ⓒ Ⓓ
88. Ⓐ Ⓑ Ⓒ Ⓓ
89. Ⓐ Ⓑ Ⓒ Ⓓ
90. Ⓐ Ⓑ Ⓒ Ⓓ
91. Ⓐ Ⓑ Ⓒ Ⓓ
92. Ⓐ Ⓑ Ⓒ Ⓓ
93. Ⓐ Ⓑ Ⓒ Ⓓ
94. Ⓐ Ⓑ Ⓒ Ⓓ
95. Ⓐ Ⓑ Ⓒ Ⓓ
96. Ⓐ Ⓑ Ⓒ Ⓓ
97. Ⓐ Ⓑ Ⓒ Ⓓ
98. Ⓐ Ⓑ Ⓒ Ⓓ
99. Ⓐ Ⓑ Ⓒ Ⓓ
100. Ⓐ Ⓑ Ⓒ Ⓓ

Reading (Parts V–VII)

101. Ⓐ Ⓑ Ⓒ Ⓓ
102. Ⓐ Ⓑ Ⓒ Ⓓ
103. Ⓐ Ⓑ Ⓒ Ⓓ
104. Ⓐ Ⓑ Ⓒ Ⓓ
105. Ⓐ Ⓑ Ⓒ Ⓓ
106. Ⓐ Ⓑ Ⓒ Ⓓ
107. Ⓐ Ⓑ Ⓒ Ⓓ
108. Ⓐ Ⓑ Ⓒ Ⓓ
109. Ⓐ Ⓑ Ⓒ Ⓓ
110. Ⓐ Ⓑ Ⓒ Ⓓ
111. Ⓐ Ⓑ Ⓒ Ⓓ
112. Ⓐ Ⓑ Ⓒ Ⓓ
113. Ⓐ Ⓑ Ⓒ Ⓓ
114. Ⓐ Ⓑ Ⓒ Ⓓ
115. Ⓐ Ⓑ Ⓒ Ⓓ
116. Ⓐ Ⓑ Ⓒ Ⓓ
117. Ⓐ Ⓑ Ⓒ Ⓓ
118. Ⓐ Ⓑ Ⓒ Ⓓ
119. Ⓐ Ⓑ Ⓒ Ⓓ
120. Ⓐ Ⓑ Ⓒ Ⓓ
121. Ⓐ Ⓑ Ⓒ Ⓓ
122. Ⓐ Ⓑ Ⓒ Ⓓ
123. Ⓐ Ⓑ Ⓒ Ⓓ
124. Ⓐ Ⓑ Ⓒ Ⓓ
125. Ⓐ Ⓑ Ⓒ Ⓓ
126. Ⓐ Ⓑ Ⓒ Ⓓ
127. Ⓐ Ⓑ Ⓒ Ⓓ
128. Ⓐ Ⓑ Ⓒ Ⓓ
129. Ⓐ Ⓑ Ⓒ Ⓓ
130. Ⓐ Ⓑ Ⓒ Ⓓ
131. Ⓐ Ⓑ Ⓒ Ⓓ
132. Ⓐ Ⓑ Ⓒ Ⓓ
133. Ⓐ Ⓑ Ⓒ Ⓓ
134. Ⓐ Ⓑ Ⓒ Ⓓ
135. Ⓐ Ⓑ Ⓒ Ⓓ
136. Ⓐ Ⓑ Ⓒ Ⓓ
137. Ⓐ Ⓑ Ⓒ Ⓓ
138. Ⓐ Ⓑ Ⓒ Ⓓ
139. Ⓐ Ⓑ Ⓒ Ⓓ
140. Ⓐ Ⓑ Ⓒ Ⓓ
141. Ⓐ Ⓑ Ⓒ Ⓓ
142. Ⓐ Ⓑ Ⓒ Ⓓ
143. Ⓐ Ⓑ Ⓒ Ⓓ
144. Ⓐ Ⓑ Ⓒ Ⓓ
145. Ⓐ Ⓑ Ⓒ Ⓓ
146. Ⓐ Ⓑ Ⓒ Ⓓ
147. Ⓐ Ⓑ Ⓒ Ⓓ
148. Ⓐ Ⓑ Ⓒ Ⓓ
149. Ⓐ Ⓑ Ⓒ Ⓓ
150. Ⓐ Ⓑ Ⓒ Ⓓ
151. Ⓐ Ⓑ Ⓒ Ⓓ
152. Ⓐ Ⓑ Ⓒ Ⓓ
153. Ⓐ Ⓑ Ⓒ Ⓓ
154. Ⓐ Ⓑ Ⓒ Ⓓ
155. Ⓐ Ⓑ Ⓒ Ⓓ
156. Ⓐ Ⓑ Ⓒ Ⓓ
157. Ⓐ Ⓑ Ⓒ Ⓓ
158. Ⓐ Ⓑ Ⓒ Ⓓ
159. Ⓐ Ⓑ Ⓒ Ⓓ
160. Ⓐ Ⓑ Ⓒ Ⓓ
161. Ⓐ Ⓑ Ⓒ Ⓓ
162. Ⓐ Ⓑ Ⓒ Ⓓ
163. Ⓐ Ⓑ Ⓒ Ⓓ
164. Ⓐ Ⓑ Ⓒ Ⓓ
165. Ⓐ Ⓑ Ⓒ Ⓓ
166. Ⓐ Ⓑ Ⓒ Ⓓ
167. Ⓐ Ⓑ Ⓒ Ⓓ
168. Ⓐ Ⓑ Ⓒ Ⓓ
169. Ⓐ Ⓑ Ⓒ Ⓓ
170. Ⓐ Ⓑ Ⓒ Ⓓ
171. Ⓐ Ⓑ Ⓒ Ⓓ
172. Ⓐ Ⓑ Ⓒ Ⓓ
173. Ⓐ Ⓑ Ⓒ Ⓓ
174. Ⓐ Ⓑ Ⓒ Ⓓ
175. Ⓐ Ⓑ Ⓒ Ⓓ
176. Ⓐ Ⓑ Ⓒ Ⓓ
177. Ⓐ Ⓑ Ⓒ Ⓓ
178. Ⓐ Ⓑ Ⓒ Ⓓ
179. Ⓐ Ⓑ Ⓒ Ⓓ
180. Ⓐ Ⓑ Ⓒ Ⓓ
181. Ⓐ Ⓑ Ⓒ Ⓓ
182. Ⓐ Ⓑ Ⓒ Ⓓ
183. Ⓐ Ⓑ Ⓒ Ⓓ
184. Ⓐ Ⓑ Ⓒ Ⓓ
185. Ⓐ Ⓑ Ⓒ Ⓓ
186. Ⓐ Ⓑ Ⓒ Ⓓ
187. Ⓐ Ⓑ Ⓒ Ⓓ
188. Ⓐ Ⓑ Ⓒ Ⓓ
189. Ⓐ Ⓑ Ⓒ Ⓓ
190. Ⓐ Ⓑ Ⓒ Ⓓ
191. Ⓐ Ⓑ Ⓒ Ⓓ
192. Ⓐ Ⓑ Ⓒ Ⓓ
193. Ⓐ Ⓑ Ⓒ Ⓓ
194. Ⓐ Ⓑ Ⓒ Ⓓ
195. Ⓐ Ⓑ Ⓒ Ⓓ
196. Ⓐ Ⓑ Ⓒ Ⓓ
197. Ⓐ Ⓑ Ⓒ Ⓓ
198. Ⓐ Ⓑ Ⓒ Ⓓ
199. Ⓐ Ⓑ Ⓒ Ⓓ
200. Ⓐ Ⓑ Ⓒ Ⓓ

THE LANGUAGE PROFICIENCY INTERVIEW

Introduction

The Language Proficiency Interview, or LPI, is a face-to-face interview conducted by a trained interviewer. The interview requires from twenty to thirty minutes to administer and for quality control purposes is usually recorded. The objective of the interview is to obtain a speech sample that can be rated on criteria set down for each of the several levels of the rating scale. The speech sample may be rated at the time of the interview—in fact, it nearly always is—or it may be rated at a later time. In most cases, when an interview is recorded it is rated twice.

The LPI tests language globally. The rating scale employs as its standard language as it is spoken by the *educated native speaker* of the language. There is no standard by profession, setting, or content. That is because native speakers are not adept in one content or professional area of language and ignorant of grammar, vocabulary, and usage as they apply to other areas. This definition of language runs counter to the often-expressed position, "My company wants me to learn English to be able to sell snowmobiles (or household appliances, or electronics), and they don't care if I can talk about an experience I had while at the university ten years ago." If that is, indeed, the case, and the speaker is charged with learning a second language only as it applies to his or her individual work activity, for levels above 1+ the LPI is not an appropriate testing procedure.

Fairness requires that anyone attempting to apply LPI ratings, whether in the workplace or elsewhere, have a clear understanding of the scale and what it can and cannot do.

There are many kinds of speakers and, for measurement purposes, all must be able to be accommodated on a common scale. Some people learn English by conversing with native speakers. Generally speaking, these people usually have excellent comprehension, a broad vocabulary, good pronunciation and fluency, and a comparatively weak control of grammar. Other people study at institutes, in schools or universities, or in environments that foster an academic approach. These speakers generally have a good command of grammar, and an adequate, if limited, vocabulary, but they are comparatively weak in comprehension, fluency, and pronunciation.

The LPI scale has clear standards for all levels, based on communication skills. The strengths and limitations of all approaches to learning are taken into account, are weighed against the effect they have on overall communication, and are factored into the rating. The purpose of this section is to clarify the requirements of the levels, for language learners and users of the LPI scale alike, and to explain the interview procedure.

The language elicited during the course of an interview does not have a narrow or circumscribed focus. Interviewers do not, or should not, have a list of questions that they ask every interviewee, or even a list from which they select questions. Rather, depending upon the experience and interests of the interviewee and the content and language requirements for the interviewee's level, the interviewer approaches the interview from a wide angle, embracing as broad a sweep of language as allowed by time and the interviewee's capability.

Because during an interview the interviewee is called upon to *produce* speech, it is difficult to confound a qualified interviewer. The interviewer is trained not to assume language capability on the part of the interviewee. If a particular level of speech is not generated and sustained, the interviewee is not to be credited with it.

There are, of course, attempts on the part of interviewees to make interviewers think they know more English than they do. For instance, interviewees may prepare a discourse on a particular topic that they think will be addressed or that they will interject into the interview. While this approach is not entirely discouraged, control of the interview must always reside in the interviewer. The effect of such a discourse, regardless of how well prepared, is not what the interviewee presumes. By it, the interviewer is alerted to the possibility that the interviewee may have limitations he or she is trying to hide. Nevertheless, within the limits of time, the interviewer will usually give the interviewee time to make his or her presentation before moving on to other matters. After all, the role of the interviewer is not to intimidate or thwart the interviewees from demonstrating their ability, but to give them an opportunity to attain their highest level of sustained speech.

Format of Interview/The Interview Setting

There are three interviewer-interviewee configurations that are possible for administration of the LPI. They are: (1) a single interviewer/rater, (2) an interviewer and a note-taker, and (3) two interviewers.

1. The first of these configurations, with a single interviewer/rater, is the most common approach and is also the most convenient logistically, if not necessarily the best one suited for providing a reliable rating. It involves a single interviewer/rater, who interviews and rates at the same time. This approach is also the most difficult of the three, from the point of view of the interviewer, as he or she must not only interview, but on completion of the interview must also provide a rating in which he or she has confidence. A recording may be made of the interview, enabling the interviewer/rater, or a second rater, to go back later to review the speech sample. Because of the expense associated with having multiple interviewers, the single interviewer approach is by far the least expensive.

   In the interview, the interviewer meets with the interviewee in an environment that is as nonthreatening as possible, perhaps sitting diagonally across the corner of a table. It is not advisable for the interviewer and the interviewee to be seated in large overstuffed chairs, or in too casual an environment, as that constitutes an intrusion on the formality and seriousness of the interview.

2. The second interview format involves two interviewers; however, in this case one is a primary interviewer and the other a secondary interviewer. With this configuration, the primary interviewer conducts the interview. Upon completion of the interview, the primary interviewer invites the secondary interviewer to address the interviewee. In this configuration, the secondary interviewer has three purposes. The first purpose is to prepare a written record of the interviewee's speech that can later be used to arrive at a consensus rating. The second purpose is to ensure that a rateable speech sample has been obtained, asking follow up

questions in situations where a rateable sample speech has not been elicited by the first interviewer. The third purpose is to participate in the interview, either as an "interpreter" to help elicit higher level speech, or as a third person in a situation. Because the second interviewer is an observer of the interview process, his or her position is that of an uninvolved third party, and therefore is considered to allow for greater objectivity.

3. The third interview format involves two interviewers, who alternate in talking with the interviewee, while carrying out the interview. This approach is rarely taken, and if not carefully orchestrated can result in an interrogation, rather than an interview. The approach is calculated to put a certain amount of stress into the interview situation, thus requiring the interviewee to perform under conditions that could have an effect on his or her speech. This introduction of anxiety is desirable when the interviewee is going to be subjected to similar stress when called upon to work in the target language.

The Interview Process

The interview requires between twenty and thirty minutes to administer. It may be shorter than twenty minutes, particularly at the lower levels, but it should not require more than thirty minutes, in any case. Nobody except personnel involved in the interview process should be present in the interview room. The ambiance and the furnishings of the interview room should be comfortable, but not plush. The room should be away from direct noise, and indirect noise should be kept at a minimum. The interviewer and interviewee should be on equal levels. This means that the interviewer should not be in a position regarded as one of authority, behind a desk or on a higher plane than the interviewee. The optimum arrangement is that both interviewer and interviewee should be sitting at a table, on which can be placed any articles necessary for the administration of the interviews, e.g., note paper, pens, interviewee lists, recording equipment, and so forth.

The Rating Scale

The scale on which the interview is rated is a specially devised eleven-point scale, beginning with a minimum rating of zero (0) progressing by whole numbers to 1, 2, 3, 4, and eventually reaching the maximum rating of 5. Each level from 0 to 4 also carries a plus (+) value. Hence, the possible ratings are 0, 0+, 1, 1+, 2, 2+ ... 4+, 5. There are no minus (–) values for any of the levels, and there is no plus (+) value for level 5, which itself is the maximum.*

For levels 0–4, the accompanying plus values indicate that the speaker is almost at the next level, but for some reason does not qualify at that level. Perhaps he is able to speak at the next level for short periods of time, on certain topics, but is unable to sustain speech at that level. Or perhaps he is nearly at the next level in all aspects of speech, but lacks the language experience that would allow him to bring all his learning

* At times, plus ratings are transcribed as .5, or mid-point ratings (e.g. 1.5, 2.5), for convenience in data processing. This accommodation to technology may have given rise to a false assumption on the part of the general public, that if there is a .5 rating, then surely there must also be other ratings, such as .4, .3, or .2. This is not the case. There are no intermediate decimal ratings.

to bear, preventing him from sustaining speech at the next level.

The meaning of the plus values will become clearer as the reader becomes informed about each plus level. For levels 0, 1, 2, plus ratings can be "compensatory," meaning that exceptional strengths in certain areas, such as control of structures, breadth of vocabulary, or comprehension, can earn for the interviewee a plus rating, although he may not exhibit plus-level strengths in all areas of speech. An interviewee can in no case be compensated *over* a threshold. For technical reasons, compensatory ratings do not apply for levels 3 and above.

The distance between the levels is not scaled as an arithmetic progression, but rather as a geometric progression, becoming progressively more difficult to pass from one level to another as a person goes up the scale. It is far easier to progress from Level 1 to Level 2 than from Level 2 to Level 3, and from Level 2 to 3 than from Level 3 to 4.

Level Descriptions

Description: Level 0

Level 0 is described negatively, in that it focuses on what the interviewee is not able to do. The 0-level speaker is one who is not able to communicate in the target language at any level. He or she may know a few isolated words or phrases, may be able to tell time, recognize numbers, and make purchases, but cannot answer simple questions or even begin to survive in the language.

Interpretation: Level 0

The Level 0 is not necessarily totally ignorant of the target language. He or she is, however, the person who has *not* achieved Level 0+ proficiency. The person may know a number of words in a language, usually in isolation of their applications. He may know some numbers, politeness formulae, and certain tourist or traveler-type language. His speech does not qualify as "communication" at any level beyond the most rudimentary, and always in very predictable circumstances.

Description: Level 0+

The 0+ speaker is able to satisfy immediate needs using learned utterances. He or she exhibits no real autonomy of expression, although there may be some emerging signs of spontaneity and flexibility. His speech is characterized by frequent long pauses and repetition of interlocutor's words still occur. He can ask questions or make statements with reasonable accuracy only where it involves short memorized utterances or formulae. Most of the 0+ speaker's utterances are short, and word endings are often omitted, confused, or distorted. Vocabulary is limited to areas of immediate survival needs. He can differentiate most sounds when produced in isolation, but when they are combined in words or groups of words, he commits frequent errors. Communication is severely inhibited, even with people used to dealing with speakers of limited ability. The speaker displays little development in stress and intonation.

The 0+ speaker is able to ask and answer simple questions, ask directions, initiate and respond to simple statements, and maintain very simple face-to-face conversations. He or she can understand simple questions and statements, allowing for slowed speech, repetition, and paraphrase.

Interpretation: Level 0+

The person at the 0+ level is unable to survive in the target language. That is to say, the person could not ask for directions and understand the reply. He could not board a bus, and tell the driver to let him know when the bus gets to his stop. He could not order a meal, knowing what food he is going to be served, and answer questions concerning it that he may be asked by the waiter. Of course, he may be able to go into a restaurant, order a meal that he always orders and has studied in great detail, and avoid starvation. That, however, is not an acceptable performance to merit a survival level rating.

Description: Level 1

The Level 1 speaker is able to formulate some questions, employing limited constructions and displaying much inaccuracy. Almost every utterance contains fractured syntax and grammatical errors. The speaker's vocabulary is inadequate to express anything but the most elementary needs. He experiences noticeable interference from his native language, particularly with regard to articulation, stress, and intonation. His limited vocabulary, his poor control of grammar, and his impaired phonology frequently cause misunderstandings on the part of the others. The interviewee exhibits little precision in information conveyed because of the tentative state of his grammatical development and the limited or nonexistent use of modifiers in his speech.

Interpretation: Level 1

The Level 1 speaker is the one who is able to survive by applying the language he or she has learned. He knows numbers, can ask and answer simple questions, can give and understand simple directions, and knows enough of the grammar to create structurally accurate simple sentences, whether questions, answers, or explanations. The Level 1 speaker translates in his mind nearly every utterance, thus he exhibits very poor frequency. To achieve Level 1 proficiency, the speaker's pronunciation must be adequate for others to understand. If it is not, and if his pronunciation renders his speech unintelligible, the quality of his speech or the breadth of his vocabulary are of no importance. Speakers may as well not know anything, if they cannot put it into an utterance that the listener can understand.

The degree to which a person understands English is very important at the 1 Level. Not commonly, people who study English are able to say quite a lot, but are unable to carry a two-way conversation because they do not understand the other person. At Level 1, the speaker can understand replies to the questions he asks, if those replies are not too elaborate. For example, at Level 1 a person should be able to ask where a post office is. He should also be able to understand a reply on the order of: "You continue on this street to the third signal. There, you turn right, and it is about 100 yards from the corner, on the right. There is parking behind the building."

The Level 1 speaker should master question words, for both production and reception. For survival purposes, it is necessary to be able to ask, to answer, and to reply to: who, what, when, where, why, how, how long/far/late/much and so forth.

Description: Level 1+

The Level 1+ speaker is able to satisfy most survival needs and limited social demands. He exhibits a developing flexibility in a range of circumstances beyond immediate survival needs. He shows spontaneity in language production, but his fluency may be quite uneven. He can initiate and sustain a general conversation, but has little understanding of the social conventions of conversation. His limited vocabulary range forces hesitation and circumlocution. In the Level 1+ speaker's speech, there is evidence of the more common structural forms, e.g., the present, past, and future forms of verbs, but errors are common. He can employ most question forms. While for simple constructions he exhibits accurate word order, errors still occur in complex patterns. The Level 1+ speaker cannot sustain coherent structures in longer utterances or in unfamiliar situations. His ability to describe and give precise information is limited. He is aware of basic cohesive features of the language (e.g., pronouns, verb inflections), but many of his applications are unreliable, especially if less immediate in reference. The Level 1+'s speaker accuracy in elementary constructions is evident, although even there it is not consistent. To that degree that it exists, his extended discourse is, for the most part, a series of short, discrete utterances. This is usually attributable to the fact that the speaker is translating as he speaks and must pause to process his translation. His articulation is comprehensible to native speakers who are used to dealing with foreigners. He is able to combine most phonemes with reasonable comprehensibility, but he continues to have difficulty producing sounds in certain positions or combinations. The Level 1+ speaker's speech will usually be labored, and he may still have to repeat utterances frequently to be understood by the general public. He is usually able to produce fairly consistent narration in either past or future.

Interpretation: Level 1+

There are different ways for a person to reach 1+ on the LPI scale. The first learner-type is the competent student of language who studies diligently and who learns vocabulary, grammar, and other elements of speech and develops aural comprehension, at something of an even pace. He does not excel in any area, but is more or less equivalent in all. This person exhibits notions of past tenses, future, progressive forms, and perhaps passive voice, but has not internalized them. He is able to begin an utterance in a structurally appropriate way that would lead him to the "problem" part of the utterance. He then backs off, applying a verb form randomly or reverting to the simple present tense. Occasionally, he will get it right, indicating that he is going in the right direction. This kind of a learner is referred to as a school or academic learner, whose approach is of the type fostered by a classroom learning environment.

A second learner type is very different from the first. This is the person who has been exposed to English in a working or living environment, outside of any classroom, and by force of time and opportunity develops excellent comprehension, fluency, pronunciation, and vocabulary. Rarely, however, under these circumstances, does the learner grow with regard to understanding or application of grammatical principles. In fact, as a rule this person disregards the role of grammar when it comes to communication. With regard to the rating, this speaker is given credit for his strong showing in areas other than grammar, hence the plus (+), while his or her control of grammar may be only at the minimum required to surpass the Level 1 threshold. This kind of speaker is very impressive and is often complimented on his speech. The problem is, however, that he will not be able to advance to 2.0 level without mastering the structures that will allow him to show sequence of events in time, or the temporal relationship of events. He is often a "terminal" learner, in that his speech patterns, as wrong as they are, become fossilized, and he is unable to correct them. His comprehension will develop, as will his vocabulary and his fluency, but his control of structures will not, and he may never achieve the requirements for 2.0 level speech.

Description: Level 2

The Level 2 speaker is able to satisfy routine social demands and limited work requirements. He can handle with confidence, but not with facility, most social situations, including introductions and casual conversations about current events, as well as work, family, and autobiographical information. He can handle limited work requirements, although he requires help in handling any complications or difficulties. He is able to get the gist of most conversations on nontechnical subjects, that is, on topics requiring no specialized knowledge. He is able to give directions on how to go from one place to another. He displays a speaking vocabulary sufficient to respond simply to most questions, although often employing circumlocution. His accent, though often quite faulty, does not render his speech unintelligible. He can usually handle elementary constructions quite accurately, but he does not have a thorough or confident control of the grammar.

Interpretation: Level 2

The Level 2 threshold is very difficult for the 1+ speaker to cross. For school learners, working in an environment where they have little opportunity to practice English on a regular basis, it requires them to *internalize* speech and be able to call it forth without having to think about it. For the street, or the non-school learner, it requires him or her to accept the role of grammar in language development, at a time when for communication purposes it appears that other factors (e.g., comprehension, vocabulary, and fluency) are of greater importance. In both instances, the learner is called upon to perform in a way that is at odds with his or her experience.

It is at this level that the learner must recognize that the effective study of a language is as much a function of a person's attitude as it is of aptitude and application. To require a one-hundred eighty degree shift in attitude is to demand a lot of the learner, which is why so many learners never go beyond the 1+ level.

Description: Level 2+

The Level 2+ speaker is able to satisfy nearly all work requirements, and is able to communicate at a high level on concrete topics relating to particular interests and special fields of competence. He often displays remarkable fluency and ease of speech, but under tension or pressure his or her language may break down. He is generally very strong in either grammar or vocabulary, but not necessarily in both. His areas of weakness range from simple constructions, such as plurals, articles, prepositions, and relative clauses. Normally, he enjoys excellent control of general vocabulary, but may occasionally show some hesitation even with regard to some high-frequency vocabulary referring to common items.

Interpretation: Level 2+

The Level 2+ speaker is able to say nearly everything he or she wants to say in the target language. Culturally he or she usually appears to be very comfortable in the second language environment, and responds appropriately in nearly all social situations.

Internally, however, he recognizes his limitations and realizes that he is something of an impostor. He understands some humor and only occasionally has to struggle to speak. His vocabulary is broad enough to deal with most, but not all, situations. It is only when discussing matters of an abstract or conceptual nature that he feels he is at a loss, or when attempting to unravel an unfamiliar, difficult, and complicated description or process. In these circumstances, he may be driven to silence because of the limitations of his control of structures, particularly sequence of tenses, and use of prepositions and adverbs, and his vocabulary. Luckily for the 2+ speaker, most everyday conversations do not concern material above his level. For the 2+ speaker, there are still "surprises" in the language. The range of his or her language experience is still incomplete, preventing him from drawing on what he *does* know to confront the unfamiliar.

It is worth noting that many native speakers fail to advance beyond this level, particularly in cases where they are never called upon to discuss abstractions or conceptualizations, where their opinion is neither offered nor solicited, and where language applications are limited to low-level employment, survival, social, and family interaction situations.

It is the rare student of English who ever achieves proficiency beyond Level 2+, and this includes many people who spend years in a native-speaker environment, at times even in academic environments.

As will be noted in the description of Level 3 speech, the Level 3 speaker is able to say everything he or she wants to say in English, without exception. The speaker may have to resort to circumlocutions, meaning a "description" of what is meant, rather than the specific language, but that is of little importance, as the message is always conveyed. Furthermore, at Level 3 comprehension is nearly 100 percent for normal everyday speech. The learner who achieves a level above 2+ is in a very select group of language learners.

Description: Level 3

The Level 3 speaker is able to speak the target language with sufficient structural accuracy and vocabulary to participate effectively in most formal and informal conversations on practical, social, and professional topics. He is able to discuss particular interests and special fields of competence with ease. His comprehension is quite complete for a normal speech. His vocabulary is broad enough so that only rarely does he have to grope for a word. His accent may be obviously foreign. His control of grammar is good, and errors virtually never interfere with understanding and rarely disturb the native speaker.

Interpretation: Level 3

The Level 3 speaker is never uncomfortable with regard to his language capability. He is able to participate in high level discussions of a professional nature, understanding nearly everything that others say—unless, of course they employ low-frequency slang terms, unfamiliar jargon, regional speech, esoteric cultural references, or slurred speech. While he may understand even some aspects of certain non-standard speech, it is not a requirement to qualify minimally for a Level 3 rating.

In most cases, this speaker has had sufficient experience with native speakers of the language that while he may not understand something that is said, he can draw on past experience to glean accurately the meaning.

The most difficult problem with regard to achieving Level 3 speech has to do with internalization of speech and structures, rather than with learning new structures. Except with regard to vocabulary, the Level 3 speaker usually does not *know* more than the 2+ speaker. The difference is that he has internalize what he knows, and does not have to think about speech to produce it. A vast array of speech is available to him without his having to concern himself with what verb tense to use, whether the verb is regular or irregular, with agreement of subject and verb, with whether a noun is countable or noncountable, singular or plural, or requires a definite, an indefinite, or any article at all. These calculations are natural to him, relieving his mind of the language task. The Level 3 speaker can devote his thinking to *what* he wants to say, rather than to *how* he wants to say it. The Level 3 speaker is able to think and speak at the same time. It is this freeing up of the mental processes, which comes at the Level 3 threshold, that enables the speaker to discuss concepts and abstractions, and to give supported opinion. At this level he also controls a vocabulary of sufficient breadth that difficult descriptions do not elude him. For instance, should he be asked to describe a boot, he could generate most of the relevant vocabulary, including: size, toe, heel, sole, laces, round, pointed, heavy, thick, stitching, leather, and rubber.

Description: Level 3+

The Level 3+ speaker is able to speak the language with sufficient structural accuracy and vocabulary to be able to use it on levels normally pertinent to professional needs. He demonstrates particular strength in vocabulary, grammar, and fluency. He may occasionally exhibit hesitancy, indicating uncertainty or effort in speech. He will most certainly display patterns of grammatical error, although his speech will impress because of its obvious strengths in pronunciation, fluency, vocabulary, and socio-linguistic cultural factors.

Description: Level 4

The Level 4 speaker is able to use the language fluently and accurately on all levels normally pertinent to professional needs. He can follow and participate in any conversation within the range of his own personal and professional experience with a high degree of fluency and precision of vocabulary. He would rarely be taken for a native speaker, but can respond appropriately even in unfamiliar situations. His errors of pronunciation and grammar are quite rare, and display no pattern of error. He can handle informal interpreting from and into the target language.

Description: Level 4+

The Level 4+ speaker displays proficiency sometimes equivalent to that of a well-educated native speaker, but cannot sustain the performance. Weaknesses may lie in breadth of vocabulary and idiom, colloquialisms, pronunciation, cultural references, or in not responding in conversation in a totally native manner.

Description: Level 5

The Level 5 speaker displays proficiency equivalent to that of a well-educated native speaker. He or she enjoys unimpeded fluency in the target language. The person's speech on all levels is fully accepted by educated native speakers in all of its features, including breadth of vocabulary and idiom, colloquialisms, and pertinent cultural references.

Conduct of the Interview

The phases of the interview:

Originally, the Language Proficiency Interview was conducted in four phases. Later, however, another phase, referred to as "the situation," was added to the sequence. The situation places the interviewee in circumstances where he or she is expected to perform a specific linguistic task, the difficulty of which is dependent upon the interviewee's level of speech.

The five phases of the interview, as it is administered today, are the following:

- Warm-up
- Level checks
- Probes
- Situation
- Wind-down

Warm-up

The interview begins with the warm-up phase, which serves several purposes. One very important purpose is to make the interviewee feel comfortable with the interview situation. It also serves to accustom the interviewee to the voice of the interviewer, his or her accent (everyone has *some* accent) and manner. A third purpose is to give the interviewer a preliminary notion as to the interviewee's level.

Any mistakes that the interviewee might make during the warm-up phase are largely ignored, as potentially the result of nervousness and not necessarily a true reflection of his speaking level. This assumes, of course, that the interviewee later demonstrates higher level proficiency. If during the course of the interview the interviewee fails to generate and sustain speech at a higher level, the warm-up phase neither adds to nor detracts from the interviewee's rating.

The warm-up phase can last from less than a minute to two or three minutes, depending upon the amount of anxiety the interviewee experiences, his level, and the ability of the interviewer to inspire trust and good feelings in the interviewee. Typical questions that a person may be asked during the warm-up phase have to do with the interviewee's name, the weather, any difficulty in finding the location, an article of clothing, and so forth. Examples of questions asked during the warm-up phase:

- What's your name?
- How do you spell your name?
- Did you have difficulty finding your way here today?
- How did you come here?
- Did you have good directions to come here?
- Your necktie (scarf, jacket, hat) is unusual. Was it a gift?
- Is it cold outside?
- Is it still raining (snowing) outside?

Of course, nobody would be asked all of these questions, and the response to any of them could serve as the basis for other questions that would either constitute additional warm-up questions, provide information for later discussion, or lead the interviewee on to the next phase.

During the course of the warm-up phase of the interview, the interviewer gets a sense of the interviewee's level. If the interviewee is hesitant in his speech, if he initiates no exchanges, and if he replies to questions in single-word responses, the impression will be that his level is low. If, on the other hand, he replies in extended discourse, if he initiates exchanges or offers information beyond what was asked, and if his speech reflects a high level of comfort with the target language, the interviewer's impression will be that the interviewee speaks at a fairly high level. Rarely, by the way, does an interviewee create one impression on entering an interview and later demonstrate that his level is more than a full point above or below that level. Initial impressions are generally quite accurate.

Level checks and probes

Level checks take up where the warm-up leaves off. If the interviewer considers the interviewee to be a 1 or a 2.0 level speaker, following the warm-up, he will proceed to address the interviewee in speech that is at that level. His intent will be to establish that the interviewee is, indeed, at that level, by a series of confirmatory exchanges. The exchanges will focus on both content and language at a level considered appropriate for a level check. For the Level 2 speaker, for instance, the interview will cover autobiographical topics, language used in the person's work, current events, or special interests, while eliciting extended discourse in the past, present, and future. If through these exchanges it is established that the interviewee speaks at that level, the interview may then go on the next phase, the probe. If, however, it is established early in the level check that the initial assessment was too high, the interviewer abandons that level and drops to a lower level. The initial level checks should serve also to give the interviewee confidence in his speech, by not taxing him at a level beyond that of which he is capable.

Following the establishment of an interviewee's level of speech through level checks, the interviewer indicates a probe, which is conversation at the *next highest level*. A probe has as its major purpose the identification of the interviewee's highest level of sustained speech. Two lessons may be learned from the probe, depending upon the earlier sequence of the interview process. The first lesson that may be learned is that the initial assessment of the interviewee's level was too low, and that it needs to be revised upward. The second lesson that may be learned is that the interviewee has demonstrated his maximum level of sustained speech, and is unable to cope with language at the next level. In the case of the former, the initial probe is followed by a series of questions or by conversation at the same level, all of which will establish to a certainty that the interviewee can sustain speech at that level. In this case, what was initially a probe becomes another level check, accompanied by a revision in the assessment of the interviewee's level. That level check is then followed by probes at the next highest level, in a stair-step fashion. In the latter case, where the interviewee fails to uphold his end of the conversation at the level of the probe, the interviewer resorts to speech at the level of the level check, seeking thus to restore the interviewee's confidence in his speaking ability.

Following the level check is another probe, followed in turn by another level check. Before the end of the interview, the number of probes that an interviewee may be given could extend to a maximum of four, if he fails on everyone. The play between the level checks and the probes continues until the interviewer is satisfied that he has both obtained a rateable speech sample and established convincingly in his own mind the speaker's proficiency level. It is here that the next phase of the interview, the situation, is introduced.

The Situation

After the interviewer arrives at his or her assessment of the interviewee's maximum level of sustained speech, a "situation" is introduced to either *confirm* the finding or betray it as being too high. The situation phase requires the interviewee to assume a role and carry on a conversation about a specific topic or concerning a particular matter. The functions, vocabulary, and structures required of the task are thought to be within range of the interviewee, judging from his performance during the level check/probe phase of the interview.

If the interviewee fails the situation, the interviewer must reassess the rating and backtrack to establish a true rating. Failure with the situation does not, as a stand-alone artifact of the interview, establish that the interviewee is to be rated at the next lowest point on the scale. In every case, there must be adequate evidence, independent of the situation, to establish the interviewee's level. It should be remembered that during the course of the interview, an interviewee must establish not only that his proficiency *is* at one level, but also that it is *not* at a higher level. Furthermore, both the interviewer and the interviewee must feel that the interviewee's language ability has been taxed to its maximum and that he has failed to meet the challenge at the higher level. This taxing of ability is referred to as "taking the interviewee to linguistic breakdown."

An interviewee should never finish an interview feeling that he has not been asked to reach with his language skills to carry his side of the interview. Given the opportunity, many interviewees reject the invitation to go beyond their level of confidence, in which case they demonstrate their limitations by their unwillingness to attempt to speak at a higher level, rather than by overt demonstration of the weakness in their speech. This phenomenon is common among speakers who monitor their speech carefully, in an attempt to avoid making errors. Such people tend to speak with remarkable grammatical and lexical precision and accuracy, but their speech exhibits a woodenness, or a rigidity, that renders it extremely bland and uninspired. Needless to say, interviewees who match this description exhibit a reduced level of expression.

Wind-down

Following the interview, interviewees often have an uneasy feeling about having being required to demonstrate the limitations of their language. To counter this negative feeling, the interview ends with the interviewer chatting with the interviewee about his day and about matters that seemingly have nothing to do with the interview. In this way, the interviewee feels relieved, speaking in simple language about simple topics, entirely unrelated to anything previously discussed. The wind-down is to let the interviewee breathe more easily, and to reinstate the interviewee's sense of dignity and control. This is important for everyone, and leaves the interviewee with a much better feeling about his performance that he would have were he dismissed after failing the last in a series of several probes.

Reasonable Expectations

People who have studied language for a while, sometimes three or four years, sometimes longer, are often offended by their rating, thinking it is too low. Language learners must be reasonable with regard to their expectations of themselves. As with any test of general proficiency, the LPI provides the learner with information about his level. When administered by a qualified interviewer/rater, the LPI is the equivalent of the thermometer that a person uses to determine whether he is well. It is only when a person knows the truth about his proficiency that he can address his problems. One should not be offended to learn that he has a long way to go to achieve his goal. Reasonable expectations with regard to progress, and an understanding of one's strengths and weaknesses, indicate the direction that the learner should take to advance to the next highest level.

Cheating

There is no way to "cheat" on the LPI, any more there is a way to cheat when playing the piano before a critical audience. Interviewees attempt a variety of ruses to make an interviewer think they know more English than they do. Sometimes this is by means of a prepared presentation. Other times it is by peppering their speech with what they assume, rightly or wrongly, to be native speaker fillers. Still other times it is by using colloquial or informal speech, to simulate familiarity. And still other times it is by refusing to discuss a variety of topics, for whatever reason, requiring the interviewer, or attempting to lead the interviewer, to find a topic on which they feel qualified to speak.

Interviewers are trained to discover a speaker's true level, through the ruses and through all of the efforts to disguise limitations. An experienced interviewer has been subjected to all of the common and to many uncommon efforts, and is not going to be fooled by the interviewee. The interviewee should understand that he will not receive credit for language he does not produce, regardless of how he approaches the interview.

Interviewees are advised to approach the interview honestly, and to demonstrate their true ability, regardless of what that ability might be. It will make the interview process more enjoyable and less anxiety-ridden, and for that may give a better result than could be had from any attempt to thwart the purpose of the interview.

The Oral Proficiency Interview (OPI) Scale

This scale was devised at Educational Testing Service* to accommodate concerns that were expressed in the schools, and among school educators that the LPI scale could not adequately classify lower-level students in categories to indicate progress at the rate common in school settings. Students found that they studied for several years and never surpassed the 1.0 level. This is to be expected, of course, as second language acquisition is extremely difficult and time consuming and, as a rule, students do not spend the time learning, nor do they have access to the learning aids and life experience necessary to advance to the higher levels of proficiency. Additionally, students, by definition, cannot achieve "educated native speaker" status (Level 5.0) or anywhere near that level on the LPI scale. The combination of lack of maturity, education, and experience, of necessity,

* The four people who conceptualized and prepared the original outline for the OPI scale were Judith Liskin-Gasparro, Protase E. Woodford, Ihor Vynnytsky, and the author, all on staff of Educational Testing Service. They later collaborated on defining the descriptions for the OPI speaking levels.

relegates them to a maximum rating of 3.0.

Realizing this, the OPI Scale was devised to measure development, while continuing to track the levels and the intrinsic thresholds of language acquisition that are inherent in the LPI scale, up to the 3.0 (Superior) level.

By referring to Table 1, it can be seen that the difference in the scales is not in the level definitions, but in the further breakout of the OPI scale with regard to levels 0 and 1. In the OPI scale, those levels have been renamed Novice (Level 0) and Intermediate (Level 1), to avoid confusion with the LPI scale.

For practical purposes, the major contribution of the OPI Scale to assessment is with Intermediate, or Level 1, speech. The differences between Intermediate Low and Intermediate Mid are in expansion of vocabulary to address content that is other than merely survival (e.g. family, school or employment, special interests), and in improved fluency and comprehension. Utterances of the Intermediate Mid speaker should be longer than those of the Intermediate Low speaker, in part as a result of the greater confidence that attends developing proficiency.

For programs in which language learners are either youths or in which fine distinctions are sought at the lowest levels of second language acquisition, the OPI scale is appropriate. It should be noted, however, that the narrower the bands employed in any rating scale, absent tight controls, the less reliable the measurement. It stands to reason that without special accommodation it would be difficult to show the same degree of interrater reliability with the OPI scale as with the LPI scale, but the differences should not be great and should not deter program managers from applying the OPI Scale when assessing proficiency at the lowest levels, especially when raters are "under one roof." That is to say, when raters work closely together in an environment that permits constant communication among raters, with exchange of audio tapes of interviews, and discussion of problem cases, the decalibration that results from isolation does not take place.

For programs for which higher levels of proficiency are either sought or acknowledged, and where such higher levels are appropriate (i.e. with mature, educated learners of English or any second language), the LPI scale should be employed.